Mythopoeic Narrative in *The Legend of Zelda*

The Legend of Zelda series is one of the most popular and recognizable examples in videogames of what Tolkien referred to as *mythopoeia*, or myth-making. In his essay *On Fairy-Stories* and a short poem entitled *Mythopoeia*, Tolkien makes the case that the fairy-tale aesthetic is simply a more intimate version of the same principle underlying the great myths: the human desire to make meaning out of the world. By using mythopoeia as a touchstone concept, the essays in this volume explore how *The Legend of Zelda* series turns the avatar, through which the player interacts with the in-game world, into a player-character symbiote wherein the individual both *enacts* and *observes* the process of integrating worldbuilding with storytelling. Twelve essays explore *Zelda*'s mythmaking from the standpoints of literary criticism, videogame theory, musicology, ecocriticism, pedagogy, and more.

Anthony G. Cirilla is Assistant Professor of English Literature at College of the Ozarks and associate editor of *Carmina Philosophiae, the Journal of the International Boethius Society*. He received his PhD in English literature from Saint Louis University and has published and presented extensively in both Boethius and videogame studies.

Vincent E. Rone (PhD, 2014, UC Santa Barbara) writes, composes, teaches, and performs. He specializes in sacred-music reforms of Catholic France and the music of fantasy, notably *The Lord of the Rings* and *The Legend of Zelda* franchises. He currently is co-editing an anthology, *Nostalgia and Videogame Music*.

Routledge Interdisciplinary Perspectives on Literature

For more information about this series, please visit: https://www.routledge.com

Mythopoeic Narrative in *The Legend of Zelda*

Edited by
Anthony G. Cirilla
and Vincent E. Rone

Routledge
Taylor & Francis Group

NEW YORK AND LONDON

First published 2020
by Routledge
605 Third Avenue, New York, NY 10017

and by Routledge
2 Park Square, Milton Park, Abingdon, Oxon, OX14 4RN

First issued in paperback 2021

*Routledge is an imprint of the Taylor & Francis Group, an
informa business*

Library of Congress Cataloging-in-Publication Data
A catalog record for this title has been requested

ISBN 13: 978-1-03-223851-7 (pbk)
ISBN 13: 978-0-367-43798-5 (hbk)

Typeset in Sabon
by codeMantra

To Camarie Cirilla and Susan Jean Rone:
  Wives of editors have it rough.
  We thank you for your encouragement, love, and support.

Contents

Acknowledgements

With an undertaking such as this, there are many people to acknowledge. First, I must thank all eleven of my contributors for their incredible work on this volume. Their dogged commitment to excellence is truly inspiring. I must also thank in particular Vincent Rone, who took on the role of co-editor and worked tirelessly and with great attention to detail to bring this volume to a higher level of excellence. My thanks are also owed to the Faculty Resources Center, especially Kyle Stevens, Jenna Hamilton, Grace Still, Laura Moore, and their supervisor Renee Crooker, for assistance getting citations into order. Special thanks to Dr. Alexander Giltner for helping to develop the vision of the project in its early stages. Finally, my thanks to Jennifer Abbott, Mitchell Manners, Nazrine Azeez, and the whole team at Routledge, for their support in this massive undertaking. And of course, our collective thanks to Shigeru Miyamoto with bringing a mythopoeic videogame into the world that has enriched all of our lives.

Introduction

Zelda, Mythopoeia, and the Importance of Developing an "Inside" Perspective on Videogames

Anthony G. Cirilla

The Legend of Zelda stands as one of the most iconic and recognizable narrative videogames in the world. Nineteen official titles make up the series, with another in production, plus additional spinoffs and the appearance of characters in other game franchises. The original installment sold over six-million copies in its initial run in 1987; 12 million copies for *The Legend of Zelda: A Link to the Past*, the third installment in 1992, and generally accepted as the burgeoning point of the series' sophisticated mythology. In total, 108.5 million units of the games have sold worldwide.[1] *Zelda* is one of the major titles exclusively owned by Nintendo, along with iconic properties such as *Mario*, *Pokemon*, and *Metroid*. All of these series, wildly popular in their own right, share with *Zelda* the basic components of avatars that players employ to engage an imagined world. *Zelda*, however, stands apart from these titles in the sobriety with which it approaches its worldbuilding. Even when it takes a more childlike aesthetic, as in *Wind Waker*, the solemnity with which the *Zelda* series regards the integrity of its own imaginary world is seldom matched by *Mario* or *Pokemon*. On the other hand, *Metroid* lacks humor almost entirely; the series follows a typical first-person shooter, isolated-warrior model of worldbuilding in more recent iterations. As a result, however, *Metroid* provides only slender hints of the society Samus Aran, the female protagonist and avatar of the game, inhabits. In *Zelda*, players encounter a civilization, its subcommunities, and the dramas in which they are embroiled, much as in the tales of *The Silmarillion* by J.R.R. Tolkien. This remark is not intended to assert that *Zelda* has no humor in its worldbuilding or even without moments that break the fourth wall, but there is—and I can find no better way to word it—a certain *reverence* with which the *Zelda* narrative approaches its mythmaking.[2]

For the reason of this earnest worldbuilding, as this introduction to the anthology argues, *The Legend of Zelda* series provides a powerful place to ground the effort to shift videogame scholarship intentionally out of its generally defensive posture. As shall be discussed, Tolkien introduced the term "mythopoeia" to describe what he regarded as a universal human impulse: imaginative creation of fantasy in order to create coherent meaning out of a painful world.[3] As a modern body of myths, I contend, *The Legend of Zelda* parallels at the turn of the 20th into the 21st century Tolkien's *Lord of the Rings* during much of the twentieth. If Tolkien was, as Shippey put it, *the* author of the century—at least as far as Mythopoeic narrative is concerned—then *Zelda* is at least the top contender for *the* mythopoeic videogame narrative. Link, whose name is a pun for his avatar function in the *Zelda* games, is modeled after Robin Hood and Peter Pan, putting him in touch with two iconic mythopoeic figures, one quintessentially medieval and the other a cornerstone image of the Victorian-turned-modern conception of childhood.[4] Moreover, *The Legend of Zelda* dwells within medieval imagery, castles, dragons, knights, dilapidated cathedrals reminiscent of Tintern Abbey's ruins, all of which evoke Tolkien's fantastic medievalism and the medievalism of the fantasy genre that followed in his wake. Just as scholars delve into Tolkien's Middle-earth with profound academic acumen, the 19 and counting titles of *Zelda*, with sprawling narrative timelines and endless opportunity for academic study, are likewise awaiting excavation for those with the will and means to do so. Just as *Tolkien Studies* constitutes a foundational component of the study of fantasy as a genre, a subfield that speaks to the larger discipline but in which one can focus entirely, *Zelda Studies* is a phrase not too indulgent to entertain, as a foundational subfield for the study of mythopoeic videogames.

The question will arise concerning why this study is significant, and I believe the answer cuts to the core of academic life. When we ask our students to write an essay or research paper, we exhort them to ask the "So what" question. Why does your paper matter? What significance does your argument have? This question comes as something of a nuisance, because the answer to that question is, in their minds, painfully obvious: The purpose of writing this paper is to get a grade from us so they can put our courses behind them. I think that part of why telling our students to ask "So what" falls flat because of our institutional failure, in academia, to answer that question on a number of levels: our classes, the institutions students attend for four or more years, the unreasonable amounts of debt that too often come with it, and the gloomy uncertainty about how readily their degree will lead to the jobs they actually want. If we do not answer the "So what" question for them concerning our courses and their general purpose in academia, if we act as though we are above that question, then it is no wonder they have a hard time answering that question for the apparent busywork of papers we put on their calendars, interrupting their lives, which are no less crowded and no less full of the drama of life than ours.

As strange as it may sound at first, addressing this problem is a driving factor behind my belief that the university must begin to incorporate videogames into the curriculum in a meaningful fashion. Humanities departments bear a major responsibility in this task, because we must connect the aesthetic and intellectual canons of the past to the organic curriculum of our modern entertainment industry. With 67% of Americans playing videogames, and half of gamers playing on more than one device, videogaming constitutes a normative mode of entertainment rather than a marginal exception.[5] As educators, we have a choice. We can respond to videogames as a lamentable blight on the intellectual engagement of our students and pit personal interest in Sonic the Hedgehog against academic interest in Shakespeare.[6] Or we can adapt innovation in media to the traditional modes of inquiry and create a bridge from their popular culture interests to the academic ones we would like them to have.[7] We can use videogames to help students learn the life of the mind, and better situate ourselves to engage their perspectives. Furthermore, we can better incorporate the perspectives of our students, if we understand them, into the needs of our disciplines.

A belief in the value of serious academic work with videogames motivated the editors to produce this anthology. Of course, this effort is not a new project: scholars have endeavored to analyze videogames intellectually at least since 1997 with the publication of Espen Aarseth's *Cybertext: Perspectives on Ergodic Literature.*[8] After all, careful thinking about any given subject is worthwhile, but that assertion perhaps underscores the value of careful thinking than any particular subject. This volume also demonstrates how videogames model and facilitate thinking. Because videogames require interactivity in ways different from the novel or the soundtrack, they require action from players to *figure the game out.* I may not understand the symbolic value of Gandalf in *The Lord of the Rings* while reading the books, but I have still read the story. If I do not understand how to interpret a videogame, however, then I do not progress through the narrative or advance the aims the game presents for my actions as the player. Understanding and progression, although required for more discerning interaction with books and films, are inextricably bound together in the player's encounter with a videogame. Although the puzzles of videogames do not always challenge players to a great extent (though in some cases they may), nonetheless they present an opportunity for modeling the process of intellectual work in unique and productive ways.

The phenomenon of the avatar in videogames generates this unique quality of the medium's mirroring of academic effort. Here, we have a protagonist who is both separated from and controlled by the player. The nervous system of the player keys into the artificial events that happen to the avatar.[9] I remember watching my stepfather play *Spyro the Dragon* on the original PlayStation. As he used the controls to guide Spyro's gliding underneath a digital obstacle, my stepfather ducked his head. My mother commented, "You actually just ducked while doing that." He laughed and said, "Did I?" An almost talismanic or superstitious way of acting can manifest itself in moments like these while playing videogames: although the controller predated motion-sensitive technology, my stepfather responded as though his ordinary responsive reflexes mapped onto the gaming world.[10]

This effect of player identification with the avatar, serving as the conduit between the player and the artificial reality of the game, becomes all the more fascinating when narrative is introduced. When a character such as Boromir dies on screen in *The Fellowship of the Ring*, we may feel an acute pain of loss; when Frodo feels the need to flee, we may feel his panicked urgency to find some means to move his plan forward. But Frodo's escape does not depend on the audience's or reader's ability to row a boat: It only depends on our attention to watch (or read about) him undergoing those trials. If my avatar is in danger, and I respond too slowly or ineptly, then the character may receive harm or even die. The weight of the narrative responsibility resides in players in a way it simply does not for readers or viewers. Consequently, those videogames that narrate a story and engage in worldbuilding—of creating an imagined reality in which the player can participate—tend to invest players in the story of the avatar and the very fabric of the world where the avatar exists. With that realization in mind, one can readily understand why videogames inspire such commitment by gamers. Often their interest does not reside only in technical skill required to play, the quality of the story telling, the sophistication of the visual images, the satisfaction of the background music, or the challenge inherent in the tasks. All of these interests intertwine concomitantly between the eyes and the screen, the ears and the speakers, and the hands and the controllers.

Overall, videogames have tended to attract the scholarship of psychologists, sociologists, and historians of technology. Philosophers, theologians, and literary critics have tried their hands at the effort as well, but there remains a tenacious scholarly resistance to videogame studies within the humanities that has baffled many videogame scholars.[11] Videogames became available for households in the 1970s, almost 50 years ago.[12] Surely, after 50 years, intellectuals have noticed that this artifice can be deemed, not only intellectually stimulating, academically worthy of attention, or pedagogically useful (many early videogames were in fact explicitly pedagogical), but also beautiful, edifying, and as engaging as other narratives we encounter. Admittedly, 50 years is not such a long time, and the nascence of videogames does not pose their only obstacle to acceptance in the humanities. They have as well associations with childish indulgence, sexism, excessive violence, and an impractical, entertainment-driven generation. Also, many videogames are badly made, poorly conceived, tedious wastes of time that can leave players feeling guilty if the tasks they make possible do not provide some meaning. As one writer put it, he likes games to have stories because "a small part" of him "is tired of having fun without knowing why."[13]

The least original response to the list of negative aspects of videogames above is still to me the strongest: Yes, of course, it is all true of many games, but it is also true of many novels, short stories, films, soundtracks, and any other media or content we may seek. "Sermonizing" describes the bad sermon with which we disagree, not the eloquent exhortation to principles we share. We call lengthy texts "wordy" often simply when they do not interest us for whatever reason. Yes, videogames can be perverse in their love for violence and failure to be mindful in the social values they promote, but if that failure is an inherently defeating argument against the videogame industry, then it is also the case that we should close shop on the George R.R. Martins, Quentin Tarentinos, and Lady Gagas of the world. Either we search for legitimate value in the media of the videogame as we do with other forms of entertainment, or we simply stare at it like Ignatius Reilly in *A Confederacy of Dunces* staring at the denizens of a bar at which he himself drinks, saying to his mother, "We must stay to watch the corruption. It's already beginning to set in."[14] But we do not wish merely to observe culture as academics; rather, we wish to participate in the game of civilization. And to do that in the contemporary landscape of aesthetic production, we must understand and appreciate the narrative of the videogame.

I say the narrative specifically because one of the most acute sources of fascination with the videogame experience arises where player identification with the avatar intersects with the narrative.[15] Many gamers also participate in Cosplay, where they dress up as characters from videogames, sometimes with incredible accuracy.[16] Without having to participate to this extent (although I cast no dispersions on the practice), we can consider how playing such a videogame facilitates meditation upon one's identity.[17] When an avatar faces a serious question, such as how meaning is made in the avatar-character's world or what is the right or wrong thing to do, the player must actually *act* within the gameworld as if that question mattered. We observe when Frodo considers keeping the One Ring and wonder what we might have done; however, a game can make possible choices and see their consequences unfold, as games like *Fable*, *Vampire the Masquerade*, and others have made possible. The problem, as I see it, lies in our tendency still to look *at* the phenomenon of videogames as a culture. As C.S. Lewis puts it in "Meditations in a Toolshed," "You get one experience of a thing when you look along it and another when you look at it. Which is the 'true' or 'valid' experience?"[18] We talk about gaming from the outside of the experience of gameplay, even if we ourselves are gamers; perhaps we admit that we play only with embarrassment or when, relieved, someone else mentions that gaming is a favored pastime. We argue *for* the videogame by stacking it up against other forms of media, as I have just been doing.[19] We nod our heads when we admit that objections to some of the deleterious qualities of videogames have some force.

But we should also look "through" the videogame perspective, if we wish to truly understand it. No interpretive model of gaming can be complete without the internal perspective of actually being a player. In "Meditations in a Toolshed" mentioned above, C.S. Lewis makes this point:

> The people who look at things have had it all their own way; the people who look along things have simply been brow-beaten. It has even come to be taken for granted that the external account of a thing somehow refutes or 'debunks" the account given from inside. 'All these moral ideals which look so transcendental and beautiful from inside', says the wiseacre, 'are really only a mass of biological instincts and inherited taboos.' And no one plays the game the other way round by replying, 'If you will only step inside, the things that look to you like instincts and taboos will suddenly reveal their real and transcendental nature.'[20]

In quite the same way as Lewis argues for a "looking along" posture adjacent to a "looking at" one, we need to position ourselves in the beam of light that falls into the world from the artificial light of the game, to see what vantage point it offers for interrogating our heuristics. Of course, as academics we are properly skeptical of only looking *through* perspectives rather than at them, for that approach can stifle intellectual inquiry. In response to this concern, Lewis goes on to write,

> Having been so often deceived by looking along, are we not well advised to trust only to looking at? In fact to discount all these inside experiences? Well, no. There are two fatal objections to discounting them all. And the first is this. You discount them in order to think more accurately. But you can't think at all - and therefore, of course, can't think accurately - if you have nothing to think about. A physiologist, for example, can study pain and find out that it "is" (whatever is means) such and such neural events. But the word pain would have no meaning for him unless he had "been inside" by actually suffering. If he had never looked along pain he simply wouldn't know what he was looking at. The very subject for his inquiries from outside exists for him only because he has, at least once, been inside.[21]

On what grounds do we ask from the outside of the gamer experience, "What is the worth of playing videogames?" but not from within that experience, "Why should videogames, an important and gripping platform for experiencing narrative and so for making meaning, be excluded from the conversation of what constitutes the life of the mind?" The sense continues that the burden of proof rests on advocates who value videogames and must demonstrate their preferred medium is not particularly more pernicious than others. But it does not, and it is not. The world is convinced—people play videogames, find meaning in them, and build relationships and lives around them. Gamers participate in a meaningful culture. If we concern ourselves with edifying participation in culture as academics, in sharing what Matthew Arnold calls sweetness and light, then we should want that participation to be as sweetened and as illuminated as it can be. If we pit intellectualism against videogames, videogames will win. And that is because a great deal of human intellect has already been absorbed into the world of videogames, which has generated products of immense human creativity of a sort that is hard to fathom even for gamers and game designers. By recruiting the videogame to the life of the mind, we consequently gain an ally rather than an opponent, one that brings unique qualities for profound contemplation.

For these reasons, we have not taken the approach in this volume of studying videogames primarily as games, although that aspect receives treatment when necessary; nor have we treated them primarily as technology, although that, too, is a reality integrated into the perspective. The essays also do not approach videogames as a medium that must be justified as part of the entertainment industry. The market of human interest and engagement has already settled that question. Instead, this volume provides what Lewis called that "looking through" approach, where we can enter into the dialogic world of meaning made possible by videogames. Indeed, precisely because videogames employ both external artifice in terms of computer technology as well as the internal artifices of music, visuals, and narrative conveyed by that technology, we have chosen Tolkien's concept of "mythopoeia" as the organizing principle for the volume. Indeed, as a major voice behind Lewis's development of his insights in "Meditations in a Toolshed," Tolkien believed that stories should be looked "through" as well as "at."[22] That shift was the powerful contribution Tolkien made to *Beowulf* scholarship with his essay "Beowulf: The Monsters and the Critics." He writes,

> I would express the whole industry in yet another allegory. A man inherited a field in which was an accumulation of old stone, part of an older hall. Of the old stone some had already been used in building the house in which he actually lived, not far from the old house of his fathers. Of the rest he took some and built a tower. But his friends coming perceived at once (without troubling to climb the steps) that these stones had formerly belonged to a more ancient building. So they pushed the tower over, with no little labour, in order to look for hidden carvings and inscriptions, or to discover whence the man's distant forefathers had obtained their building material. Some suspecting a deposit of coal under the soil began to dig for it, and forgot even the stones. They all said: 'This tower is

most interesting.' But they also said (after pushing it over): 'What a muddle it is in!' And even the man's own descendants, who might have been expected to consider what he had been about, were heard to murmur: 'He is such an odd fellow! Imagine his using these old stones just to build a nonsensical tower! Why did not he restore the old house? He had no sense of proportion.' But from the top of that tower the man had been able to look out upon the sea.[23]

Scholars fail to understand the edifice of the poem when they only take it apart for information; the poem is understood when it is put back together by the reader and *experienced* as the poem it was intended to be. The mythopoeic videogame stands vulnerable to similar critical treatment at the hands of critics, if we are not careful first to ascertain the value of these productions from a mythopoeic standpoint, which generations of scholars failed to do when assessing *Beowulf* prior to Tolkien's seminal recovery of the poem's aesthetic worth.

For Tolkien, mythopoeia, or myth-making, transcends a cerebral process, constituting a means by which we discover our interior disposition to search for meaning in the world:

The heart of man is not compound of lies,
But draws some wisdom from the only Wise,
and still recalls him....
Whence came the wish, and whence the power to dream,
or some things fair and others ugly deem?
....All wishes are not idle, nor in vain
fulfilment we devise—for pain is pain....[24]

We do not have a choice about whether life will impose experiences upon us that exhibit meaning. But the meaning we can find can be nasty, brutish, and short. Fairy tales and myths, genres on the same spectrum for Tolkien, express through narrative the process of imagination by which he believes humans find the comfort of a life informed by value deeply felt as well as conceptually understood. This notion of comfort resulting from the comingling of emotion and understanding is what Tolkien terms Joy:

The consolation of fairy-stories, the joy of the happy ending.... This joy, which is one of the things which fairy-stories can produce supremely well.... Giving a fleeting glimpse of Joy, Joy beyond the walls of the world, poignant as grief.[25]

For Tolkien, "Fantasy is a natural human activity,"[26] and the fairy-tale, the effort of mythopoeia, is fantasy employed for the sake of that Joy.

It is therefore those videogames that engage in mythopoeia, which Tolkien might have argued touches on the central role of story itself: to produce in those who engage it a genuine sense that existence is worth the trouble.

The 12 pieces in this volume thus endeavor to make the overall argument: *The Legend of Zelda* series facilitates our assessment of the intellectual and academic merits of the videogame from the inside; and we can adopt the inside posture best through a mythopoeic interpretive stance, even when that stance is subverted, critiqued, or strained to its limits, as some of the essays show. A single volume or even a very many number of volumes cannot provide a concluding word on the dignity of the mythopoeic reach for meaning and the potential of videogames to refine the grasp of that reach; however, the essays in this anthology are included with the hope that soon we will stop asking whether videogames are art and begin focusing on how the artistry of videogames can yield valuable returns when approached with the tools at the heart of humanism and its scholastic endeavors. This volume consequently includes a breadth of the humanities: art history, literary criticism, theology, philosophy, musicology, as well as a number of subspecialties in this investigation into the *legendarum Zeldae*.

The first section of the anthology, "Foundations: Myth-Makers and Myth-Players," sets the tone by investigating the mythopoeic methods and practices of those involved with *Zelda* from both the sides of production and consumption. Alicia Fox-Lenz insightfully inquires into surprising resonance between the progenitor of *The Legend of Zelda*, Shigeru Miyamoto, and Tolkien, two classic examples of myth-makers in spite of the difference in their preferred media. Thomas Rowland provides an essential foundation in videogame scholarship per se, explaining the way in which the intromersive capacity of videogames provides a particular access into aesthetic experience. Ethan Smilie investigates how some players, called speedrunners, upend the mythopoeic aspect of games like *Zelda* by trying to complete them as quickly as possible; however, in so doing they assimilate to themselves a heroic status in the spectacle of the gaming community.

The second section of the anthology, "*The Legend of Zelda*: Entrance into Mythopoeic Structure," builds upon the foundational discussion of makers, medium, and players by developing a posture of "looking along" the mythic structure of *Zelda* to perceive the conceptual posture its interactive narrative enables. I argue for a synthetic understanding of the Campbellian Hero's Journey and Tolkien's *On Fairy-Stories* as it unfolds in *The Ocarina of Time*, putting the videogame's interactive component by means of the avatar into conversation with the grammar of worldbuilding and its capacity to illuminate identity, thereby communicating the satisfaction of meaning found in the phenomena of our primary world. Vincent E. Rone investigates how music of *Zelda* functions inside and outside the games, particularly within *Twilight Princess*, as signifiers of nostalgia essential to the Tolkienesque aesthetic, defending thereby the noetic value of nostalgia for its mythopoeic power to help make meaning. Michael Elam concludes the section with a close reading of the Hero's Journey in *Wind Waker*, examining how its resonances with other sea-faring epics including *The Odyssey* and *The Aeneid* lend dignity to the domestic spaces in the game. Elam thus qualifies, through *The Wind Waker*'s mythopoeic domesticity, the Campbellian emphasis on the journey at the expense of return and homecoming.

The section "There's Something Mything Here: Problems of Counter-Structure or Contra-Structure in *Zelda's* Mythopoeic Methods" contains essays, which, in different ways, contend for possibly subversive or alternative approaches to *Zelda* mythopoeia while retaining the perspective that the presence of the myth yields productive insight into assumptions that bear interrogation. Nathan Schmidt interrogates the often-assumed binary between human agency and nature as revealed by evil's disruptive influence, identifying an anthropocentric impulse in myth, which is manifested in *Zelda* even as it is undermined by the very myths that posit it. Matthew Sautman investigates a different yet no less salient component of hermeneutic unrest within *Zelda*: the perennial and convoluted issue of *Zelda*'s timelines and how they queer our relation to time's apparent stability. Tying these themes together, Damian Asling analyzes how *Majora's Mask* uses horror to invite players to question their own memories.

The final section, "The Legend of Pedagogy: Theory and Practice", initiates a conversation about the *Zelda* series from pedagogical perspectives, as a body of texts we can teach and a body of texts we can use to teach other subjects. Chamutel Noimann codifies the value of understanding *The Legend of Zelda* as children's literature and the engagement it provides for children to begin conceptualizing narrative at an early age. David Boffa provides an account of an Art History class he designed around *The Legend of Zelda*, documenting both his methods in teaching *Zelda* games as texts worthy of artistic examination, as well as how he used study of the games to teach methods in the field of art history. The final essay, collaboratively authored by Farca, Lehner, and Navarro-Remesal, demonstrates the inherently pedagogical nature of the most recent installment of the series, *Breath of the Wild*, and provides a fitting conclusion for the volume as a whole.

We offer this volume in the hope it will inspire new forays into *Zelda Studies* and its adjoining field of the mythopoeic videogame, with the belief that looking along the experience of players of such worldbuilding, narrative games harbors great potency for the concerns of all who believe in the work of the humanities.

Notes

1 See Video Game Sales Wiki: The Legend of Zelda. https://vgsales.fandom. com/wiki/The_Legend_of_Zelda.
2 Explicit homages to other games, especially Mario, can be found in the games which gently undermine the otherwise careful worldbuilding.
3 For Tolkien, the only distinction between the great myths and the nursery fairy tale is stature, status, and stakes, where gods are grander than pixies, kings better known than accountants, and saving the cosmos more impressive than saving one's dog. But the desire to treat these all with the fantastic power of imagination all have potential for the dignity of mythopoeia, in Tolkien's view. Myth as narrative-driven meaning making, rather than as historical bodies of myths from world religions, is the emphasized connotation of the term invoked in the volume, though the overlap in usage is vital.
4 Of course, players can opt to choose names other than Link, but this is his official appellation. His connection to Peter Pan in particular becomes more explicit in games such as *Ocarina of Time* and *Majora's Mask* where he acquires Tinkerbellesque fairy companions. Link is also technically a rebel fighting against prevailing powers, however unjust (as when Ganondorf takes over Hyrule), and so his virtuous outlawry puts him in touch with the Robin Hood mythos. Aside from rupees in pots, however, thievery is not typically something with which Link is associated. See Chamutal Noimann's contribution to the volume for further discussion.
5 The Entertainment Software Association. "Industry Facts," accessed 17 August 2019, www.theesa.com/about-esa/industry-facts/.
6 A reaction noted by James Newman in "Everybody Hates Videogames," *Playing with Video Games* (London, UK: Routledge), 1:

> Videogames have not enjoyed an easy ride in the popular press which has long concerned itself with the negative influences of their representations and the consequences of play. For many commentators, if videogames are worth considering at all, they can be easily and readily dismissed as little more than inconsequential trivialities. Indeed, so pervasive is this discourse of videogaming as worthless diversion that many gamers recount the experience to which they devote many hours of puzzling, dedication and creative effort as shameful, guilty pleasures … two types of story have come to dominate. The first centres on the apparently universally violent nature of videogames … the second type of story … treats these experientially, technologically and structurally identical 'videogames' as both symptomatic of and the partial or even sole cause of social, cultural, and educational decline. From standards of child literacy through sociality to imagination and creativity, videogames are seen to exert a singularly deleterious effect
>
> (1–2)

It is worth noting, however, that eight years have passed since *Playing with Videogames* was published; scholarship has advanced and the entrenched negative opinion toward videogames is perhaps not as pervasive as Newman noted nearly a decade ago.
7 Fundamentally, this position operates on the paradigm provided by Gerald Graff in his book, *Clueless in Academe: How Schooling Obscures the Life of the Mind*. Graff contends that popular culture can be leveraged to refine students' capacity for understanding the intellectual moves necessary in academic writing; I go further and argue that certain subsets of popular

culture can be adopted as academic interests on their own merits. Videogames hold our attention here, although this argument can be productively applied elsewhere too.

8 See Thomas Rowland's contribution to this piece for a fuller investigation into the history of videogame scholarship.

9 Although what one ought to think of this is a matter of much debate, that it happens is undisputed. See Tung-Chen Lin, "Effects of Gender and Game Type on Autonomic Nervous System Physiological Parameters in Long-Hour Online Game Players," *Cyberpsychology, Behavior, and Social Networking* 16, no. 11 (2013) for an example. This particular study finds some gender differences in the phenomenon:

> Long-hour online game playing resulted in the gradual dominance of the parasympathetic nervous system due to physical exhaustion. Gaming workload was found to modulate the gender effects, with males registering significantly higher sympathetic activity and females significantly higher parasympathetic activity in the higher gaming workload group
>
> (1)

10 If this was an effect then, one wonders how much more powerfully motion-sensitive and virtual reality-based games impact the nervous system.

11 An example of this critical disdain can be seen in Joshua Gibbs, "Should Classical Students Play Video Games?" *The Cedar Room*, 2019, www.circeinstitute.org/blog/should-classical-students-play-video-games Negative views are not always so explicitly articulated as that presented by Gibbs (a high school educator), but I have encountered reservations among my co-workers, and many of my colleagues involved in gaming scholarship have reported similar bias against the pursuit within a classical model of education. I make no scientific claim as to how pervasive the attitude is: but that the potential for videogames as a tool of initiating students into the life of the mind generates resistance in some quarters appears true. The hope is that this volume can help us move past that debate and into practical questions of how to use videogames to do serious, life-of-the-mind work.

12 See Rusel Demaria and Johnny Lee Wilson, *High Score! The Illustrated History of Electronic Videogames* (New York, NY: McGraw-Hill Osborne, 2002), for more on the subject of the history of videogame ownership and play.

13 Mike Buckler, "A History of the Videogame Narrative," Arts & Living in *The Amherst Student* (31 October 2012): 142–148, https://amherststudent.amherst.edu/article/2012/10/31/history-videogame-narrative.html.

14 John Kennedy Toole, *A Confederacy of Dunces* (New York, NY: Grover Press, 1980), 17.

15 See James Newman, "Videogames and/as Stories," *Playing with Videogames* (London, UK: Routledge, 2008), 46–68.

16 See James Newman, "Things To Make and Do: Fanart, Music and Cosplay," *Playing with Videogames* (London, UK: Routledge, 2008), 69–88. Newman writes,

> A contraction of 'costume' and 'roleplay,' cosplay describes the act of dressing up as characters from popular animation, film, and videogames… cosplay's playful fusing, synthesis or even juxtaposition of the real and the virtual present a rich site within which the extraordinary characters of videogames may be lived and seen in the most ordinary of places and situations
>
> (83–88)

17 The goal here is not to suppress what videogame scholars term the *ludic* element of games, that is, task-oriented play which requires development of gameplaying, but to connect that development of player skill with the storytelling impulse in videogames. See Graham H. Jensen, "Making Sense of Play in Video Games: *Ludus, Paidia*, and Possibility Spaces," *Eludamos: Journal for Computer Game Culture* 7, no. 1 (2013): 69–80 for a discussion of this facet of gameplaying.

18 C.S. Lewis, "Meditations in a Toolshed," in *God in the Dock: Essays on Theology and Ethics*, ed. Walter Hooper (Michigan: Eerdmans, 1972), 213. Lewis's own thought, as he reiterates in numerous places, was profoundly shaped by Tolkien's view of myth, both in *On Fairy-Stories* and *Mythopoeia* and the conversation which led to their composition. These remarks thus aptly set the tone for the present volume.

19 I make no claim that this move is exclusive to defense of videogames or the study of them, only note the problematic nature of the move.

20 Lewis, "Meditations in a Toolshed," 213.

21 Lewis, "Meditations in a Toolshed," 214.

22 Famously, when C.S. Lewis referred to myths as "lies breathed through silver," Tolkien retorted with the view that myths were a lens for apprehending certain truths that could be discovered no other way, an argument that was instrumental to Lewis's reconversion to Christianity. Tolkien wrote "Mythopoeia" to enlarge upon his insights from that discussion.

23 J.R.R. Tolkien, "Beowulf: The Monsters and the Critics," in *An Anthology of Beowulf Criticism*, ed. Lewis E. Nicholson (Chicago, IL: University of Notre Dame Press, 1963), 54–55.

24 J.R.R. Tolkien, "Mythopoeia," in *Tree and Leaf*, ed. Christopher Tolkien (New York, NY: HarperCollins, 2001), 87–88.

25 J.R.R. Tolkien, "On Fairy-Stories," in *Tree and Leaf*, ed. Christopher Tolkien (New York, NY: HarperCollins, 2001), 68–69.

26 Ibid., 55.

Foundations

Mythmakers and Myth-Players

1 Digital Mythopoeia

Exploring Modern Myth-Making in *The Legend of Zelda*

Alicia Fox-Lenz

Two Masters at Play

"It began…well, it began as you might expect. In a hole in the ground…"[1] but instead of a hobbit, this hole in the ground led to Hyrule. During the late 1950s post-occupation Japan, a young Shigero Miyamoto lived in the rural village of Sonobe. An adventurous child, he often walked the countryside without a map and discovered new places. One day, when he was seven or eight, he happened upon a small hole in the ground while exploring the wooded mountains by his home. He peered inside and saw only darkness. Intrigued, he returned the next day with a lantern, squeezed inside, and opened a subterranean world of caverns, which he explored all summer. Miyamoto returns to this story often when explaining how *The Legend of Zelda* came to be. It has become his personal legend, as much as Tolkien's scribbling "[i]n a hole in the ground, there lived a Hobbit" on an exam sheet has become part of his "biographical legend."[2] *New Yorker* writer Nick Paumgarten likens Miyamoto's cultural and commercial success to Walt Disney, suggesting Miyamoto mastered play the same way Disney mastered sentiment and wonder.[3] Though an apt surface-level comparison Disney adapted folk tales, whereas Miyamoto *subcreated* an entire fictional world. A subcreation is an internally consistent, imaginary, and relatively self-contained secondary world, not simply existing as a symbolic representation of real life, the primary world.[4] Tolkien coined the term in "On Fairy-Stories," his treatise on the cultural importance of fantasy where he likens the human drive to subcreate to divine creation. Miyamoto compares more readily to Tolkien, who has similar cultural and commercial success as Disney yet creates a deeper level of worldbuilding.

Biographical legends aside, many similarities exist between the two subcreators. Both Tolkien and Miyamoto became entranced by the countryside of their youth and retained that sense of natural wonder as their cultures underwent rapid and technology-focused urbanization—Tolkien lived during the rise of mass production in Britain and Miyamoto during Japan's high-technology economic growth—hearkening back to that lost natural world in their work.[5] When designing a new game, Miyamoto tries to capture the feelings of wonder he experienced as a child exploring nature, since these experiences are harder to encounter in a "paved and partitioned world."[6] With *The Legend of Zelda*, he sought to create "a miniature garden you can put into a drawer" filled with the memories of his childhood, from the expansive natural world ripe for exploration to the dungeons reminiscent of the maze of sliding screens in his childhood home.[7] In her biography, Jennifer deWinter states Miyamoto's fascination with the natural world is based in Japanese Shintoism, the belief in an active, spiritual natural world, full of nature spirits or *kami*. This belief system becomes manifest in *Zelda*, especially in the forest spirits, fairies, and the Deku tree, sentient nature itself.[8] Tolkien similarly has been accused of druidism for his treatment of nature, such as Caradhras, a mountain that blocks passage with malice, and the Ents, essentially anthropomorphic trees.

The natural world is most present in both of their worlds by an intense focus on landscape and setting. As the *Zelda* franchise has grown, the adventure has grown up—no longer simply a string of "quirky perils and hidden delights," the narrative's stakes have been raised, but the expansive landscape and its exploration remains a central theme in its gameplay.[9] A similar arc occurs within Tolkien's works: the evolution from *The Hobbit*, a children's adventure, to *The Lord of the Rings*, an adult tale grimmer in tone. The narrative matures, but Tolkien still meticulously details the landscape as the fellowship travels through different lands, and he later uses landscape as a character within its own right to convey the spread of evil.

Miyamoto and Tolkien also create to their own exacting standards, often at the expense of deadlines. Tolkien was a famous perfectionist, only publishing *The Hobbit* and *The Lord of the Rings* in his lifetime due to his tendency to become lost in minutiae and to restart at the beginning when he had made a mistake. Miyamoto is also known for perfectionism, something deWinter ties to his Japanese background. Miyamoto has joked in a 2007 Game Developer Conference keynote that his development team quakes in fear when they hear him approach, afraid he will upend the tea table and has been credited with saying a "delayed game is eventually good; a bad game is bad forever."[10]

Perhaps the most important similarity between Miyamoto and Tolkien is their effect on popular culture. Tolkien gave us Modern Fantasy as a genre.[11] His influence surfaces clearly in literature and popular culture today, from immersive fantasy literature such as George R.R. Martin, to the depiction of elves in RPGs such as *Dungeons and Dragons*. Miyamoto has had a similar influence on the gaming industry. When he began in the early 1980s, videogames appeared primarily in arcades and were high-score driven. *Donkey Kong,* his first foray into videogame design, introduced the character Mario, *the* most recognizable videogame character, and revolutionized the industry with its narrative focus.[12]

Ian Bogost asserts that videogames always were storytelling media, but before Miyamoto disrupted the industry this was not widely true.[13]

With the Mario-related franchises, Miyamoto created platformers, and with *Zelda* he created an open-world, savable, nonlinear game, laying the foundation for action-adventure and role-playing games. GameSpot listed *The Legend of Zelda* among the 15 most influential games of all time; and 9,000 videogame developers named Miyamoto their "ultimate development hero" in 2009. Will Wright, developer of *The Sims*, said, "[a]t the end of the day, most of the designers out there now grew up playing his games."[14] Similar to how Tolkien's influence spread from literature to games, Miyamoto's influence spread via adaptation of his work into games and other media, including television and graphic novels.

Miyamoto's renown for his work is somewhat surprising, however. Videogames are seen as commercial products, as opposed to creative works, produced by a team of developers and designers who labor in relative obscurity, though this is slowly changing.[15] Not many can name their favorite game designer like they can their favorite author, but Miyamoto challenges this trend. He is one of the industry's few *auteurs*, his mark indelible and unmistakable.[16] Even as he stepped back from his central role in the development of recent games, Miyamoto's approval remains coveted and his word is the last on matters of lore and gameplay.

Crafting the Miniature Garden

Furthermore, Tolkien and Miyamoto similarly developed their worlds and the relationships among their individual works. The events of *The Hobbit* comprise one episode within the broader context of Tolkien's legendarium, the overarching mythological framework for Middle-earth, which he began developing more than two decades prior. With the publication of *The Hobbit* and then *The Lord of the Rings,* Tolkien was forced to finalize some parts of his yet-unpublished legendarium and to rework other parts of it to fit with content published in those volumes. Eventually, many of these reworked, finished writings were published as *The Silmarillion*; however, in *The History of Middle-earth* and *Unfinished Tales* we catch a glimpse of these revisions. For example, Tolkien inserted new characters into his histories such as Galadriel— who first appeared in *The Lord of the Rings* and gradually rose in prominence throughout his revisions until she became a chief character within Middle-earth. Tolkien also tended to use paratext, his forwards and appendices specifically, to apply retroactive continuity or *retconning. The Lord of the Rings*, for instance, seeks to ground *The Hobbit* further into the larger legendarium by adding "previously missing" detail regarding the nature of the ring and Bilbo's relationship with it.[17] The development of the *Legend of Zelda* franchise is similarly episodic. Yet instead of the games pulling from an existing, background framework that necessitates refitting, the framework develops alongside that of the games.[18] Each game deepens the metanarrative and retcons details as necessary, operations that continue within the paratext, which includes multiple volumes of books published by Nintendo that collect and canonize details of the universe.

Similar processes but very different effects: with Tolkien, two published works operate under a specific timeframe within his larger world, and his revisions focus on adding details to its history to ensure everything fits together. Miyamoto conversely chooses to move each episode through time until they relate to each other satisfactorily and then retcon when necessary.[19] This process has led to a complex timeline, and it helps to speak of the games first in order of their release and then their placement within the chronology of the subcreation.[20] Moreover, the fourth game released in the franchise but third in the chronology, *Ocarina of Time*, features a time-control component integral to the story line. The hero, Link, receives the eponymous ocarina, which grants him the ability to time travel between childhood and adulthood. Link's time travel splits the chronology into three timelines, where the hero fails, the hero wins but fades into legend (the adult timeline), and the hero wins and travels back in time to prevent the events of the story from happening (the child timeline).[21] Thus, the original *Legend of Zelda* of 1986 occurs at the end of the timeline spawning from the hero's failure, while *Skyward Sword* of 2011 takes place at the beginning of the timeline, predating the events of all other games.[22] *Breath of the Wild* (2017), the most recent game in the series, presents a difficulty because Nintendo has placed it at the end of the timeline without specifying which one. Fans continue to debate its placement as either ending one timeline— likely the child timeline—or in the future when all three timelines somehow have converged.[23]

Retroactive continuity can apply to more than altering the narrative or timeline. *Skyward Sword* stands as the best case-study of this sort of retconning, as the entire game functions as a retcon for the earlier game installments. Much like how the foreword to *The Lord of the Rings* changed the nature of the One Ring from a magic invisibility ring to an artifact of great terror and power, *Skyward Sword* similarly nuances and signifies existing items in *The Legend of Zelda* canon, many recognizable from *Ocarina of Time*. *Skyward Sword* traces the red bird of the crest of the royal family of Hyrule, present on the Hylian Shield, to Link's red loftwing, a large bird used for transportation in the sky realm. *Hyrule Historia,* the Nintendo-published volume most concerned with the lore of the in-game *Zelda* universe, also hints at the Ocarina of Time being crafted from a time-shift stone excavated in ancient times before the events of *Skyward Sword*, which can explain its ability to control time.[24] The harp in *Ocarina of Time*, which Zelda plays while disguised as Sheik to teach Link sacred melodies, emerges in *Skyward Sword* as an ancient artifact of the Goddess Hylia. The harp can warp Zelda to new locations as it does in *Ocarina of Time* when Sheik teaches Link.

Tolkien and Miyamoto both blur the line between their secondary and primary worlds via their paratext. Much like Tolkien's foreword to *The Lord of the Rings*, *Hyrule Historia* boasts pseudo-historicity. *Historia* does not claim to be a found manuscript as *The Lord of the Rings* does with the Red Book of Westmarch, but it does treat its content with textbook-like reverence, which connotes its historical authority. Tolkien's use of this conceit is tied to his scholarly work; in working with medieval manuscripts, translating a found historical document occurs often, and his use of the author-as-translator enables him to add authenticity to his subcreation. There exists in *Hyrule Historia* no idea of the separation between primary and secondary worlds and therefore no reason to link them together. Tolkien felt compelled to push readers into a willing suspension of disbelief to engage in his fantasy properly. Based on the integrated treatment of *Hyrule Historia,* however, modern readers do not need such cajoling, possibly due to a gradual cultural acceptance of the consumption of fantasy. Yet it is likely tied to the hybrid nature of videogames—the player is embedded simultaneously both mentally and emotionally in the narrative of the secondary world while physically present in the primary world interacting with the game in ways readers do not need to be.

Mythopoeia

So many similarities exist between the men and their creations, it is a wonder Miyamoto never named Tolkien as an influence. Prior to 2001, readership of Tolkien in Japan was limited, but Japanese translations of Tolkien's work have appeared since 1969, and at least one of the designers who has worked alongside Miyamoto, Takashi Tezuka, is reportedly a Tolkien fan.[25,26] Although from disparate cultures and times, Tolkien and Miyamoto lived through similar cultural shifts that shaped their creative output. Tolkien and Miyamoto gained immense commercial success and cultural influence; both are enamored of nature and have created expansive fictional worlds through episodic storytelling, made cohesive through intelligent retconning. Assisted by the digital means of distribution, the immersive world of Hyrule is Miyamoto's subcreation. Subcreation is, as Tolkien writes in "On Fairy-Stories":

> What really happens is that the story-maker proves a successful 'sub-creator'. He makes a Secondary World which your mind can enter. Inside it, what he relates is 'true': it accords with the laws of that world. You therefore believe it, while you are, as it were, inside.[27]

Thus, the nature of *The Legend of Zelda* as a videogame series assists in the immersion requisite for Tolkien's idea of subcreation. Far from passive bystanders, players engage in the world and story in ways more difficult to achieve than for readers. Players through their avatars live within that subcreation, and they interact directly with them as if in the primary world. Tolkien also said of subcreation:

> Every writer making a secondary world wishes in some measure to be a real maker, or hopes that he is drawing on reality: hopes that the peculiar quality of this secondary world (if not all the details) are derived from Reality, or are flowing into it.[28]

The subcreation of Hyrule grounds itself in reality by including a well fleshed-out mythology that unfolds with each new installment of the series. This mythology poises *The Legend of Zelda* franchise as both subcreation and a work of mythopoeia.

Tolkien introduced the term mythopoeia in the 1930s, which literally means "myth-making," though it runs deeper than evoking mythic themes or a well-ordered history in a fantasy world. Mythopoeia imitates the creation of real-world mythology through an author or small group of collaborators in a short period of time instead of a cultural group through centuries of oral tradition. It contains dense self-referentiality lacking in many works that only invoke mythic elements.

To Tolkien, mythopoeia is entwined with subcreation. He presents mythopoeia in "On Fairy-Stories," alongside Faërie and the Cauldron of Story, forming the critical foundation upon which his subcreation is built. *Faërie* is a subcreated land of the fantastic and the everyday, created via the author's interaction with the Cauldron of Story, the well of experience and reference through which a subcreation is fashioned. The removal of the everyday into a fantastic realm facilitates something Tolkien refers to as Escape and Recovery: the ability for readers to enter secondary worlds and review and possibly alter assumptions from an outside perspective.[29] Mythopoeia then functions as the mechanism through which a subcreation achieves recovery for readers.

Tolkien's legendarium contains myths of origin and creation myths, epic-poetry cycles based on these existing mythological frameworks, as well as fictive linguistics, geology, and geography; this fully realized world serves as the benchmark for subcreation and its relationship to mythopoeia. Tolkien's Letter 131 reveals his subcreation goals: to make a body of "more or less connected legend, ranging from large and cosmogonic to the level of romantic fairy story—the larger founded on the lesser in contact with the earth, the lesser drawing on the splendor from the vast backcloths" of the larger; he asserts legend, myth, and fairy story contain elements of moral truth which we can absorb through this mode of storytelling.[30]

Ascribing the literary term mythopoeia to videogames may seem counterintuitive, as many regard the latter as commodity and entertainment, yet it remains necessary and accurate. Popular culture can evolve eventually into something more palatable to academia, examples including craft into art or novels into literature. The discipline of Tolkien Studies has emerged because people thought he was worth serious study despite his writing fiction. Pioneers of Tolkien Studies fought for his inclusion in the academy; Tolkien's work thus has elevated to the status of literature. *The Legend of Zelda* can follow suit, an expansive work of digital storytelling embedded within the cultural conscious, although the place of narratological versus ludological study of videogames is a contentious topic in digital humanities.

In 2006, Ian Bogost considered if video*games can* produce stories while questioning if they even need to, a statement seemingly incongruent with the current sophistication of videogame production.[31] Amy Green argues that videogames increasingly tell "powerful, culturally relevant stories," while simultaneously indicting the academy for neither embracing videogames as narrative vehicles nor positioning them for study within the digital humanities.[32] Videogames have narrative, conflict and tension, dialogue and characters, and they cover complex, culturally relevant issues—very little can distinguish a modern videogame from a film regarding storytelling other than player interactivity. If arguments exist about the literary merit of film, then they can and should extend to include videogames. Contrary to merely wasting time, videogames pioneer digital literature, storytelling in an increasingly technological world, and are considered the most lucrative, fastest growing medium of our age. Jordan Weissmann notes that a Pew Research Center poll in the mid-2000s revealed the number of non-book readers in America has tripled since 1978, suggesting this cultural shift further necessitates digital storytelling.[33] As videogames become more ubiquitous while book readership falls, it will become increasingly important to engage with all types of digital media, including videogames, as a vehicle for story within the academy.

If mythopoeic literature endeavors to bring the underlying truths Tolkien describes to a modern audience, and modern audiences increasingly interact with digital literature and interactive media, then mythopoeia will become more present in these media. The interactivity of videogames immerses players in the subcreated world, allowing the mythopoeic elements to act upon them as mythology does in the primary world. Mayra states that games emphasize ludosis as opposed to semiosis, respectively, meaning-making through player action to create interactive cultural systems and meaning-making through decoding messages and representations in media. This notion insinuates that though the vehicle for engagement differs, the goals of storytelling in videogames and literature align.[34] A current multidisciplinary movement, metamodern classicism, seeks to create a "living mythological tradition: interactive, dynamic, evolving—and relevant" through collaboration among artists and writers, further broadening the scope of mythopoeia.[35] But is *Zelda* mythopoeic?

The Miniature Garden to a Pocket-Sized Universe

The Legend of Zelda has many of the same features Tolkien sought with his subcreation: a creation myth for Hyrule, an origin myth for the Hylians, and a legend about the cyclical nature of the incarnations of the hero, the princess, and evil. RPGs often include interactive mythological elements for players, but *Zelda* goes further.[36] Hyrule has a fully realized geography and internal cultures for its various peoples—complete with distinct writing systems, ceremonies, traditions, and songs—much like Tolkien's subcreation.

The mythology of Hyrule evolves throughout the series as the technology allowed for more narrative gameplay. In the original *The Legend of Zelda*, the foundation for the mythology is laid. Zelda enters as a princess in peril, kidnapped by the demon Ganon. Ganon holds the Triforce of power, stolen during an attack on Hyrule. And Link must rebuild the Triforce of Wisdom from the fragments Zelda scattered throughout Hyrule to thwart Ganon's recovering both Triforces. The third piece of the Triforce does not appear until the second game, *The Adventure of Link*, which centers upon Link's recovering the Triforce of courage to awaken Zelda from a curse of endless sleep. The franchise began to develop its mythological underpinnings with the next title, *A Link to the Past*. We are introduced to two notions. One is the Golden Goddesses who created the Triforce, now contextualized as the legendary relic whose power holds Hyrule together and grants the desire of its holder. The second is the root of evil in Hyrule: the desire to harness the power of the Triforce for personal ends, specifically Ganon's desire to wield the Triforce to dominate Hyrule. The mythology deepens in *Ocarina of Time*, where the Golden Goddesses receive individual names and complementary temperaments. Din, the goddess of power, created the land of Hyrule; Nayru the goddess of wisdom, created law and order; and Farore, the goddess of courage, created all life.[37] The Triforce emerges as an artifact of three golden triangles, each containing the essence of a goddess: power, wisdom, and courage. Before departing from their creation, the goddesses magically sealed the Triforce away in a place hidden from the rest of Hyrule, the Sacred Realm.

The conceptions of creator spirits and a sacred realm are features held in common between *Zelda* and Tolkien's writing. In *The Silmarillion*, Middle-earth is shaped by the Valar, angelic beings who have humanized names and personality traits, as well as dominion over specific natural phenomena and elements. The Valar settle within Middle-earth in Valinor, the later known as the Undying Lands, where they reign as deities. Valinor eventually becomes magically separated from the rest of Middle-earth as a consequence of the greed of men, who, listening to Sauron, attempted to steal immortality from the Valar. Only certain people can reach Valinor by the time of *The Lord of the Rings*.[38]

Middle-earth as well as Hyrule both have sacred relics central to their legends, the Silmarils and One Ring for the former and the Triforce for the latter. The nature of the Triforce and its ability to grant wishes also becomes apparent in *Ocarina of Time*: Only someone with the three virtues of the Triforce in balance can make a wish. If those with unbalanced virtues touch the Triforce, it will split and grant them the virtue most dominant within them—the other parts of the Triforce then manifest within two others who exhibit their corresponding virtues. Only the Triforce intact will yield its true power. Once whole, the Triforce indiscriminately will grant a wish whether for good or evil, and the nature of the wisher's heart will change the nature of the Sacred Realm into either paradise or hell.

Tolkien's conception of "lesser" stories drawing upon the larger cosmogenic ones finds a parallel in Ganon's descent into darkness, first suggested in *A Link to the Past* and shown in the events of *Ocarina of Time*. He begins as Ganondorf, leader of the Gerudo, a tribe of almost exclusively female desert-dwelling thieves. Ganondorf desires the power of the Triforce and travels to Hyrule castle and feigns allegiance to the king to take the Triforce by force. Princess Zelda guesses his plan and convinces Link, at this time a mere boy, to access the Sacred Realm and claim the Triforce first. Link thus gathers the spiritual stones, which act as the Sacred Realm's keys: Kokiri Emerald, Goron Ruby, and Zora Sapphire—all held by the forest-dwelling Kokiri, the rock-dwelling Gorgons, and the water-dwelling Zora, respectively. After acquiring the stones, Link then must pull the master sword from its pedestal in the Temple of Time to enter the Sacred Realm. Ganondorf, however, had followed Link, sneaks into the Sacred Realm after him, claims the Triforce for his own, and turns the Sacred Realm into a realm of darkness. When Ganondorf touches the Triforce, it splits due to his unbalanced virtues. Only the Triforce of power remains, which enables Ganondorf to conquer Hyrule until Link returns from the Sacred Realm as an adult to defeat him. During the battle, Link defeats Ganondorf as a human, but he transforms into the demon king Ganon, the villain from the earlier installments. The story of Ganondorf's fall and the Hero's rally to defeat him encapsulates the basic form of the cyclical nature of the legend of light and darkness in Hyrule, this installment focusing on a mortal man finding his destiny and entering a supernatural sphere. This journey from mortal to supernatural happens most frequently with Zelda in games including *The Wind Waker* and *Skyward Sword*.

The interplay between human drama and mythical elements in *Zelda* also occurs in Tolkien's work, specifically the Fëanorian saga within *The Silmarillion*. Fëanor, an elf prince of great skill, fashioned three jewels that harness the light of two trees that illuminated Middle-earth before the sun and moon. When the evil Vala Melkor leads Ungoliant to kill the trees, Fëanor was asked to give up his jewels. He refused out of greed and pride, unaware Melkor already had stolen the jewels and murdered Fëanor's father. Fëanor then vowed revenge and took a group of elves into exile with him to battle Melkor until the curse of his and his sons' greed over the Silmarils extinguishes his line and nearly destroys Middle-earth. With Ganon, a mortal character is removed from his mortal concerns and thrust into a supernatural life; with Fëanor, a nearly god-like being becomes a slave to his mortal desires. Both stories humanize the supernatural but in opposite ways.[39]

While Melkor embodies ultimate evil in Middle-earth, which Sauron later reflects, Ganon did not originate evil in Hyrule. In *Skyward Sword*, we journey to the birth of the cycle of light and dark. The goddess Hylia—apparently a sort of lesser goddess to the three creator goddesses—guards the Triforce from demons who have appeared in the world. One demon, Demise, emerges as the root of evil and claims the Triforce for his own. Hylia manages to seal away Demise but cannot eradicate him fully without the Triforce; only humans can harness its power. Hylia thus chooses death and human reincarnation when the seal weakens and Demise threatens to return. Hylia leaves within the Temple of Hylia a sword able to seal away darkness, and she transports the part of the temple with the sword and its surrounding land into the heavens. Thus she forms Skyloft, the city in the clouds where Link later resides. Hylia's rebirth awakens the sword, which then chooses a hero to wield it.

The goddesses of Hyrule are interventionist—in *The Wind Waker*, the King of Hyrule appeals to the goddesses to seal away the evil of Ganon, as the hero does not awaken alongside him. They oblige by submerging the entire land, forcing subsequent generations to live isolated on islands or nomadically upon ships. Multiple tiers of divine beings also exist in Tolkien's world, as angelic beings living in Middle-earth, the Ainur, are split into two levels of power: the god-like Valar, the less powerful Maiar, and the supreme god, Eru Illúvatar, who lives outside of the circles of the world. Although conceived as a representation of the Christian relationship among God, archangels, and angels, Eru's typical lack of intervention results in the Valar acting as de facto gods as opposed to messengers.[40] When things went ill for the Elves following Fëanor's revolt, the Valar, not Eru, intervened and defeated Melkor, whom they imprisoned in the void. Similar to *The Wind Waker*, by imprisoning Melkor the geography of the world changed and disrupted entire cultures.

Hyrule's creation myth and its legends of the nature of good and evil compare well with the cosmogony in Tolkien's Middle-earth. The Ainulindalë in *The Silmarillion* details the creation of the world by the performance of music created by Eru Ilúvatar, which he and the Ainur sing. The root of evil in the universe comes from one of the Ainu, Melkor, who wishes to create for his own and not follow the will of Ilúvatar, manifest in the form of harmonic dissonance during the music. Nevertheless, the song, the Great Music, shows the Ainur a vision of the creation of what will become to be known as Middle-earth. Ilúvatar then speaks the world into being and tasks the Ainur with creating the vision they had seen. There are parallels between the creation of the worlds by the direct work of divine beings and their interventionist nature, especially of the Ainur in the First Age of Middle-earth mentioned above.

In Hyrule's creation myth, Hylia is reborn as the human Zelda, daughter of the headmaster of the knight school in Skyloft. When the evil of Demise pulls her to the surface world below, the sword awakens and sets Link upon the path of the Hero. He journeys to the surface to track Zelda as she purifies herself in sacred springs so to awaken as Hylia. She falls under an attack from which Link cannot save her, causing her to escape by traveling to the past. Link then must temper his sword with the sacred flames to activate the Gate of Time and journey to the time when Hylia chooses to die. Zelda greets him as the mortal incarnation of Hylia. She then instructs Link to command the Triforce to destroy Demise, so she may awake in their proper time, the Sky era. Link wishes for the eradication of Demise with the Triforce in the Sky era, awakening Zelda; but Demise's servant Ghirahim kidnaps and brings her back in time to sacrifice her soul to break the seal upon Demise. Link travels back in time and defeats Demise, who curses the descendants of the Hero and the Goddess to be reincarnated in a cycle without end alongside a being born from his hatred. Back in the Sky era, Zelda decides to remain on the surface instead of returning to Skyloft, where she founds the kingdom of Hyrule and the Hylian royal family. Thus, the blood of the goddess runs in the royal family, granting them special powers to fight the recurring evil that awakens the hero and princess in whom dwell the courage and wisdom of the Triforce. The nature of evil in the two universes differs but remains pervasive: Evil plays an integral role in Middle-earth's creation, sung into being by Melkor, whereas in *Zelda* evil recurs through cyclical manifestations of the Melkor-like Demise's curse.

Crafting Cultures

Tolkien and Miyamoto do not focus only on cosmogony, as they have built entire discrete cultures for their worlds. The peoples within Hyrule live in developed cultures with their own legends about creation and cycle of light and darkness. The Gerudo, for example, live communally in a fortress built into cliffs on the edge of the desert, very similar to the cliff dwellings of the Native Americas in Mesa Verde. According to Gerudo legend, every century a male is born among them destined to become their king—Ganondorf in the era of *Ocarina of Time*. Their society represents the opposite to that of the Hylians, and both likely have developed independently of each other to account for these differences. Gerudo seem to live in a quasi-communist warrior society with shared housing and little by way of commerce in their town, as opposed to the market feudalism of the Hylians. The Gerudo, likely due to their gender homogeneity do not observe stereotypical gender roles for men born outside their tribe. The most striking difference lies in the belief system of these two groups: Instead of worshipping Din, Nayru, and Farore, the Gerudo worship the Goddess of the Sand. No evidence exists of her outside the Gerudo-built Colossus that houses the Spirit Temple, suggesting that she is a reinterpretation of one of the three goddesses, likely Din, who has associations with creating the earth and also Triforce of Power that Ganondorf holds. In *Breath of the Wild*, the Gerudo have fallen away from religion and defaulted to ancestor-worship. They also evolve from thievery into masters of trade and are no longer isolationist, though they still ban men from entering their dwelling even more strictly than before. The Gerudo language also has its own writing system— consisting of 26 letters, 2 numerals, and 4 punctuation marks—similar to but differing from the written Hylian language and with more elongated glyphs.[41]

Hyrule mimics but does not capture completely Tolkien's development of culture. Tolkien began with linguistics: Each of his peoples has at least a minimally developed language and adopts one of two writing systems. Elves have the most developed culture, especially upon considering the notes and drafts contained within *The History of Middle-earth*. Tolkien's Elves have two different languages, one an ancestor of the other that shows real-world characteristics of a descendent language, and they developed two universal writing systems used by every language in Middle-earth. The Elves have similar cultural shifts as well: first as great craftsmen, then as mighty warriors, and ending in *The Lord of the Rings* as isolationists and academics. Although several groups under the umbrella of Elves react to the events within Middle-earth differently, this trajectory generally holds true cross-culturally. Likewise, Hylians receive the greatest development in Hyrule's culture, with cultural elements of other races, such as Gerudo, Gorons, Zoras, and Deku Scrubs receiving some development as well.

Tolkien does not focus on economics, a necessary focus in *Zelda* due to the player's need to acquire items. So little information exists about the economic activity of Elves outside some being gifted craftsmen; they seem mostly to be nobility and warriors. Elves in Middle-earth and

Hylians in Hyrule register as the default "good" characters, the former having a similar rivalry with a morally ambiguous people, the Dwarves, as compared to the latter and the Gerudo. The Gerudo and Dwarves share secretive and isolationist traits, though the Dwarves also are great traders. They also have a competing creation myth, eschewing the Elvish myth of the Great Music and Eru. They worship their creator, Makar, who carved them from stone within a sacred mountain. In *The Silmarillion*, the Elves believe Makar to be the Valar, Aulë. This disagreement exemplifies real-life religious contention, like those who practice Abrahamaic faiths and have differing opinions on the identity of Jesus as the incarnation of God or as a prophet. *Zelda* hints at this as well, but not quite as deftly as Tolkien does.

As in Tolkien's Legendarium where music is an instrument of creation, music figures importantly into *Zelda* stories; musical instruments often have magical properties integral to the advancement of the plot, a ludic element dating from the original *Legend of Zelda*'s recorder.[42] It defeats the boss of one dungeon, reveals the entrance to another dungeon, and allows players to warp via whirlwind. Beginning with *Ocarina of Time* in the console games, musical instruments become central to the plot and gameplay: powerful heirlooms that push the narrative forward by opening sealed areas, assisting in puzzle-solving, and allowing fast travel through summoning horses or warping. The peak of music's ludic importance occurs in *The Wind Waker*, where three different musical instruments are central to the plot. Early in the game, Link receives the Wind Waker, a magical baton once used by the King of Hyrule to conduct the sages. The Wind Waker enables the game map to open, as it can control the direction of the wind and allow Link to traverse the map via sailboat in any direction. It also can unlock the temples the dwelling places of the sages, those who hold the power of the master sword. Once in the temples, Link meets the shades of the previous sages, who teach him the song to awaken their heirs: Medli the Rito holds the sage's sacred harp, gifted to her from the Rito royal family; and Makar the Korok holds Fado's violin, a family heirloom. These two instruments restore power to the master sword and create a direct link between the water-dwelling Zora of earlier games and the bird-like Rito, as well as the Kokiri fairy children and the tree-like Koroks, all because of the inherited nature of the instruments.[43]

This use of music is used both by Tolkien and *Zelda* to fashion a motif of meta-subcreation. In *The Lord of the Rings*, Tolkien assigns different metrical patterns to each of the peoples, so Hobbits sound different than Elves who sound different than Dwarves. Tolkien also gives examples of legendary songs, such as Aragorn's singing the Lay of Lúthien, or Bilbo's performing his song about Eärendil—both based on the events of the First Age. One may argue that *The Lord of the Rings* and *The Silmarillion* themselves are meta-subcreations; the frame story to *The Lord of the Rings* specifies it as a translation by the narrator of a found copy of Bilbo's Red Book of Westmarch and *The Silmarillion* a translation of Bilbo's Translations from the Elvish. *Breath of the Wild* features a traveling bard, Kass, who sings and plays on the accordion legendary songs while visiting settlements of the various sundered people following Ganon's return. Kass's relationship to music differs from what we experience in earlier games. He uses music as a means of in-game storytelling, something rarely encountered in earlier games, where music is more atmospheric, adds mythological depth by harkening back to legend, or is integral to the gameplay. Players often can see Kass near stables and shrines. Kass endeavors to finish a song by his teacher, the former court poet of the royal family of Hyrule. He is knowledgeable in history and legends captured in the ancient verse passed down from his teacher. Kass shares those verses with Link, which allows him to unlock shrines. At stables, Kass offers to sing a legendary song of Ganon's defeat 10,000 years prior to the events of *Breath of the Wild* and will play other ancient tunes featured in previous games. In the second downloadable content pack, The Champion's Ballad, Kass comes into his own as a creator by finishing his old master's song, inspired by Link's adventures. Kass represents a meta-subcreation much like Tolkien's, where characters draw from underlying mythological elements to begin creating self-referential works.[44] This meta-subcreation furthers the case that *The Legend of Zelda* operates not only as a game with mythological elements but as a work of mythopoeia. A world lacking the depth necessary for mythopoeic consideration cannot support this level of in-world creativity.

Zelda makes mythopoeia relevant to a new generation via a richly crafted world with its own cosmogony and legends created by Miyamoto and his team of developers. The overarching mythology has analogs in the primary world, as does the secondary world's development of cultures, legends, and myths. In this way, Miyamoto follows in Tolkien's footsteps, a subcreator of digital mythopoeia within the land of Hyrule, fully immersive to players in a way Tolkien, critical of film and stage-fantasy depictions, could only imagine due to its medium: videogames. Unlike Tolkien's era of film and stage, videogames have only the limit of the imaginations of the development team for depictions of the supernatural, and, instead of assuming the role of passive bystanders, players actively engage in the medium, building the story as they play in a fully immersive secondary world. Due to their interactive nature, mythopoeic videogames have strong potential to assist in Escape and Recovery, Tolkien's concept recontextualizing the everyday by placing it in a fantastic environment and allowing readers to reevaluate preconceived notions.[45] Play is escape, and *Zelda* mimics the enchantment of Tolkien's Faërie.[46] Given these considerations, *The Legend of Zelda* may have been the narrative-visual use of the videogame medium to convince Tolkien that fantasy can live outside illustration and the written word.

Notes

1 *The Hobbit, an Unexpected Journey.* Directed by Peter Jackson. Produced by Peter Jackson, Carolynne Cunningham, Zane Weiner, and Fran Walsh. By Fran Walsh, Philippa Boyens, and Guillermo Del Toro. Performed by Ian McKellen, Martin Freeman, and Richard Armitage. United States: Warner Bros., 2012. DVD.
2 Dimitra Fimi, *Tolkien, Race, and Cultural History: From Fairies to Hobbits* (Basingstoke: Palgrave Macmillan, 2010), 7.
3 Nick Paumgarten, "Master of Play," *The New Yorker*, 19 June 2017, accessed 31 December 2018, www.newyorker.com/magazine/2010/12/20/master-of-play.
4 J. R. R. Tolkien and Christopher Tolkien. "On Fairy-Stories," *The Monsters and the Critics and Other Essays*, ed. Christopher Tolkien (London: Harper Collins, 2006), 112.
5 Humphrey Carpenter, *J.R.R. Tolkien: A Biography* (Boston, MA: Houghton Mifflin, 2000), 20–21.
6 Paumgarten, Nick. "Master of Play."
7 Ibid.
8 Jennifer deWinter, *Shigeru Miyamoto: Super Mario Bros, Donkey Kong, the Legend of Zelda* (New York, NY: Bloomsbury Academic, 2015), 14.
9 Paumgarten, "Master of Play."
10 deWinter, *Shigeru Miyamoto*, 14.
11 T.A. Shippey, *J.R.R Tolkien: Author of the Century* (Boston, MA: Houghton Mifflin, 2002).
12 Ibid.
13 Amy M. Green, *Storytelling in Video Games: The Art of the Digital Narrative* (Jefferson, NC: McFarland & Company, 2018), 7.
14 Nick Paumgarten, "Master of Play: The Many Worlds of a Video-Game Artist," *The New Yorker*, 20th & 27th December 2010.
15 deWinter, *Shigeru Miyamoto*, x, xi.
16 Ibid.
17 Fimi, 7.
18 Philip Tallon. "The Birth of Gaming from the Spirit of Fantasy: Video Games as Secondary Worlds with Special Reference to The Legend of Zelda and J.R.R. Tolkien," *The Legend of Zelda and Theology*, ed. Jonathan L. Walls (Los Angeles, CA: Graymatter, 2011), 57.
19 See Hunter Justus, "On Hylian Virtues: Aristotle, Aquinas and the Hylian Cosmogenesis," in *The Legend of Zelda and Theology*, ed. Jonathan L. Walls (Los Angeles, CA: Graymatter, 2011), 111–112.
20 See Matthew Sautman's contribution to this volume concerning the role of time in *Zelda*'s mythopoeia.
21 Sean C Duncan and James Paul Gee, "The Hero of Timelines," in *The Legend of Zelda and Philosophy: I Link Therefore I Am*, ed. Luke Cuddy (Chicago, IL: Open Court, 2008), 89.
22 Gombos, Michael, Takahiro Moriki, Heidi Plechl, Kumar Sivasubramanian, Aria Tanner, John Thomas, and Akira Himekawa, *The Legend of Zelda: Hyrule Historia* (Milwaukie, OR: Dark Horse Books, 2016), 71.
23 Sean C. Duncan and James Paul Gee, "The Hero of Timelines," in *The Legend of Zelda and Philosophy: I Link Therefore I Am*, ed. Luke Cuddy (Chicago, IL: Open Court, 2013), 86.
24 Ibid., 53.
25 Roberto Arduini, "Japan: Reception of Tolkien," in *J.R.R. Tolkien Encyclopedia: Scholarship and Critical Assessment*, ed. Michael Drout (New York, NY: Routledge, 2007).

26 Robert Ellwood, "The Japanese Hobbit," *Mythlore: A Journal of J.R.R. Tolkien, C.S. Lewis, Charles Williams, and Mythopoeic Literature* 1, no. 3, art. 2, (1969), https://dc.swosu.edu/mythlore/vol1/iss3/2.
27 Tolkien and Tolkien, "On Fairy-Stories".
28 Ibid.
29 Ibid.
30 J. R. R. Tolkien, *The Letters of J.R.R. Tolkien: A Selection*, ed. Christopher Tolkien (London: HarperCollinsPublishers, 2006), 144.
31 Ian Bogost, *Unit Operations: An Approach to Videogame Criticism* (Cambridge: The MIT Press, 2006), 70.
32 Amy M. Green, *Storytelling in Video Games: The Art of the Digital Narrative* (Jefferson, NC: McFarland & Company Publishers, 2018), 1.
33 Jordan Weissmann, "The Decline of the American Book Lover," *The Atlantic*, 14 January 2014, accessed 5 March 2017.
34 Frans Mayra, *An Introduction to Game Studies* (London: Sage Publication, 2008), 19.
35 "About," *[R]econstructionist Art - Art, Ecology, Metamodernism*, accessed 31 December 2018, www.reconstructionistart.com/about.html.
36 Zelda is not the only videogame that might be considered mythopoeia; Skyrim and it's 338 books of in-game lore certainly also comes to mind.
37 Patrick Dugan, "A Link to the Triforce: Miyamoto, Lacan, and You," *The Legend of Zelda and Philosophy: I Link Therefore I Am*, ed. Luke Cuddy (Chicago, IL: Open Court, 2008), 209.
38 Both of mythological systems are similar to real-world mythologies such as those of Greece and Rome, with large groups of named deities who dwell in sacred areas difficult or impossible for a mortal to penetrate.
39 To revisit an earlier comparison to real-world mythology, the end result is similar to Zeus's base character flaw of unbridled lust and the human drama the unfolds due to it.
40 Exceptions to Eru's non-interventionism exist: In addition to providing the power for the shaping of Arda, Eru awakens Men and Elves, reshapes the world into a sphere, drowns Númenor, and sent Gandalf's Maia spirit back to Middle-Earth after his death in the fight with the Balrog. These exceptions are, however, rare.
41 *Breath of the Wild* expanded greatly on the Gerudo language: coining the greetings *Sav'aaq, Sav'saaba,* and *Sav'otta,* and the farewell *Sav'orq*; also *Sarqso* for "thanks;" *Vure,* which likely means "bird;" *Vai* and *Voe,* "female" and "male," respectively; and *Vaba* and *Vahvi,* meaning "grandmother" and "child."
42 See Vincent E. Rone's discussion of the music of *Zelda* elsewhere in this volume.
43 This macro-evolution is mostly alien to the universe Tolkien, a devout Catholic, created. While cultural evolution occurs in Middle-earth, the interbreeding of Men and Elves or orcs and goblins represent the closest examples of biological evolution. The evolution of peoples lends Zelda's universe grandeur and a sense of scientific accuracy, even if those evolutionary choices seem whimsical—as when the aquatic Zora evolve into the avian Rito.
44 Vincent E. Rone and Matthew Sautman discuss the music of *Zelda* in depth later on in this volume.
45 Tallon, 54, 59, 62.
46 See Anthony G. Cirilla's contribution to this volume for a discussion of the element of recovery in *Zelda*'s fairy-tale fantasy.

2 Extrapolative Silence in Mythopoeic Spectacle, or, Why Does Link Look So Bored?

Thomas Rowland

Videogames go unrecognized amidst the national echelon of literary award systems (Pulitzers, Oscars, Emmys, and Tonys); they are omitted from economic success indicators (such as weekend box office announcements or bestseller lists); they are routinely and persistently left off the syllabi and research agenda of academics. This collection touches upon another problem in our academic culture: Literary experts tend to overlook or understudy videogames. Many critics avoid videogames either because the learning curve is too steep (a particularly important indicator of the changing nature of 'literacy') or because of the unfortunate idea that they are, like comic books or pulp novels, merely the entertainment *inter populum vulgum*.

Admittedly the detractors are not entirely wrong. Videogames require a substantial investment of technology and time, and often the more time the player is willing to invest, the more complex and rich the videogame experience. The videogame audience has become a highly specialized one, and the videogame experience has provoked too little academic interpretation and attention. This is a shame, given the complex and mythic qualities that videogames have to offer us as our distinctive, modern literary landscape. We need more researchers like those in this volume who are well-versed in videogame literacy and critical analysis to emphasize the rich potentialities and subtleties that videogames offer.

Videogames offer an experience that is deeply intromersive and personal, and they accomplish this through literary mechanisms that are absent in the films and novels that precede them. Specifically, videogames such as the *Zelda* series can benefit from looking more deeply into historical literary interpretative heuristics and finding in them the vocabulary useful to explain how games such as these create a deeply personal experience in which the reader comes to identify closely with the protagonist through as much in moments of isolation, silence, boredom, inactivity as in moments of action, characterization, and conflict. These quiet moments result in an extrapolative silence that bring the reader and Link, even in those moments when he seems 'bored', in a closer alignment than happens in many other traditional forms of literature.

Ergodic Play, Intromersion, and Narrative Layering

Historically literary academics have ignored the narrative elements of videogames for several reasons. While the "first" videogame, *Tennis for Two* (1958) made little splash, the videogame industry by the 1970s did, and the market for videogames had its own nearly fatal bubble that popped in the early 1980s, just when Nintendo branched into home console units. Through the 1980s and 1990s, videogames were considered programs, and not literary texts, and the nascent Internet prompted enthusiastic interpretations for its promise of hypertext language and chatroom culture. Though the discussion around hypertext and chatroom culture has subsided, videogames continue to be mostly ignored by the top journals and academics.[1]

Videogames were not entirely overlooked, however. Espen Aarseth introduced a foundational theory for understanding videogames by highlighting the ergodic nature of reading them.[2] His work proposed that videogames operate as a text by mechanical interactions, which require a substantial (ergodic, or "work-based) effort to accomplish. He introduced a field of interpretation known as ludology, which is characterized by a focus on the game qualities of these texts.

Ludology supposed that videogames, as "cybertexts," were more "game" than "story," and as such their nonlinear textual sequences opposed those who saw in videogames a relevant narrative thread (a "narratological" interpretation).[3] The concept polarized an already skeptical academic audience. The few media scholars working on videogames chose sides, and the issue developed into a fruitless period of videogame criticism, where the two hermeneutics competed for dominance.[4] A few insightful scholars, such as Henry Jenkins and James Paul Gee, argued that videogames had a place in culture as literary texts and educational tools,[5] but the debate between the ludologists and the narratologists reinforced an old bias of defining a text by the standard of the novel.[6] Consequently, literary scholars, used to working with more established but limiting interpretative systems, made little progress in analyzing videogames.

Around 2002 and again around 2012, advances in internet communication and graphic processing resulted in a burst of new, engaging games that introduced more complex mechanisms of character development, which players quickly embraced and exploited to realize new levels of self-identification within the game system. Videogames encouraged players to develop unique characters in online worlds, follow stories punctuated by richly rendered cutscenes, and explore multiple branches of completion in games.

Building from Aarseth's concept of ergodism, I have pointed out how videogames demonstrate an ergodic quality by requiring readers to be actively engaged (at least with hands, but sometimes with the whole body) in negotiating the text. Likewise, the possibility of "death" in a videogame text incentivizes the reader to progress through each sequence ("chapter," to use a novel-centric term), even difficult ones.[7]

In *Zelda*, the reader is ergodically engaged with Link, the avatar, through the interface of the Nintendo controllers, which themselves have changed over the history of Nintendo systems. The change in controllers and the sophistication of the subsequent games challenge the reader to relearn, and thus reinvest in each iteration, producing a serial interest in the game, and a subsequent identification with the character. The physicality of the controller interface is rewarded by the game-world physicality of Link's adventures, whether in exploring dungeons, sailing a flooded kingdom, shape-shifting, time-shifting, lycanthropy, or archery.

For Aarseth and for many who followed him, ergodism separated the reader from the text and precluded a literary interpretation of videogames. Aarseth wanted to isolate the idea of story from the idea of a game, but this is an insufficient foundation for videogame studies. In fact, the intersection of game and story is the foundation not only of videogames but also of much historical literature, and specifically the ability to control the virtual body of the avatar through the physical body of the reader deeply connects the reader with the character. The connection of reader and character requires a world to explore, and the virtual realization of an exploratory space constitutes what I have termed "intromersion."

In another essay, I proposed that videogames innovated a new connection with the reader by providing a virtual space wherein the reader could not only inhabit but also explore (in the literal sense of moving through).[8] I suggested that while cinema developed the *immersive* world, which like a panoramic photograph provided the viewer an ability to view the constructed environment, videogames pushed further by situating the avatar within a cinematic virtual landscape the player is able to explore, connected through the ergodic nature of the game. Intromersion results from the combination of these two precedents, the realization of a virtual environment and the ergodic connection of reader and character. In this essay, I argue that this combination furthermore produces another distinctive experience of the videogame: the moment of extrapolative silence, by which the reader connects to the character in moments of isolation, loneliness, inactivity, and boredom.

Aarseth's theory of ludology met resistance from narratologists who emphasized the narrative elements in videogames, elements that were not negated by their ergodism or intromersion. *Zelda* exemplifies and complicates a discussion of narrative in games, since the various games do not exist as "sequels" in the sense that they continue a persistent narrative (or develop new narratives around existing characters), nor do they remake existing narratives.

Tracing the narratives of the various *Zelda* texts requires a substantial effort, and the result presents a complicated mythology of Good against Evil in the form of Zelda and Ganon, respectively.[9] The various iterations of Link and Zelda are *not* the same story, but rather a layered sediment of parallel stories, interconnected yet distinct. This narrative layering emerges from game design (narrative) with intromersion (extradiegesis): Readers (in control of the characters) have an ergodic "experience" (an extradiegetic narrative) by exploring a virtual environment within the constraints of a designed videogame story (a diegetic narrative).

The complicated nature of the narrative layering complexifies the idea of *linearity*, the interpretation of the sequence of events to establish a continuous cause-effect chronology. The study of narrative belongs to the field of narratology (which is not restricted to videogame texts), but while these studies of linearity allow for different patterns, the complicated dual narrativity (a ludic linearity) of videogames has not had much attention. Yet the narrative layering results in an essential quality of videogames: the simultaneous experience of ergodism and intromersion with designed diegetic narrative—both of which we can define through Aristotle's concept of *spectacle* ("opsis," another oft-neglected literary function) —to explore why videogames merit the designation as the new literature of the digital generation.

Linearity and Aristotelian *Opsis*

Narratology as a field has been dominated by the question of what constitutes the essential nature of story. The answer to this question provides a rationale to link many different types of texts without neglecting essential differences in medium and genre, and the field holds the promise to carefully delineate a history of reading through its various iterations (and not, as is common, through novelcentric assumptions of reading).

While narratology dates back to Enlightenment ideas of literature, its first modern iteration came in Saussurean semiology in the West and Russian Formalism in the East. Structural narratology in these cases intended to catalog forms of narrative that might provide productive cross-cultural examinations, such as in the efforts of the Aarne-Thompson Index,[10] while formalists such as Vicktor Shklovsky and Vladimir Propp focused on defining the essential characteristics of literature.

Their work was picked up by later critics such as Roland Barthes, Tzvetan Todorov, and Gerard Genette, who deconstructed literary texts or else compiled data on literary building blocks. While early efforts in narratology focused on classifying narrative in the forms in which it occurred (print, film, radio, oral culture, and performance), later efforts moved toward deconstructing narrative, which by then had become a rather wide-ranging and ambiguous conceit.

This decentralization of narrative prompted a wave of responses by the end of the 20th century: In some, narratology became a quest to rediscover a centralized definition that allowed for productive investigation. Often this focus was located disparately in often unrelated disciplines, including "psychology, education, social sciences, political thought and policy analysis, health research, law, theology, and cognitive science."[11] Media critics, such as McLuhan and Ong, looked at the presentation of narrative to extrapolate key cultural characteristics. Later (digital) narratologists, such as George Landow, David Herman, Henry Jenkins, or Marie-Laure Ryan, looked at specific forms of digital discourse and interaction in the emerging world of new technologies and electronic communication, such as hypertext and computer-mediated conversation (online chat).[12]

The quickly changing world of electronic communication facilitated a new wave of theorizing, though it hardly kept abreast with the rate of change in popular habit and in technology, and more surprisingly it rarely considered videogames. The latest book on topic x seemed woefully outdated only a few years after its publication: so too were comprehensive studies on character and avatar design after only a few new games rendered the older designs old fashioned, ugly, or unpopular.[13] Even Marie-Laure Ryan, who is largely considered a leading narratologist, failed to recognize the growth of videogames and the decline of other forms of electronic communication.[14] The scenario in 2019 was not as the textual critics had imagined it in 1999, and the trends that many casual videogamers recognized went unnoticed by the critics until long after the fact. Hypertext receded as a new medium for storytelling, and the old semiotic methodologies for discussing narrative in electronic media had subsided. Consequently, much of the literature of this period has fallen off and left current critics with few precedents upon which to build.[15] As both a videogamer and a literary critic, I have felt all too sharply the disconnect between the expression of critical theory with the actual, enjoyable experience of the videogame. Part of the problem is in how modern narratological approaches tend to focus on elements that are not well developed in videogames.

I recommend that we return to a recurring influence in literary theory to remedy that deficit: Aristotle's original conclusions on literature.[16] His early perspective, being as it was on literature expressed orally and theatrically, refocuses on elements again important in digital literature. For the present purpose, I contend that we should turn to one of those elements, one perhaps most often neglected, *spectacle*, to edify our discourse on the videogame medium in general and to access *Zelda* more fully especially.

Aristotle adopted the term for spectacle from Plato's discussion on self-rule and justice in *The Republic*. In it, Plato uses the word *opsis* to discuss the reliability of the visual image (*opsis*) as a representation of reality, scorning its reliability in his cave allegory. In the familiar allegory, prisoners set within a cave can only perceive the shadow (*opsis*) of reality—that shadow is *opsis*—that deceives the prisoners into a sense of understanding of reality. Experience of that reality, however, is greater still, and Plato contrasts *opsis* to *noeton topon* (the knowable world). Aristotle reintroduces *opsis* as a reliable sense of perception, though he maintains some of Plato's reluctance to give too much credibility to sight, which was too easy to deceive. Aristotle presents *opsis* as elements of visual drama that fool the audience into understanding the action of the play: the costumes, scenery, and masks that cue the observer into the path of emotional catharsis. But because the literary heart of the Greek tragedy lies with the playwright, though he has little control over staging, or spectacle, of the play, speech (*lexis*) pre-empts sight in the power of literature.[17]

The tension of speech and sight in literature provides a reliable metric for understanding the changes in reading modes, from oral epic recitation and Greek tragedy to manuscripts, print, film, and digital. The videogame, borrowing elements of both drama (the ergodic performance of narrative) and cinema (the visual presentation of narrative), refocuses literature on *sight*—and thus, on spectacle. In some games, especially *Zelda*, the emphasis on sight is nearly complete, as recorded dialogue or voice acting are instead substituted for dialogue presented visually on-screen.[18] When we consider that multiple elements of the game—visuals, auditory cues, and the framing through a screen—invite the readers to engage intromersively, we realize just how critical the visual nature of the videogame is to the experience, even while simultaneously it potentially accommodates the Platonic warning not to get too accustomed to the intromersive world, which deceives us and makes us forget the revelation that the sun brings.

Thus, the tension between sight and speech can imply deceit and understanding. Because spectacle engaged those elements intended to persuade the audience into believing themselves to be in a setting that was not real, sight was implicated in deceiving the reader. Speech, the vehicle for delivery of the narrative, was more trustworthy and reliable than sight, and that tension carries into the videogame today. The visual, intromersive setting is an illusion for the benefit of the narrative, but the actions engaged by the reader are the narrative that in its essence is indisputably real. Put another way, the world in which Link moves and acts may be illusory, but the story that Link participates in is real.[19]

The tension of the real and the illusory is critical to understanding narrative and linearity. Because we perceive linearity as a sequence of events defined by logical cause-effect relationships, and because the number of cause-effects sequences we can keep in memory are limited, most texts keep these sequences simple and short, with a limited cast of characters and a few hours of narrative. But to enhance the economic appeal of videogames, many designers pad their stories to incentivize slow, deliberate, and multiple readings. And so, the *Zelda* game *Breath of the Wild* presents the reader with a massive open world suitable for many days of exploration.[20] Videogames often last far longer than movies, television programs, or books, with more than 60 hours of designed gameplay. To accomplish this, many videogames provide multiple routes to accomplish objectives, alternate or open endings, and sub-narratives to follow. As a result of these tangled web of diegetic narratives, videogames can appear to be a- or nonlinear.[21]

Spectacle in videogames therefore challenges our notions of linearity. It cannot be the diegetic narrative that the reader supposes is happening, but is more about the *perceived* sequencing of events. Linearity and spectacle combined create a highly personal perception of narrativity: Consider the extradiegetic ergodic and the diegetic narratives simultaneously occurring for the reader, and we can begin to glimpse the innovative nature of the videogame experience.

Spectacle, ergodic, intromersive, and linear confusion are common to most videogame literature. But the *Legend of Zelda* series complicates these elements further by its constant reinvention of parallel stories. Its mythos means we cannot easily trace even a ludic linearity onto it. And so we turn to two mythologists to help decipher this series.

The Mythological Linearity of the *Zelda* Series

The Legend of Zelda series of games features the common linearity confusion arising from the intromersive integration of spectacle in the text, but it also complicates the serial chronology by failing to link (no pun intended) the games together.

On the surface, specific elements indicate the *Zelda* mythos is mythological—the stories often include a brief narration of cosmic genesis, as well as a timelessness of its characters. The stories unfold in large themes rather than in character development, despite considerable relationship-building between Link and Zelda. Link and Zelda of the various texts may or may not be the same individuals across the texts: The events of one text seem to contradict others, or else replay the cosmic struggle of another text. Nintendo's sponsored compendium *Hyrule Historia* attempts to rectify the incongruent storylines into a comprehensive chronology, but so doing requires diverging from a central timeline, establishing multiple universes. In what appeared a flagrant disregard to establish a narrative coherency, *Breath of the Wild* confounded fans' attempts to position it within the serial chronology. Any discussion of the chronological linearity of *Zelda* raises unanswered questions: Are the individual characters Link and Zelda the same persons across games? Is it the same Hyrule kingdom in each story? Why don't the various geographies match? And why doesn't anyone else seemed concerned enough to resist Ganon?

The series resists readers' attempts to resolve the chronology issues; however, the same confusion encourages readers to view these stories mythologically. Mythology has long been a contentious term in academic and popular circles, but I cannot overstate the universal importance of mythology to literature. Hence, we can find in the medievalist J.R.R. Tolkien's discussion of fairy-stories and classicist C.S. Lewis's comments on Greek mythology a productive interpretation of *Zelda* mythology. The two began a dialogue on myth, debating the merit of myth in faith and philosophy. Each of them developed these early ideas into unique works of fiction and of interpretation, which remain highly influential in literature and Christian faith.

Tolkien, whose work preceded that of Lewis, predicted the forthcoming trend to give over literary interests to more social scientific research.[22] He pushed back by recognizing the basic human reactions to the powerful work of fairy tales. Tales of "Faërie" presented encounters of wonder and enchantment; a mere mortal suddenly thrust into the midst of Faërie would have an experience that by definition was extraordinary:

> The realm of fairy-story is wide and deep and high and filled with many things: all manner of beasts and birds are found there; shoreless seas and stars uncounted; beauty that is an enchantment, and an everpresent peril; both joy and sorrow as sharp as swords. In that realm a man may, perhaps, count himself fortunate to have wandered, but its very richness and strangeness tie the tongue of a traveller who would report them. And while he is there it is dangerous for him to ask too many questions, lest the gates should be shut and the keys lost forever.[23]

Tolkien uses Faërie as a means to represent the human need to step into a land steeped in wonder, and his language strongly approximates our description of intromersion in both space and time. In *space* because the description of Faërie suggests the presence of flora and fauna, lands and peoples that have yet to be encountered, drawing the reader into the text *in order to explore*. In *time* because the illusion of a history in the story presents a feel of agelessness, a timelessness that this land has existed beyond the count of men and will continue to do so. Tolkien in his moment in history was most familiar with the prose works of literature of his day: were we to translate his written descriptions for Faërie onto visual experiences, we would find ourselves neatly describing the effect of the best of videogames.

For example, *Breath of the Wild* challenged both designers and readers by pushing the sheer size of the world to be greater than any previous *Zelda* game. In it the reader walks, hikes, climbs, glides, rides, and teleports to various kingdoms that contain ruins, temples, villages, cities, and hinterlands occupied by predatory wildlife. The experience is intended to produce the same sense of wonder and exploration that Tolkien identified in Faërie. More extensively than other *Zelda* titles, *Breath of the Wild* included special elements that do not pertain to the primary narrative thread. For instance, several areas contain memorials to previous *Zelda* texts, suggesting a temporal longevity contributive to a sense of wonder and cohesion to the disparate texts of the series. Traveling bards point to lore from ages past (often established in past games). In one place, a small pond shadowed by a cherry tree is a site of wonder: On certain nights, a ghostly glowing stag appears. In another place, ethereal dragons ride upon the night breeze. The effect on the reader is to produce a sense that this land has existed for much longer and with various creatures who have inhabited it, and that the *reader*—being a wanderer—is the one out of place.

Tolkien closely links the fairy-story with myth and language, indicating that the power of myth lies in its ability for man to express "fantasy"—highly aesthetic and expressive language to craft a new form of reality—through an act he terms *sub-creation*.[24] That power of sub-creation, he affirms, is not in some vain effort at scientific reasoning before modern empirical methods but rather at crafting narrative that has a specific effect on its audience, a sense of being pulled into something *old* and *wonderful*.[25]

Tolkien and Lewis briefly quarreled about the usefulness of myth as an indicator of *truth*, and Tolkien's response, a poem entitled *Mythopoeia*, which gives this book its theme, asserted that myth was more than a contrast to truth (science): Myth allowed man to exercise his desire to create, an act of faith in imitation of his own Creator. The wonder inherent to (sub)creation was, we might suppose, an echo of man's original experience in the Garden of Eden. Eventually Lewis also began to champion myth as a story with more power than its immediate narrative significance. Myth provided a solution to the intellectual dilemma that we as humans cannot experience and reflect on experience simultaneously: "in the enjoyment of a great myth we come nearest to experiencing as a concrete what can otherwise be understood only as an abstraction."[26]

The power of myth and myth-building thus lies in its ability to establish an intromersive world of wonder, one in which we are compelled to enter, and in so doing we can discover an understanding extending beyond the immediate situation. The encounter with the other reveals our own façade; the decisions reached in the other world reveal our own thought processes. If this world is ergodic, then the revelations reached in the other world are tested in real time: If, once you enter this world, you come to understand yourself as *x*, will you confirm it by behaving like an *x* once given the choice?

The world of Hyrule certainly embodies some of the "higher mythology" Tolkien describes. Hyrule contains, but is not contained by, the Manichean struggle of Good and Evil of Zelda and Ganon. This central struggle is retold in various semi-parallel iterations, using recurring but not necessarily identical characters. But that returns us to the problem of linearity confusion: For if each text is an iteration of the same mythological struggle, how can they present a single linear narrative thread throughout the series?

I would suggest, following Tolkien and Lewis, this is the wrong question. For as myth is tied so closely to language (and in this case *language* includes the visual representation of event, the *opsis*, and not just the printed word), then the ebullient wonder of Faërie *requires* a variation in language to represent it adequately. Myth is revealed in the multitude of tellings, and the Truth, as Lewis suggests, can avoid falling into mere allegory or abstraction only if the tension of its language—of its sight and speech— ambiguously reveals and conceals its principles simultaneously. Put another way, myth reveals truth(s), but once revealed, it hides it (them) once again.

The nature of myth challenges notions of linearity. If we expect to find examples of historical chronology (following semiotic and formalist expectations) in literary narrative, myth disappoints, and the *Zelda* series lacks a "proper history" in its presentation. But the intromersive, wonder-esque nature of Hyrule suggests that returning to the central struggle and reading it as hints, allusions, and allegories of human truths establishes a decentered linearity that moves spirally. The careful attention to detail provides the reader a deliberate sense of narrative cohesion, which in turn presents an experienced linearity that allows the reader to re-engage with the mythological principles presented therein. Each text continues this pattern, but because they are not just revisions of the same story, the readings do not move circularly, but spirally, over the same mythological points but not at the same nodes. The details are the same *kinds* of details, but are not the same in their specifics.

The mythological spiral linearity of *Zelda* matches other common modern mythologies, such as our superhero narratives, which, when taken altogether, result in a confusing chronology due to the contributions of multiple graphic novel authors, directors, and actors over several generations. The various iterations of comic books, movies, television programs, books, and fan fiction move around and around the same points, but spirally over the same characters, events, and resolutions.[27]

So far, we have seen how mythology challenges our expectations of diegetic ludic linearity, and how spectacle and ergodism challenge our notion of extradiegetic linearity. The combination of the two produces an experience much more intimate than some other forms of literature. Now we come finally to the point where we can test this idea. If, as we say, the videogame reading experience is so highly personal, then we should be able to see it manifested in the concurrent experience of the reader and the spectator. I suggest that we can find this nowhere more poignantly expressed than in narrative moments of silence.

The Ludic Linearity and Extrapolative Silence

Since academic literature prioritized finding cohesive, linear narratives using intermittent information, one might understand why early videogames fell through the cracks of literary studies. The issue of linearity, as we have seen, derives from the complicated simultaneity of diegetic and extradiegetic narrativity through ergodic intromersion. Linearity can be difficult to decipher because readers are accustomed to being given explicit cause-effect events in the narrative, or units of information referred to as *lexia* in many theories of digital interpretation. In this case, a problem of finding linearity is not in the absence of information, *lexia*, or connective tissues, but in the surplus of it. When we consider, furthermore, the capability of multiple players to both experience and guide the narrative, we find it nearly impossible to trace a consistent narrative thread.

Zelda famously has never featured multi-player capability, but that does not much reduce the multiplicity of linearity possible in a game. Although a single reader *plays* the text, there is the possibility of another person *watching* the text, much as one might watch a film. And the rise of internet videos has facilitated a popular category of videos of plays-through.[28] The ergodic experience (mediated through the game controller) clearly separates the reader-player from the reader-spectator, and branches our discussion in two.

The reader-spectator experiences the text more like a film than a videogame, and as a result has less success achieving an intromersive engagement with the protagonist. The character of Link is always separate from the reader-spectator, whereas he is intimately associated with the reader-player. Since the videogame is structurally different from the film, especially in terms of pacing and characterization, watching a game can be tedious (a characteristic that is both revealed and avoided by the ability to skip forward in online videos).

The identification of the reader-player and reader-spectators challenges our understanding of audience and reveals the solitary nature of videogames. The reader-player is removed from their physical community (as least mentally) and virtually set into an intromersive environment, where they are encouraged to visualize themselves in the form of the avatar, to explore, and to reside. That process isolates the reader-spectator who can only observe this phenomenon. Therefore, if the ergodic and intromersive experiences of the reader-player and the reader-spectator differ, then we should expect the experience of linearity (both diegetic and extradiegetic) to vary. To demonstrate this, we may look at one particularly tedious moment of the videogame experience: the idling of the avatar.

Several videogames, including the *Zelda* series, program idle behavior for the avatar. That is, in moments when the reader-player is not actively controlling the avatar, the character features simple actions. Sometimes these are directed to the reader-player; sometimes they indicate boredom. For instance, sometimes Link as the avatar waves, yawns, lies down, shuffles, or swings a weapon. Horses paw the ground, fairies flit, boat-heads flex jaws. These are moments of narrative silence—moments when the plot is not developing, although the text is not paused, the reader-player continues to engage with the character. These moments of inactivity occur for various reasons involving the reader-player, but they resemble similar moments of tedium that occur whenever the reader-player has to travel to another point in the gameworld. This is particularly endemic to *Zelda* texts because they tend to avoid, at least for a period, fast travel systems that cut out sequences of simply moving from one point to another.

These moments create tedium for reader-spectators, precisely because there is no action, no development of the plot. In film production, these are the moments that are cut or edited into montage sequences, which provide information of repetitive and essential actions but without the redundancy or boredom of watching it unfold in real time or sacrificing the energy of the storytelling.

But for the reader-player, these moments of tedium can be exhilarating. The experience of moving across long distances and exploring new areas is part of the experience of encountering the intromersive Tolkienesque wonder of the fantasy world, and it becomes part of both the diegetic and extradiegetic narratives of the reader-player. Sitting still and remaining idle can often mirror the feelings of the reader-player, as well.

Time spent traveling, planning, or simply idling create moments of narrative (but not necessarily auditory) silence do not develop or advance the narrative thread. They provide critical moments to the experience of the game by elongating the linear structure of the narrative with small intimate moments wherein the character reflects feelings of the reader-player, like a mirror, back onto him, and in turn consequently allows the reader-player to reinforce an association of identity with the character. These moments of narrative silence are shared only between the reader-player and the text and confirms the reader's identification with the character. This space is therefore *extrapolative*, creating a discourse of reader and character while separating each from its context: the reader from his immediate environment (including other non-readers nearby) and the protagonist from its essential narrative thread. In the crucial moments of plot and characterization, therefore, the reader-player projects his identity into the narrative and creates an intromersive experience of both plot and spectacle through both time and space.

This is one of the defining elements of ludic texts. The moment of extrapolative silence does not distance the reader-player from the avatar, though it might for the reader-spectator. In *The Legend of Zelda*, the reader-player can spend intimate moments with the character. The reader-player stays with Link when he rides a horse, when he fishes, or when he goes to sleep or breaks pots. We appreciate the idle amusement of leaving the trail to explore some corner or new area of the map, confident of our chance to return to the essential narrative thread shortly. These moments create a period of narrative silence, a silence which reveals (extrapolates) the tension inherent in Spectacle of the real and the deceptive, the solitary spectator and the non-participant, the intromersion into the mythological.

The combination of Aristotelian spectacle with Tolkienesque mythopoeia through videogames highlights the bright future of videogames as literature. Despite the academic neglect of videogames as a significant and important source of new literary experiences, we can rest assured that videogames like *Zelda* reinvent pre-modern forms of storytelling to good effect. By highlighting elements such as intromersion, extrapolative silence, ergodic narrative, and mythological linearity, I believe we can more effectively recognize the elements that make videogames work as literary texts within the long history of reading, and trace new lines connecting digital media with other types of narrative both contemporaneous and historical.

Notes

1 This situation is evident by the example of the primary writing style handbooks which struggle to identify which essential elements to use in citations.
2 Espen Aarseth, *Cybertext: Perspectives in Ergodic Literature* (Baltimore, MD: Johns Hopkins University Press, 1997).
3 Espen Aarseth, "Nonlinearity and Literary Theory," in *The New Media Reader*, ed. Noah Wardrip-Fruin and Nick Montfort (Cambridge, MA: The MIT Press, 2003).
4 Jesper Juul, "Games Telling Stories: A Brief Note on Games and Narratives," *Game Studies* 1, no. 1 (July 2001).
5 See David Boffa's essay for a recent application of James Gee's argument.
6 The debate itself only existed because the literary cadre had effectively separately the idea of "game" and "story", despite the useful work of new media theorists like Huizinga, McLuhan, and Ong. Later, medieval scholars would question the distinction of "game" and "story" even further: medieval texts seem not to operate with that distinction.
7 Thomas Rowland, "'And Now Begins Our Game:' Revitalizing the Ludic Robin Hood," in *Robin Hood in Outlawed Spaces: Media, Performance, and Other New Directions*, ed. Lesley Coote and Valerie Johnson (Abingdon, UK: Routledge, 2016), 175–178.
8 Thomas Rowland, *Reading Games and Playing Stories: Intromersive Literary Spaces in the Long History of Reading,* Dissertation (Saint Louis University, 2014).
9 This systematizing effort has been attempted in *Hyrule Historia*.

10 The Aarne-Thompson Index attempted to identify specific themes in folklore and mythology, which themes could then be traced and compared across different cultures and corpora.

11 Matti Hyvärinen, "Towards a Conceptual History of Narrative," *The Travelling Concept of Narrative*, ed. Mari Hatavara, Lars-Christer Hyden, Matti Hyvarinen (Amsterdam, Netherlands: John Benjamins Publishing Company, 2013), 20.

12 "The feature that enables hypertext to "reconfigure narrative" on the discourse level is, evidently, the interactive nature, or ergodic dimension of the medium" states Marie-Laure Ryan in "Beyond Myth and Metaphor – The Case of Narrative in Digital Media," *Game Studies* 1, no. 1 (July 2001).

13 It is hard to overstate this phenomenon. Dated videogames are often shunned by readers because they appear ugly (often with *uncanny valley* problems), or are re-released with new high-definition graphics. Videogames as a mode of presentation have gone through radical growth spurts in three phases: genesis (late 1970s to the crash in the mid-1980s), adolescence (mid-1990s to around 2005), and ubiquity (since around 2005). Each wave barely resembles the previous as advances in technology allowed designers to radically redesign from the ground up, especially as new physics engines, such as Unreal Engine, Source, AnvilNext, Cryengine, and Unity were developed. New iterations of these engines significantly altered the look and visual sophistication of videogames.

14 Marie-Laure Ryan, *Narrative as Virtual Reality II* (Baltimore, MD: Johns Hopkins University Press, 2015). In this text she addresses the changing conventions of videogames which rendered her own previous book on the matter outdated, but surprisingly still managed to err on understanding the rising role of VR and physical interactions through systems like the Wii, which approximate VR experiences.

15 George Landow, *Hypertext 2.0 The Convergence of Contemporary Critical Theory and Technology* (Baltimore, MD: Johns Hopkins University Press, 1997); Michael Joyce, *Of Two Minds: Hypertext, Pedagogy, and Poetics* (Ann Arbor: University of Michigan Press, 1995); Janet Murray, *Hamlet on the Holodeck: The Future of Narrative in Cyberspace* (New York: The Free Press, 1997).

16 It is perhaps important to emphasize that Aristotle's ideas rarely leave our literary meditations, as seen in the French theatre of the 18th century, or in Neo-Aristotelianism of the 1920s, or in the New Critical approach exemplified by scholars like Wayne Booth more recently.

17 "Spectacle is the least artistic of all the parts, and has least to do with the art of poetry," Aristotle, *Poetics*, book 6 (1450b, 17–21) (pg. 232). See also the discussion in "Spectacle," Theories of Media online presentation, csmt. uchicago.edu/glossary2004/spectacle2.htm.

18 A third category, that of music (and we add sound effects), falls outside the scope of this essay and is better addressed by Vincent Rone in this volume.

19 We are frequently misled by declarations about "real stories", in the sense that a movie about Abraham Lincoln has a greater claim to authenticity because its protagonist actually existed in real life. The authenticity of stories is not based on their antecedent in living figures, a truth that ancient and medieval storytellers understood. Link's story is real not because someone named Link lived it once, but because it authentically engages its reader and brings him through the experience of identifying with the protagonist in the story. This statement describes another fundamental Aristotelian notion, that of *mimesis* in narrative.

20 Regarding the basic narrative, the game suggests around 20 hours to complete. To complete the extraneous activities, some users report spending
upwards of 100 hours.

21 To clarify: non-linear follows a sequence of events, but shuffles the events
outside of normal temporal expectations. Alinear entirely removes an expectation of a sequential events.

22 As evidenced in his landmark essay, "The Monsters and the Critics", in
which he identified the monsters as those who would mine the poem of *Beowulf* solely for worthwhile evidence of historical value, while ignoring its
primary effect as a piece of literature.

23 J.R.R. Tolkien, "On Fairy-Stories," *The Tolkien Reader* (New York, NY:
Ballantine Books, 1966), 33.

24 Tolkien, "On Fairy-Stories," 49.

25 Ibid., 56.

26 C.S. Lewis, "Myth Became Fact," in *God in the Dock*, ed. Walter Hooper
(Michigan: William B. Eerdmans Company, 1970), 66.

27 I am not ready to commit to the metaphor of a coiled spring as mythology,
but if we visualize many spiraling iterations of a *muthos* we do end up with
that kind of shape. This model of interpretation I have from studies of the
Book of Revelation, which tends to summarize the mythological reiteration
of historical circumstances happening repeatedly until the spring itself is
snapped by the reintroduction of Christ into history.

28 Admittedly this phenomenon, as well as the cinematic trope of arcade games
played in front of adoring fans, challenge the idea that viewers and readers
enjoy very different levels of engagement and satisfaction. But I believe these
experiences to be overhyped and significantly less common than the normal
tedium experienced by someone watching a videogamer at work, as many
significant others can attest.

3 *Curiositas* and Critical Glitches

Speedrunning *The Legend of Zelda*

Ethan Smilie

The *Zelda* series has drawn and continues to draw gamers for many reasons, not the least of which is its compelling mythic narrative. In an era of streaming platforms, such as Twitch, speedrunning—the pursuit of completing a game in a short as time as possible—also has become a significant means of generating knowledge and attracting interest in the series.[1] Speedrunners are among the most skilled and experienced players; their live broadcasts attract thousands of viewers and their videos even greater numbers of views. Nonetheless, the art of speedrunners—their skill and strategy—can pose an antithesis to the art of the *Zelda* games. Their techniques, analogous to those literary critics typically employ on texts and akin the vice of *curiositas* as defined by medieval thinkers, largely side-step the immersive aspects of the games and, therefore, often disrupt the narratives of the games, diminishing the wonder they can produce. Paradoxically, though, the artistry and skill of speedrunners invoke their own wonder in audiences and can, therefore, bring some part of Tolkienesque *Faërie* into the real world.

The processes and effects of the speedrunner ostensibly mirror those of the sort of critic J.R.R. Tolkien warns of in his essay "On Fairy-Stories." Tolkien begins his now-authoritative work by disclaiming his own authority, admitting "I have not studied [fairy-stories] professionally. I have been hardly more than a wandering explorer (or trespasser) in the land, full of wonder but not of information."[2] Indeed, Tolkien depicts the analysis of such stories as something of a dangerous quest for explorers/trespassers (whether they go alone or not), for critics may discover information about tales in general, but, in doing so, they may lose the wonder such tales produce.[3]

Tolkien then describes a key danger a critic encounters: the "rationalization" of fairy-stories, which anticipates speedrunning in its textual impact. Tolkien believed that rationalization of fairies occurred to some extent in England, where "fairy" was coming to mean merely "diminutive size" to account in narrative for the empirical imagination's inability to envision a space for such beings.[4] Ultimately, such rationalization "transformed the glamour of Elfland into mere finesse, and invisibility into a fragility that could hide in a cowslip or shrink behind a blade of grass."[5] However, one cannot rationalize or explain *Faërie* fully; it "cannot be caught in a net of words; for it is one of its qualities to be indescribable, though not imperceptible. It has many ingredients, but analysis will not necessarily discover the secret of the whole."[6] Though the fullest appreciation *Faërie* always contains non-rational elements that cannot be mined from a text, this fact does not prevent critics from seeking secrets—various facts—about stories, nor does it prevent them from thinking that they have indeed discovered "the secret of the whole."

In many ways, such illegitimate seeking of facts, of rationalizing fairy-stories or capitalizing on videogame glitch lore, recalls the medieval view of what we today call curiosity, which medieval thinkers termed *curiositas*. Today we generally regard "curiosity" as a virtue; indeed, curiosity is praised and fostered in school children. In the Middle Ages, philosophers, theologians, and poets classified *curiositas* as a vice. Augustine, Bernard of Clairvaux, and Thomas Aquinas, echoing pre-Christian warnings, defined *curiositas* as illicit intellectual pursuit, which could take a variety of forms.[7] *Curiosi* could seek knowledge of illicit objects of knowledge, including secrets or trivial and useless information. Moreover, whether licit or not, they pursue knowledge by illicit means, for instance—to use a Thomistic example—by means of conjuring demons.[8] Finally, *curiosi* pursue objects of knowledge for illicit ends: They could obtain knowledge in order to commit a sin—for example, by learning how to pick a lock to steal or, for the sake of pride, of boasting one's learning. Ultimately, knowledge in some way should increase our knowledge and love of God; seeking knowledge for any other end constitutes *curiositas*.

No doubt medieval thinkers would classify a good deal of contemporary literary criticism with its numberless books and articles about trivial concerns as *curiositas* (a charge that could be laid against this essay). The ends of literary criticism are not always pure, as some authors write for personal gain or glory through publication. Moreover, such ends are occasionally mercenary, at least to the extent that publications can lead to promotions and better academic positions. And, recalling Aquinas, critics rarely refer their knowledge to its due end—God. Or, as Augustine would put it, critics often enjoy (*frui*) our acts of criticism they should instead use (*uti*) as a means to enjoy the Trinity, and they seldom pursue scholarship for the sake of knowing and loving God to a greater degree.[9] In many cases critics do not even refer their knowledge to a more proximate end. Often scholarship focuses on the minutiae of a text, without any significant reference to the text as a whole and, consequently, destroys the wonder a text evokes. Speedrunners, I hope to show, encounter these same pitfalls.

Literary critics, and in an analogous way speedrunners, can avoid such pitfalls by means of a legitimate form of criticism, the sort that enables critics to experience more fully the wonder of a text—what Thomas terms *studiositas*.[10] "On Fairy-Stories," for many, has just this effect. It does not rationalize the mystery of fairy-stories, and Tolkien's analysis leads to a greater appreciation and wonder of its subject. Tolkien, thus, inquires into the origins of fairy-stories with the goal of pursuing other wonder-instilling explorations into the origins of stories *per se*, of language, of the mind. Ultimately, this sort of intellectual pursuit refers the acquired knowledge to God. As Tolkien indicates at the end of his essay, this sort of criticism can help us to discover the "joy" that is "the mark of the true fairy-story" or "the seal upon it" and better recognize the fairy tale quality—the *eucatastrophe*—God has written into creation.[11]

Tolkien explains that in such investigation, critics can examine the "many elements in fairy-stories" to great benefit including comparing motifs across cultures, provided they avoid such *curiositas*.[12] However, one can study all these elements "without tackling [the] main question" of origin. According to Tolkien, the *curiosi* studying fairy-stories in a rationalizing or "scientific" manner use "the stories not as they were meant to be used, but as a quarry from which to dig evidence, or information, about matters in which they are interested. A perfectly legitimate procedure in itself—but ignorance or forgetfulness of the nature of a story (as a thing told in its entirety) has often led such inquirers into strange judgments."[13] Such judgments result from criticism devolving into curious analysis and losing sight of the bigger pictures, including the fairy-stories themselves, the origins of those stories, and the origin of the fairy-story of God's creation. By not referring objects of knowledge to God, curious critics cut themselves off from the Creator of creators. Necessarily, then, the knowledge gained from a given site of inquiry will be limited, skewed, one-sided, and it will no longer invoke wonder: The *curiosi* may observe, for instance, that *Beowulf* contains elements found in a number of Norse myths but fail to be awestruck by the hero's magnificence.[14]

Tolkien makes two analogous points about the wonder-destroying effects of curious scholarship. The first occurs during his discussion about the suitability of fairy-stories for children. Whereas children are likely to *read* them, Tolkien observes that some adults will *study* them as curios.[15] Children, who so easily find things wonderful, are not nearly as susceptible to *curiositas* as some jaded adults. Tolkien's discussion of magic in "On Fairy-Stories" also illuminates the potential for criticism to destroy wonder. Magic, Tolkien explains, "is not an art but a technique; its desire is in this world, domination of things and wills."[16] Curious critics, instead of wondering at a text, often dominate and abuse it, transforming it into a vehicle to advance an ideology not clearly relevant to the text. As suggested above, critics can exhibit the magician's "greed for self-centered power," working their magic on texts for mercenary reasons or for the sake of self-aggrandizement.[17] The actions and skills of both magicians and curious critics are antithetical to wonder; one is interested in the discovery facts, the other in producing them, both for their own power, and both can destroy "the primal desire at the heart of Faërie: the realization, independent of the conceiving mind, of imagined wonder."[18]

As essays in this volume argue, games in the *Zelda* series can lead one into *Faërie* just as a text can. These games at their best fully immerse gamers into an imaginary, wonderful world.[19] As such, the identity of gamers merge with that of Link via the narrative, abetted by the spectacle of sight, sound, and the gamer's ability to write, at least in a small part, some of the narrative by their decisions. Typically, gamers become more skilled as they play. Just as Philip Sidney claims that poetry leads to the "enriching of memory, enabling of judgment, and enlarging of conceit," gameplay produces the same effects.[20] So, it is unsurprising that games usually increase in their difficulty as one proceeds through them. Literary critics can progress in an analogous fashion: Their increased familiarity and experience with a text should lead to increased, more significant insight. Yet as expertise increases, so does the temptation of *curiositas*, searching for minutiae to overcome the possible contempt of an overly familiar text. Pride, too, can result, as one's mastery of a text can produce a desire to boast.

I contend that some of the most expert gamers of the *Zelda* series—speedrunners—tend to exhibit the traits possessed by curious critics and Tolkien's "laborious, scientific, magician[s]." As such, they can miss the forest for the trees and loss a sense of wonder of the game's narrative, as the techniques remove them from the immersive game experience. That speedrunners are experts in the games they play is not difficult to establish. These gamers exemplify Malcolm Gladwell's dictum that it takes 10,000 hours of committed practice to achieve mastery of a skill. Indeed, many of the speedrunners have logged their time—during online streams—of their gameplay. More commonly, they tally their number of attempts that they have played a game to reach a certain goal. Not uncommonly, these tallies number in the 10,000 or 20,000 range or beyond. For example, the current world records for *The Legend of Zelda* and *Ocarina of Time* were set, respectively, on the 15,840th and 11,740th attempts of the holders.[21] Consequently, top speedrunners can in a matter of minutes complete games that typically require 40 or more hours to finish.[22]

To achieve such mastery of the game, speedrunners scientifically examine games similar to how curious critics examine texts. Just as the latter scour texts for tensions, contradictions, and ambiguities, speedrunners scour games for glitches. In both texts and games, such loci can be exploited to the discoverer's advantage—critics can make a novel claim, speedrunners a new time-saving strategy. Additionally, their motivations can be equally suspect: One may seek to discover a new glitch or strategy for the sake self-aggrandizement, beating an opponent or setting a new world record. Regardless of the intentions of speedrunners, the same type of negative effect can occur as does with curious critics: Speedrunners can lose sight of the wonder-producing narrative of the game.

Speedrunning tends to destroy the wonder of a game because, by the nature of its strategies, it eliminates the time and space in which a game's immersive narrative exists. The quest to beat a game as quickly as possible renders the story an enemy. Although immersive games like those of the *Zelda* series ideally allow players to escape from what Tolkien calls Primary World into the Secondary World, speedrunners strive to remain as much as possible in the Primary World, the clock of which is usually very visibly ticking onscreen. For instance, Thomas Rowland argues that the "alinearity" of *Zelda* is key to the "intromersive" experience of the player.[23] Anthony G. Cirilla likewise has shown how the heroic progression of Link "allows for a transformative synthesis of the player's imagination with the story's *Faërie* perspective."[24] Examining the immersive aspects of games, Katie Salen and Eric Zimmerman observe that they can "sensually transport the participant into an illusory, simulated reality... so complete that ideally the frame falls away so that the player truly believes that he or she is part of an imaginary world."[25] Mark Hayse has further suggests that, as both the player and Link grow in skill and prowess throughout the game, "The experience of Link and the player can be described as a shared journey of self-transcendence."[26] Speedrunners, however, attempt to evade the game's immersive features.

In order to more fully immerse gamers, game designers, Rowland observes, utilize elements such as large, wide-open maps "so that readers will seek out prolonged experiences with the text" and provide gamers "with multiple options for pursuing different goals."[27] While making the case for the pedagogical usefulness of games, Sasha A. Barab, Melissa Gresalfi, and Adam Ingram-Goble argue "games are transactive, enlisting narrative story lines and interactive rule sets that support a dynamic (transactional) unity of person, content, and context in which all are transformed through participation."[28] They also note, however, that "merely playing a game does not ensure that one is engaged in transformation play" but involves, among other things, "taking on the role of a protagonist."[29] While the most obvious means of narrative immersion comprise visual spectacle and player interactivity, other elements including sound and music contribute to the same effect.[30]

Speedrunners avoid feelings of nostalgia, assuming the protagonist's role, and the wide-open spaces conducive to immersion but that take far too much time to traverse. Speedrunners cannot allow aimless, nonessential wandering in their singled-minded drive to complete the quest as soon as possible. As such, alinearity and protagonist-identification are undesirable, detracting Siren's songs to the speedrunner. Instead, the speedrunner is on a hyperlinear, often truncated path to the end of the narrative. In a speedrun, players calculate every input and make no room for the "narrative moments of silence" and assuming the role of the hero.[31] Speedrunners never lose sight of the frame, for they strive to break out of it as soon as possible.

In an attempt to complete a game as quickly as possible, speedrunners violently disrupt narratives in various ways. David Snyder notes, a speedrunner's "route has no sense of story continuity nor duty to plot."[32] Rainforest Scully-Blaker likewise explains, "speedrunners do not relate to games in the same ways [typical] players do."[33] Speedrunning is "deconstructive" in that it "dismantles narrative boundaries by transgressing both the literal narrative and the narrative implied by the design of the gamespace....The player arguably 'does violence' to the narrative contained within the gamespace and finds a narrative for himself."[34] Besides completing a game as quickly as possible, speedrunners have also established dozens of other categories of competition (all of which, nonetheless, are embarked upon in the fastest possible way). For all categories, the time stops with the last of the player's input in a controller. Hence, the game ends with the last action of the player, not with the denouement after the defeat of Ganon. Speedrunners disrupt a game's narrative in all categories, some examples of which follow:[35]

> 100%: Since this category requires speedrunners to complete the narrative ending of the game while completing tasks and acquiring items typically necessary to do so, it retains the most immersive qualities. However, 100% speedruns skip over actions and items that have been designated as "non-essential" for fully completing the game by the speedrunning community. Speedrunners may, for instance, skip over an earlier item that would typically be replaced later by a superior item. For example, they may obtain a magic boomerang but not the standard version, the longshot, not the hookshot, etc.
>
> Any%: This category is the quickest possible way to beat the game. For instance, speedrunners can beat *Ocarina of Time* in under seventeen minutes. Consequently, these speedruns are highly destructive of the game's narrative.
>
> Low%: In this category, the speedrunners beat the game by obtaining as few items as possible. They cannot obtain items not necessary to beat the game. In *Ocarina of Time*, this means that many items (such as heart containers) and upgrades (such as double magic) cannot be obtained.
>
> Ganonless: This is a category in *Ocarina of Time* in which speedrunners exploit a glitch that cues the credits of the game without having to complete the final narrative action of defeating Ganon.
>
> Swordless: This is a category used in the first *Zelda* game, in which the speedrunner cannot obtain a sword. Hence, the game

cannot even be completed; instead, the timer stops when Link enters Ganon's chamber.

Miscellaneous Categories: There are a number of other various categories that do not complete a game's narrative. Instead, only certain actions must be accomplished and/or items gained in order to complete the run. In *Ocarina of Time*, for instance, there are the following categories: All Gold Skulltulas, All Fairy Rewards, All Medallions, All Songs, All Chests, All Child Dungeons, Reverse Dungeon Order, All Cows (obtain Epona's song and milk all 16 cows), Loach % (catch the Hylian Loach).

Glitchless: All of the above allow for the use of glitches—no holds barred—but there are glitchless categories. Even so, many (so called "non-essential") narrative elements are skipped in this category as well.

Additionally, speedrunners often compete in two categories of racing utilizing many of the same techniques, rather than: randomizer races and bingo races:

Randomizer races: This method of playing the game requires altering the game's code, such that what lies behind an entrance differs from that which appears in the original code.[36] For instance, in the original NES game, the first door that leads to a room where Link receives his wooden sword could lead to Level 7, a shop, the money-making game, etc. Speedrunners often race against one another in this category, which adds new challenges to a possibly too familiar game. Necessarily, the random relocation of elements lends itself to a non-linear, incomprehensible narrative. But this fact is irrelevant to speedrunners; after all, the goal is to defeat Ganon as soon as possible. Replacing Link's avatar with those of other characters, including those of *Zelda* and of enemies, is a particularly narrative-destroying aspect of randomizer races.

Bingo Races: These races constitute another popular type of race for speedrunners. Typically, twenty-five accomplishments—items gained, locations unlocked, bosses defeated—are randomly placed on what looks like a (electronic) bingo card. Players win by completing five tasks that comprise a bingo or in a game of blackout all of them. In *Ocarina of Time*, a winning row might look like this: defeat King Dodongo, collect all four Lon-Lon Ranch area Skulltulas, collect the Goron Tunic, obtain three swords and three pairs of boots, and win the Bombchu Bowling Prize. Obviously, such races destroy the game's narrative and rarely does a competitor, even one winning a blackout, complete the game.

To accomplish any of the above feats (except for glitchless runs) as quickly as possible, skilled speedrunners use a number of glitches. These glitches sometimes take years to discover and require analysis of the game's code. Speedrunners share knowledge and suggestions in community forums, produce and study tutorial videos, and test theorized glitches. Accidental time-saving discoveries occur frequently. Speedrunners practice new glitches endlessly, often with the help of emulators, which allow players to practice a specific skill repetitively. Though by no means conjuring demons (as Thomas warned against), speedrunners conjure aberrant means unintended for gameplay. Akin to the laborious, scientific, magical literary critics, speedrunners mine curios from the game for the sake of mastery. Though they are "immersed" in parts of the games, players practicing these strategies and techniques regard narrative as at best irrelevant and at worst an obstacle to their gameplay.

In games like *Ocarina of Time*, the most time-saving techniques and glitches skip the narrative-dense scenes, times, and places, including, as mentioned above, the concluding scenes of the game, for the timer stops with the player's last input. Indeed, spectacle loses its role in aiding the wonder produced by narrative, becoming a tool instead. Rarely does the game's "regenerative counter-space" instill astonishment, curiosity, and terror in speedrunners.[37] Though speedrunners do pay excessively close attention to sight, sound, and music, they do so for the sake of visual and audio cues indicating when they should produce certain controller inputs to execute glitches. Speedrunners are immersed in the game but not the story. Though they keenly observe those elements aiding their goals, these goals lie outside the game's narrative. When discussing the importance of internal consistency in Secondary Worlds, and consequently *Zelda*, Philip Tallon notes, "glitches in video game play, stemming from bugs in the code or an incomplete system of rules and rewards, shatters the world of the game, annoying the players, perhaps causing them to quit."[38] For speedrunners, however, the prospect of further shattering the game's world motivates their continued play.

In contrast to typical players who emulate Tolkien's ideal reader who experiences wonder and avoids asking too many questions, speedrunners resemble the magicians Tolkien critiques. James Ash asserts, "Videogame users do not achieve a sense of mastery and control over the space [of a game]; they are encouraged to lose themselves in the space through the proxy of their avatar."[39] Ash further notes that gamers typically do not notice spatial limitations when enmeshed in the narrative and spectacle of the game; ultimately, those he studied "did not exhibit a detached mastery over the space; they were actively shaped by it."[40] Speedrunners clearly perform the opposite; they are masters of the game by actively shaping it. Expanding on Tim Rogers's distinction between a "player" and "gamer," Seb Franklin states,

> The gamer looks to explore every possibility within the game world, and as Rogers significantly notes, this is because he does not only

"think within" this world, which would entail the completion of only essential components of the story [as does the "player"], but considers every statistical possibility as a component of the game, irrespective of impact on its plot or completion. The speedrunner, in contrast to both player and gamer, thinks the game world from outside the technology, or rather sees the technical makeup of the game, both interface and code, as part of the overall diegesis. The speedrunner sees the game as coded space, not only seeking every conventional diegetic possibility, but every exploit that is achievable through the game's standard control interface and that can redefine the possibilities of gameplay.[41]

In the rigorous pursuit of quickly completing games and consequently abandoning their narratives, speed runners are, as Kaitlin Elizabeth Hilburn observes, engaging in "transformative play."[42] In a similar fashion, Kristina Drzaic and Peter Rauch analyze the play of speedrunners by applying Roger Callois's distinction between *ludus* and *paidia*. *Ludus* entails "following the designed rules of the game" in pursuit of "the ultimate game goal."[43] In contrast, with *paidia* players create "their own game rules and goals and [play] outside of the game's story, and outside the moral structure of that story....The player can even be described as aspiring to godhood, since she is not merely playing with Link, but with every element of the game."[44] Speedrunners typically eschew *ludus* for *paidia*, and, like Tolkien's scientific "magician," they seek to dominate and abuse the narrative and rules of the game. Drzaic and Rauch claim,

> often, *paidia* goals involve doing things the designers did not even intend to be possible. Unsurprisingly, the *paidia* game—which, after all, requires a great deal more time, skill, creativity, and dedication than the *ludus* game—is considered to be a more elite form of play by many gamers. In gaming culture, secrets are equated with mastery: the more (and better) secrets, the better the player.[45]

As such, speedrunners perform feats with games analogous to those Tolkien describes scientific "magicians" as performing on texts. Drzaic and Rauch argue, "the path intended by the designers is merely a starting point, too easy and not secretive enough to generate true esteem among elite players,"[46] so speedrunners and "magicians" may also share intentions, especially self-aggrandizement.

The masterful feats of speedrunners disrupt narrative and diminishes wonder. For example, Snyder, in his overview of speedrunning, notes that because of common techniques such as "the use of awkward camera angles to reduce lag, and skips and shortcuts that render much of the plot irrelevant, speedrunning can seem like an irreverent way to play games.

White knuckle boss battles are reduced to anti-climactic instant TKOs."[47] *Zelda* speedrunners utilize a variety of narrative disrupting techniques and glitches. For instance, speedrunners of *Ocarina of Time* prefer to use a Japanese version of the game because, during cut scenes with dialogue, the Japanese text takes less time to scroll onto the screen than English characters. Hence, for non-Japanese speakers, comprehension of narrative is severely limited. Regardless of language, when naming the avatar, *Ocarina* speedrunners will use a name comprised of a sole textual character, as each character takes a fraction of a second to appear in the dialogue box, consequently limiting the player's identification with the protagonist. Glitches common to many *Zelda* games allow Link to perform feats such as walking through walls, crossing other boundaries without the boons typically required to do so, warp (without a warp whistle or ocarina) in space and time, moving very quickly and jumping higher (without special boots), and producing more damage with weaker weapons.

In learning to execute such feats, speedrunners master their skills by reading advice posted on specialized websites and watching live and recorded video of skilled speedrunners. Often, they utilize emulators for learning, practicing, and discovering glitches. Recordings of tool-assisted speedruns (TAS) also aid in their study. TAS creators produce these speedruns via computer to input commands at rates and times impossible for human to achieve. Thus, TAS videos show the limit of a game's completion time by illuminating new possible glitches. Even with the aid of computer, these runs take enormous amounts of time and study. As speedrunners continue to improve, their times reduce closer to the best possible TAS times. Scully-Blaker notes that deconstructive runs among top runners "show that speedrunning is continually narrowing the list of ludic feats that can only be seen in a TAS."[48] Indeed, Franklin's account of TAS videos shows the similarities between their production and the process of top speedrunners as they optimize their play: "Ironically, for a practice that ultimately involves the fastest possible completion of a game, the production of a high-quality run is an extremely slow and painstaking process, involving reverse engineering and the close examination of source code and algorithms followed by the assembly of sequences, often frame-by-frame."[49]

Although speedruns tend to deconstruct a game's narrative, a speedrunner's feats provide a narrative for the speedrunner. Drzaic and Rauch rightly note that masterful players' "strange and varied accomplishments have no narrative meaning in the gameworld, nor do they have moral meaning: Link cannot be said to be a good person for achieving them."[50] Nonetheless, speedrunners are lauded for achieving them. Thousands watch the best speedrunners. They become the spectacle, heroes of their own stories external to the games. Viewers do not watch livestreams and videos of world-record runs and attempts (or even just players practicing) for the sake of the game's narrative. They tune in to see the quest of speedrunners, to see if they can set a new world record by executing a series of seemingly impossible tasks. Speedrunners become heroes, able to accomplish through glitches feats that Link should only be able to accomplish after legitimately earning boons during his quest. As Hilburn observes about speedrunning *Ocarina of Time*, "instead of venturing through Hyrule on a series of quests, the Link in this speedrun narrative warps straight to the end, fighting the final boss in a matter of minutes. Yet, the tension and challenge of beating the game feels just as gripping, especially among longtime fans of the game."[51] Snyder similarly describes the experience of watching a speedrun: "The tension of whether a runner will nail a difficult trick builds over the course of a run, and in the last minutes this pressure boils over as runners must perform perfectly, over and over again, and do so better than ever before if they hope to obtain a world record."[52] The "heroic" quality of speedrunners accounts for the fact their gameplay is an exception to the rule Rowland identifies concerning the boredom typically experienced by audiences of gameplay.[53] The viewer cares not (as does the casual gamer) whether *Link* will accomplish the required feats but whether the speedrunners can accomplish their required feats. Speedrunners journey on quests for a personal best times or world records, and the viewer watches with anticipation whether they can do so by means of magical feats (glitches).

Speedrunners become the heroes of their own narratives, documented cinematically during live streams and archived videos. Henry Lowood has chronicled the history of machinima, noting that early speedrunning of *DOOM* and *Quake* was instrumental in producing this "new narrative medium."[54] Speedrunners exemplify "the metamorphosis of the player into a performer" and "competitive play into theatrical play."[55] Machinima makers, "beginning as players...found that they could transform themselves into actors, directors and even 'cameras' to make...animated movies."[56] Utilizing the work of Lowood, Gabriel Menotti cautions us not to classify TAS speedruns as cinematic but as "non-narrative machinima."[57] Nonetheless, in the case of live-steaming and recorded videos of speedruns there is a narrative present, though external to the game's. After all, in most cases the speedrunner's face (and sometimes hands and controller) is prominently displayed on screen with a timer and splits (and sometimes simultaneous footage of his or her personal best run) along with the live footage of the game. As Hilburn describes, this display is a type of performative, transformative play:

> Speedrunning a video game, which involves attempting to complete a game in the shortest amount of time, might sound obsessive or isolating, but this overlooks the inherently performative and communal nature of playing video games. Speedrunning emphasizes

high performance play, working to add these additional player-made challenges in order to re-create the initial satisfaction of beating a game. However, arguably much of the satisfaction of these additional challenges comes from sharing and performing for a community.[58]

The audience has a fairly clear idea of at least the maximum amount of time a particular run will take, for speedrunners often display times and splits from previous runs. Additionally, the majority of runs among top speedrunners end early due to their making mistakes. But such mistakes themselves are part of the spectacle. Viewers tune in to see how far a speedrunner can go, which glitches and strategies he or she can execute and which will ruin ("RIP") runs. And when viewers have regularly watched speedrunners and have seen them practice glitches and attempt countless runs, they know the speedrunners' strengths and weaknesses, which allows for moments of suspense and expectation during the run. Viewers are thus engaged in narrative spectacle, but it is not the game's. When successful, speedrunners become something like the legendary Link, and their narrative can even eclipse his in evoking wonder.

Speedrunning, like critical inquiry, is a double-edged sword. Whereas wandering through a wide-open map can facilitate immersion and increase the wonder of its mythos, wandering through a game's minutiae (and code) can destroy narrative as can the curious seeking of the literary critic. Snyder concludes his book on speedrunning with this warning: a game can be

> ripped open and revealed for what it really [is], a computer program. The same dull collection of algebra that calculates a company's payroll. With enough prodding the immersive video game worlds we grew up exploring become nothing more than a collection of ones and zeroes. Speedrunners take a brilliant, electric magic show and peek behind the curtain, desperate to know the magician's secrets. This curiosity is natural, but if we want video games to thrill and surprise us as they did when we were children maybe it's better not to know all the tricks.[59]

What, then, should we make of the value of speedrunning games in the *Zelda* series, which attracts countless viewers? At their worst, speedrunners murder to dissect, and as Gandalf warns, "he that breaks a thing to find out what it is has left the path of wisdom."[60] At best, they are a means of drawing new audiences to the games and ultimately their narratives. After all, even a bowdlerized Disney version of a fairy tale or a critical analysis of minutiae of a tale might lead a viewer or reader to a renewed, wonderful experience of the real thing. Speedrunners' prowess can attract new players to the games, novices who may yet be transported to wander, and thus wonder, through Hyrulean *Faërie* and catch a glimpse of the universal *eucatastrophe*. Any other wonder speedrunners evoke will be external to the narrative of the games, whether that is instilling wonder in viewers by means of the skill and beauty of a speedrun or themselves experiencing wonder at the inner workings and glitches of a game. That is, both speedrunners and their audiences can refer their seemingly minute and often obscure objects of knowledge to their due end, God: Critical glitches can foster the *studiositas* described by Thomas. Though it employs tactics and goals largely conducive to *curiositas*, speedrunning *Zelda* can nonetheless produce the intuitive perception of *eucatastrophe*.

Notes

1 The *Zelda* series, especially *Ocarina of Time*, has been vital in promoting interest in speedrunning. It is likely that the most watched speedruns are those of *Ocarina of Time* performed by a speedrunner known formerly as Cosmo (now known as Narcissa) in 2013 and 2014. The most detailed discussion of speedrunning is David Snyder, *Speedrunning: Interviews with the Quickest Gamers* (Jefferson, NC: McFarland, 2017). Synder presents a history of speedrunning, an overview of typical speedrunning processes (glitches, the use of emulators, speedrunning categories, timing methods, community involvement), and interviews with some of the most-watched speedrunners.
2 J.R.R. Tolkien, "On Fairy-Stories," in *The Tolkien Reader* (New York, NY: Ballantine, 1966), 3.
3 Ibid.
4 Ibid., 4.
5 Ibid., 6.
6 Ibid., 10.
7 Thomas, as he is synthesizing earlier thinking on *curiositas*, offers the most convenient and concise account of the vice. See *Summa Theologiae* II–II, q. 167.
8 Often Ganondorf and his minions involve themselves in such necromantic activities (often, where his minions are concerned, *Ganon* is the demon being summoned). One could thus read evil in *Zelda* as *curiosi* who glitch the gameworld from the inside, where speedrunners do it externally.
9 For Augustine's distinction between *frui* and *uti*, see *de doctrina christiana* I.2–4.
10 For Thomas's discussion of *studiositas*, see *Summa Theologiae* II–II, q. 166.
11 Tolkien, 70.
12 Ibid., 17.
13 Ibid., 18.
14 Cf. Tolkien's "Beowulf: The Monsters and the Critics."
15 Ibid., 33.
16 Ibid., 53.
17 Ibid.
18 Ibid., 14.
19 See also Tallon, 47–69. Tallon identifies "childish wonder"—"*the wonder of exploration, the discovery of new worlds*" as the animating principle of *Zelda*, which occupies a portion of the "secondary world" of Faërie.
20 Philip Sidney, *The Defense of Poesy*, in *Classic Writings on Poetry*, ed. William Harmon (New York, Columbia University Press, 2003), 124.
21 These records were current as of 20 August 2019, on speedrun.com.

22 Tallon, 62, argues that the "escape" Tolkien observes fairy tales provide is equally afforded by videogames like *Zelda* but that such escape is a double-edged sword: "Though many hours of joyful escape often are opened up through videogames like *Zelda*, any honest gamer knows the feeling of 'desertion,' abandoning duties for more play. No matter the age, desertion of duty, large and small, happen for the avid gamer: skipping class, dodging chores, neglecting family, or even neglecting other pleasures (good food, outdoors, reading books)—all for the sake of 'more.'" Such "desertion" was considered a detrimental effect of *curiositas* by medieval thinkers. For the best example of this, see Dante's portrayal of Ulysses, who neglects his family in order to seek out knowledge to which he is not privy (*Inferno* 26).

23 See Rowland's contribution to this volume.

24 From Cirilla's contribution to this volume.

25 Katie Salen and Eric Zimmerman, *Rules of Play: Game Design Fundamentals* (Cambridge, MA: The MIT Press, 2003), 450.

26 Mark Hayse, "The Mediation of Transcendence within *The Legend of Zelda: The Wind Waker*," in *The Legend of Zelda and Theology*, ed. Jonathan L. Walls (Los Angeles: Gray Matter Books), 90.

27 From Rowland's contribution to this volume.

28 Sasha A. Barab, Melissa Gresalfi, and Adam Ingram-Goble, "Transformational Play: Using Games to Position Person, Content, and Context," *Educational Researcher* 39, no. 7 (2010): 525.

29 Ibid., 526.

30 See included in this volume Vincent E. Rone, for instance, who examines how the nostalgic effects of music enhance the immersive mythic qualities of *Twilight Princess*.

31 From Rowland's contribution to this volume.

32 Snyder, 29.

33 Rainforest Scully-Blaker, "A Practiced Practice: Speedrunning Through Space with de Certeau and Virilio," *Game Studies: The International Journal of Computer Game Research* 14, no. 1 (2014), http://gamestudies.org/1401/articles/scullyblaker.

34 Ibid. In contrast to "deconstructive," Scully-Blaker defines a "finesse" speedrun as one that completes a game speedily while it follows the narrative of the game.

35 The best source for rules, routes, and records for each category is speedrun.com, which contains such information about not only all of *The Legend of Zelda* series, but also hundreds of other games.

36 Speedrunning and races are by no means the only reasons hackers alter a game's code. The multitudinous uses of Game Genie codes suggest as much. An interesting example of the purposes and effects of code alteration is *Hack 'n' Slash*, a *Zelda* inspired game that requires altering code to win, or, as the developers put it, "The only way to win is not to play...by the rules!" www.hacknslashthegame.com/.

37 See Farca, Lehner, and Navarro-Remesal's contribution to this volume for "regenerative counter-space."

38 Tallon, 59.

39 James Ash, "Teleplastic Technologies: Charting Practices of Orientation and Navigation in Videogaming," *Transactions of the Institute of British Geographers*, New Series 35, no. 3 (2010): 419.

40 Ibid., 423–424.

41 Seb Franklin, "On Game Art, Circuit Bending and Speedrunning as Counter-Practice: 'Hard' and 'Soft' Nonexistence," *Resetting Theory* (2009), https://journals.uvic.ca/index.php/ctheory/article/view/14760/5632.

See Tim Rogers, "The Literature of the Moment: A Critique of Mother 2," https://web.archive.org/web/20131022032055/http://www.largeprime numbers.com/article.php?sid=mother2.

42 Kaitlin Elizabeth Hilburn, "Transformative Gameplay Practices: Speedrunning through Hyrule," (M.A. Thesis, University of Texas at Austin, 2017), 31, https://repositories.lib.utexas.edu/bitstream/handle/2152/62782/HILBURN-MASTERSREPORT-2017.pdf?sequence=1&isAllowed=y

43 Kristina Drzaic and Peter Rauch, "Slave Morality and Master Swords: *Ludus* and *Paidia* in *Zelda*," in *The Legend of Zelda and Philosophy: I Link, Therefore I Am*, ed. Luke Cuddy (Chicago: Open Court, 2008), 70.

44 Ibid., 70–71.

45 Drzaic and Rauch, 71.

46 Ibid.

47 Snyder, 10.

48 Scully-Blaker.

49 Franklin. See Manuel Lafond, "The Complexity of Speedrunning Video Games," 2018. 9th International Conference on Fun with Algorithms 27 (2018): 1–27. Lafond details the "profound algorithmic problem"—in an extremely technical fashion—of optimizing speedrunning techniques such as damage boosting and routes.

50 Drzaic and Rauch, 71.

51 Hilburn, 39–40.

52 Synder, 11.

53 See Rowland's contribution to this volume.

54 Henry Lowood, "High-Performance Play: The Making of Machinima," *Journal of Media Practice* 7, no. 1 (2006), 25.

55 Ibid., 30, 34.

56 Ibid., 26.

57 Gabriel Menotti, "Videorec as Gameplay: Recording Playthroughs and Video Game Engagement," *Game: The Italian Journal of Game Studies* 1, no. 3 (2014): 83–85.

58 Hilburn, 38–9.

59 Snyder, 228.

60 J.R.R. Tolkien, *The Fellowship of the Ring*, 2nd ed. (Boston, MA: Houghton Mifflin), 272.

The Legend of Zelda
Entrance into Mythopoeic Structure

4 The Hero of Faërie

The Triforce and Transformational Play in Link's Mythopoeic Journey

Anthony G. Cirilla

Nintendo's strategy guide to *Ocarina of Time* (*OoT*) states,

> Much of Hylian lore has faded with the passing of years, but one story that still shines bright is *The Legend of Zelda*.... Link always seemed destined to be a hero.... his fate was bound to the fate of the Triforce.[1]

This opening assertion interprets the player's gameplay as Link in terms of the hero's journey. Joseph Campbell argues that the heroic journey's mythic sequence is required to join the audience's psychology to the symbolic significance of any literary structure. *OoT* awakens the player's imagination to Link's version of the hero's journey by communicating concepts of power, wisdom, and courage through fairy-tale worldbuilding, so that the player can experience transformational play when performing the hero's journey of the avatar.

Barab, Gresalfi, and Ingram-Goble provide the paradigm deployed here for understanding how videogames "are a powerful medium that curriculum designers can use to create narratively rich worlds for achieving educational goals."[2] According to their model, videogames offer the opportunity for "transformational play," where players adopt "the role of a protagonist who must employ conceptual understandings to transform a problem-based fictional context and transform the player as well."[3] Link and the player become united through the handheld controller's interface; thus, character-avatar and player *together* constitute the "person with intentionality" of the game. This person of intentionality seeks to embody and protect the values encapsulated by the Triforce. The game thus has as well the third aspect of videogames that targets transformational play, a built in "content with legitimacy," making necessary "the application of academic concepts" (power, wisdom, and courage in this case), in order for players to "resolve the game-world dilemmas."[4]

Zelda's status as a fairy-tale may seem to undermine its capacity to teach "content with legitimacy." Tolkien's *On Fairy-Stories* provides the framework for perceiving how the gameworld communicates concepts of power, wisdom, and courage to the player's imagination through a journey of authentic transformation by means of the Faërie atmosphere suffusing gameplay. As conceived by Tolkien, Faërie is a literary experience constituting an epistemic posture toward the self's relationship to the world. As I argue, in *OoT* the player-avatar dyad becomes incorporated into this Faërie perspective, and so learns that to be a hero of Faërie is to make oneself subject to the effects of sub-creative imagination. This process allows players to identify more deeply with Link's Hyrulean value system, most tightly codified in the Triforce talisman.

To establish the Triforce as the game's "content with legitimacy," the first section of this chapter discusses the overall structure of *OoT* as it manifests Link's in-world development of power, wisdom, and courage. The second section examines how *OoT*'s Faërie aesthetic produces the game's "context with consequentiality," while the third gives a localized analysis of Link's Deku Tree quest in terms of how the hero's journey elements of the sequence integrate the player into the avatar's intentionality. This tripartite analysis provides insight into how the player potentially transforms through gameplay into a participant in Link's identity as a hero of Faërie.

The Virtues of the Triforce and *Ocarina of Time*'s Structure

According to the transformational play theory, "content with legitimacy" involves "positioning the understanding and application of academic concepts as necessary if players are to resolve the game-world dilemmas successfully."[5] The Deku Tree defines the legitimating content of the Triforce to Link before sending him into the world:

> Din, the goddess of power... Nayru, the goddess of wisdom... Farore, the goddess of courage... Din... With her strong flaming arms, she cultivated the land and created the red earth. Nayru... Poured her wisdom onto the earth and gave the spirit of law to the world. Farore... With her rich soul, produced all life forms who would uphold the law.... And golden sacred triangles remained at the point where the goddesses left the world. Since then, the sacred triangles have become the basis for our world's providence.[6]

Wisdom, power, and courage are pinnacle concepts within a hierarchy of value concerning how to act in the world—in other words, they are virtues, a classically academic concept.[7] The structure of the game models proper and improper manifestations of relations amongst the three virtues.[8] Because the goddesses embed their virtues in the created order exemplified by the Triforce, the noetic value of each constituent "force" manifests itself in the structure of nature, society, and the individual's interaction with these values in myriad ways. The fabric of the imagined gameworld thus deeply mediates interaction with wisdom, power, and courage, an interplay exhibited both in the relatively linear structure of the game and in cyclical encounters with talismans or archetypal figures that guide Link into the Triforce's tripartite unity of virtues. The three acts of the game (child Link excavating three dungeons, adult Link cleansing five temples, and Link's final confrontation with Ganondorf) progress in order thematically from courage, to wisdom, to power as the focus of Link's transformational education in mastering the unified virtues of the Triforce. The balance among wisdom, courage, and power therefore becomes the implicit, transcendent value Link must learn, and so the player must learn those values through him.

Link navigates three elemental dungeons, sacred sites of their nearby tribes: the Deku Tree, sentient tree, and guardian of the Kokiri; Dodongo's Cavern, from where the Gorons derive their source of food; and Lord Jabu Jabu, a giant fish venerated by the Zora people. Link obtains three spiritual stones from these locations, making accessible the sacred realm wherein the Triforce resides. As conduits to the Triforce, the spiritual stones serve as elemental embodiments of the Hyrulean virtues, a notion reinforced by their color scheme. Given that wisdom, power, and courage have higher-order manifestations in the form of the Triforce and lower-order manifestations in the form of the Spiritual stones, this means that hierarchy exists within the values themselves: Thus courage, for example, must regulate *courage* as much as it must regulate wisdom and power.

Courage

Link lays the foundation of courageous unity he brings to the Hyrulean virtues in the first act of the game. Farore, as the divinity of courage, produces the impulse of life itself; indeed, her power is at the core of the verdant plenitude somberly guarded by the Deku Tree. The Spiritual Stone of the Forest therefore stands as a talisman of courage. The Deku Tree gives "the green and shining stone" to him at the outset of his quest to find Zelda, an omen that he will eventually bear that same Triforce of Courage. Similarly, Link travels into the depths of Dodongo Cavern to defeat the King of the Dodongos, thereby receiving the Spiritual Stone of Fire from Darunia, king of the Gorons. Din's element is fire and so her color is naturally red, and the Goron's Ruby possesses the sympathetic magic of her virtue, power. Finally, Link receives the sapphire jewel of the Zoras, the spiritual stone of water; Nayru puts the softening color of blue into the sky and lays the groundwork for Farore's gift of a green world.

Each of these preliminary trials emphasize the Hyrulean virtues: Link must bravely walk into the cavernous Deku Tree and fight spiders under the cover of subterranean shadows; he must become strong enough to lift heavy bombs to break open the rock blocking Dodongo Cavern; and he must discern that feeding Lord Jabu Jabu grants him access to the belly of the beast. The first act of the game concludes with Link using the three spiritual stones to open the Door of Time by means of the Ocarina of Time, which he receives from Zelda as she flees Ganon. This culmination of Link's childhood adventure suggests that he has reached a pinnacle of the adventure: He has mastered the Triforce's values to the degree that they are reflected in the Spiritual Stones, and, via his playing of the ocarina to literally harmonize their power, Link demonstrates sufficient mastery of their mutual integration that he can move to the next stage of his journey. Courage defines the first act: Entreating Link to undertake his quest, the Deku Tree says, "Thou art courageous,"[9] and when preparing to cross the threshold to adulthood, Link demonstrates that courage by opposing Ganondorf, although ill-equipped to do so. In this initial sequence of the game, therefore, Link masters courage as a principle organizing courage, power, and wisdom.

Wisdom

The second and longest act of the quest requires Link to master five temples, a variety of sub-dungeons, and side quests to develop wisdom within his courageous identity. Link's magical growth to adulthood at the outset of this sequence indicates his increased power, but also a psychological maturation. Fittingly, the insightful figure of Shiek appears to give Link counsel, giving his courageous intentions direction and teaching him new music, developing the same skill, which allowed Link to tap into the harmony of the elemental "triforce" of the spiritual stones. After awakening in the Temple of Time, Link journeys through five further temples, abandoned sites of ancient wisdom where he combats the ill effects of Ganondorf's power by awakening the Sages. The first three temples reiterate Link's youthful trials, but with a greater emphasis on the pro-social capacity unique to wisdom among the virtues. Breaking the Forest Temple's curse, a more developed version of the Deku Tree, frees Kokiri Forest of monsters and makes possible the new life of the informative Deku Sprout, the offspring of the Deku Tree. Likewise, in clearing the Temple of Fire of a dragon causing volcanic eruptions (mirroring Dodongo Cavern), Link befriends the Goron child named after him and releases Gorons from imprisonment, highlighting Link's socialization into the persona of the hero. Clearing the Water Temple, similarly, removes the curse of drought from Lake Hylia and, eventually, thawing the frozen Zora Domain. Link's heroic activities have increasingly positive ramifications for his community, and his journey through the value system of the Triforce advances. The Forest Temple's ghosts, including Phantom Ganon, require Link to affirm his courage; the battle with Volvagia requires Link to wield the power of the Megaton Hammer; the challenging Water Temple requires Link to use his wisdom to overcome the dungeon's notoriously difficult puzzles. Because the Water Temple is the capstone trial of Link's reiteration of his childhood lessons, he meets here the manifestation of his personal abyss in the form of Dark Link.

But adult pursuit of wisdom pushes Link further than an expansion of the three virtues in the Shadow Temple, a reminder of Hyrulean mortality and capacity for malice. Link encountered death early in the loss of his father figure, The Deku Tree, and other morbid enemies appeared before, such as Phantom Ganon or skeletal warriors. But Link encounters here Death's most gruesome expression. Indeed, the Shadow Temple is the first one that requires Link to travel backwards to his childhood, forcing him to face primordial fears present at life's wellspring, and therefore a visit to the bottom of a literal well. This time the far more disturbing images of death highlight the threatening face of the Hyruleans, the side for which Link fights. The Shadow Temple exemplifies the negative, potentially disunifying aspects of the Triforce virtues. Courage becomes foolhardy in the Shadow Temple where false floors are enchanted to drop the overly bold into zombie-infested tunnels; the Eye of Truth reveals ghastly sights, which implies that knowledge can be pursued rashly; and the life-destroying potential of power displays everywhere as oversized guillotines and hostile skeletons. Apparently beheaded for misuse of the Eye of Truth's wisdom, Bongo Bongo darkly mirrors Link as a musician. By having exposed himself to this abyss of the Hyrulean virtues, Link can ascend into the Spirit Temple to integrate those virtues more completely.

Link's progression through the Spirit Temple highlights the positive, cooperative principle necessary to unify the Hyrulean virtues, a site of wisdom beyond wisdom where the mirror shield pragmatically symbolizes the power of reflection. Link saves the Gerudo princess and future sage Nabooru, and receives acknowledgement from Kaepora Gaebora, his wise childhood mentor, that Link no longer needs his guidance. Link's cooperation with Nabooru while a child enables him to clear the dungeon as an adult, and his strategy of turning the twin witches Kotake and Koume against each other with the mirror shield reflects the principle of unity they fail to manifest in their bickering relationship (even in the state of death). The witches are the first temple bosses with real personalities and with the ability to combine their powers, yet their lack of compassion for one another in defeat shows the limits of the authenticity of their integration. By discerning their weakness, Link obtains the wisdom that unites wisdom to power and to courage. When Link has completed this trajectory, Shiek regards him as prepared to know "his" true identity as Zelda, bearer of the Triforce of Wisdom. Act two thus begins with hidden wisdom (Zelda disguised as Shiek) and ends with revealed wisdom (Zelda, too, is a sage). This revelation signals Link's readiness to encounter Ganondorf's vicious abuse of power.

Power

Although Zelda's disclosure leads to her capture, she endows Link with the Arrow of Light's power, allowing him to undermine Ganondorf's strength and ultimately defeat him in battle with the help of Zelda and the other Sages. Ganondorf's magical ambush on Zelda, an uncourageous display of power toward Zelda, motivates Link to save her and so become wisdom's hero, too. Just as a triangle is more than its points, Link must be a hero of the Triforce's complete hierarchy of values, not merely the corner of the Triforce that is his primary association. Link attains the golden gauntlets that allow him to lift tremendous rocks, and subsequently he receives an upgrade to his life power from a Great Fairy. Having mastered power with courage and wisdom, Link can overcome Ganon's power and subject him to the force of Zelda's wisdom, who seals him in the Sacred Realm.

Link must relinquish the Master Sword's power, for clinging to it would liken him to Ganondorf in his hunger for dominance. Link surrenders as well a Zelda who knows him and Navi who has guided him. Restored to his childhood, Link returns to a world that does not know him as a hero. Link and the player now share a secret, transformative enrichment in their understanding of the Triforce's virtues. But understanding the player's affective bonding with the avatar requires more than this structuralist reading of the story's discourse on virtue.

Fairy-Tale Context and the Consequentiality of Imagination

The affective experience of Faërie fuses the heroic virtues of power, wisdom, and courage into Link's avatar symbiosis with the player and into the emotive, conceptual experience of the gamer's world.[10] Tolkien's conception of the fairy-tale style fantasy elucidates how *Zelda*'s genre accesses the aspect of transformational play conceived of by Barab et al. as "context with consequentiality." In *On Fairy-Stories*, Tolkien writes, "The human mind is capable of forming mental images of things not actually present. The faculty of conceiving the images is (or was) naturally called Imagination."[11] The power of imagination is essential to every individual because perceiving patterns in the world around us is basic to our attempt to make sense of the world and to interface our knowledge with language: "The human mind, endowed with the powers of generalization and abstraction, sees not only green-grass, discriminating it from other things (and finding it fair to look upon), but sees that it is *green* as well as being *grass*."[12] Imagination is indispensable for recognizing that the green in grass and the green in Link's tunic are the same color; imagination, too, connects green in Link's tunic to the life-giving principle of Farore's courage, thus making possible the meditations on virtue of the preceding section.

When imagination is recognized as essential for basic attempts to learn about and act in the world, the consequences of fantasy's real-world value becomes more apparent. For Tolkien, fantasy is the application of rational contemplation to the "arresting strangeness" of "images of things… which are indeed not to be found in our primary world at all, or generally believed not to be found there."[13] Just so, when Link first emerges from his treehouse to survey Kokiri Forest, a chalk drawing of a small hero with a sparkling companion facing some sort of reptilian beast decorates the base of his house, possibly a Dodongo or even Ganon in his monstrous form. This depiction of the initial fantastic image of arresting strangeness gestures at the grammar of the whole myth (a boy faces a monster with sword, shield, and fairy friend) within the enchantment of the game's sub-creation writ large. Tolkien explains that "the inner consistency of reality" achieved in compelling fantasy is "Art, the operative link between Imagination and the final result, Sub-creation."[14] More potent in Tolkien's view than the art which compels our "willing suspension of disbelief," sub-creation is art, "which commands or induces Secondary Belief."[15] We do not believe in the existence of the Deku Tree in our world; instead, we react with belief toward the presence of the Deku Tree in the game *as if he were real*, or, in other words, with secondary belief. The success of sub-creator depends upon articulating a reasonable world for the fantastic image conceived by the artist. Tolkien writes, "Fantasy is a natural human activity. It certainly does not destroy or even insult Reason…. On the contrary. The keener and clearer is the reason, the better fantasy it will make."[16] Adult knowledge makes fantasy satisfying, both because we apprehend more clearly the symbolic reason for the fantasy surrounding the arresting image and the rationale for imaginative alterations in the operation of the Secondary World made by things not present in our Primary World. For example, it makes sense for forest children, who never grow up, to have a forest parent such as the Deku Tree, who can last for ages. The artistic achievements of fantasy generate the context for the consequentiality of imagination.

The opening of *Ocarina of Time* displays this distinction between the fundamental faculty of imagination and its rational fulfillment as artful, compelling context. In his purview as a guardian spirit, the Deku Tree explains to Navi that an evil threatens the land and he so must speak with Link. Here the gamer is not a player but a reader of the Deku Tree's words and a viewer of the images relayed by the cutscene: "In the vast, deep forest of Hyrule…. Long have I served as the Guardian Spirit… I am known as the Deku Tree."[17] These words appear on a black screen with no audio. The Deku Tree, a voice of authority, virtually speaks *directly to the player*, more significant in a videogame than in the address to the reader of a novel, because the Deku Tree's words define the nature of the player's choices and attitudes about them. As the scene cuts to Link's bedroom within a hollow tree, he continues, "The children of the Forest, the Kokiri, live here with me. Each Kokiri has his or her own guardian fairy. However, there is one boy who does not have a fairy."[18] The game here sets the stage for the player to imagine a fantasy world where forests have guardian spirits and Kokiri have guardian fairies. Immediately, the gameworld develops into one where an ancient being like the Deku Tree can have knowledge about how the myth operates. The narratorial voice of the Deku Tree connects his unfamiliar world to something with which we are familiar: a boy without a fairy. The game deftly flips normal and abnormal: We do not, in this world, typically have fairy companions, but will have one in the game; individuals within Kokiri Forest normally do have fairy companions, and the protagonist who will be our avatar has been inactive because he has not had one. The arrival of Navi as his fairy companion raises his status to the expected norm of the community in his fantasy world, helping the player to accept more easily this Secondary Belief. Our normal state, uncompanioned by fairies, becomes in the fantasy of *Ocarina of Time* an oddity, which identifies us with Link. At this point, we hear Link shiver in his sleep, and the cutscene transitions into his dreamscape.

The transformational power of fantasy generates context, provided particularly through Navi, compelling players to invest in Link's identity. Link's dream foretells his eventual confrontation with Ganondorf, as well as his alliance with Zelda and Impa. In his dream, a defenseless Link encounters Ganondorf, who threatens the unarmed boy. The screen then turns white, and the Deku Tree summons Navi. As the first moment of dialogue in the game, it also provides the first opportunity for player agency: pressing "A" continues the dialogue. The fantasy instantiates a basic, crisis-laden story to care about, and *then* gives the player a chance for interaction within that story. Not incidentally, the player's first interaction occurs through Navi, the fairy shortly to be assigned to Link. By accepting this dialogic interaction, the player receives the first visual of the Deku Tree, whose tremendous, deciduous face cannot fit on screen. Navi hovers before him as the audience of his speech, and the player, who was already heeding the Deku Tree, links to the game's world initially through her.

Navi provides for gamers what Tolkien terms the *recovery* experience of the fairy tale: "Recovery....is a re-gaining—regaining of a clear view... We need... to clean our windows; so that the things seen clearly may be freed from the drab blur of triteness or familiarity."[19] Adulthood sometimes harbors a cynical tendency to take the basic aspects of life as a given, where we treat the surprising facts of existence as wearisome. But Navi empowers us to do basic things with wonder again; holding conversation with others, reading signs, or examining an object all become filtered through the whimsical fairy's capering presence. The Deku Tree exhorts Link, "When Navi speaks, listen well to her words of wisdom." Through Navi the narrative of *OoT* recovers "the potency of the words, and the wonder of the things, such as stone, and wood, and iron."[20] Throughout the game, we see Link reacting with awe at new things he learns or finds, discovering a map or learning a new song, and Navi's presence mediates all of this wonder. The recovering light of her wisdom lends the player courageous insight into the use of Link's power. She manifests wonder, which leads the player into identification through "context with consequentiality" with the intentional personality of Link—and so with his hero's journey.

The Hylian's Journey: An Enchanted Person with Recovered Intentionality

I employ Campbell's understanding of the hero's journey here to show how *OoT* constructs a "person with intentionality" who engages concepts of Hyrulean virtue and the contextualizing consequentiality of Faërie, thus creating a transformational experience of play.[21] The intentionality provided by Link's journey into a heroic personality constitutes the means by which the Faërie perspective on imagination and mythmaking enchants the reader in order to help the value system of the game's story, discussed above, transform the player's own attitudes about those concepts. An analysis of the Deku Tree quest, the initial stage of Link's journey, suffices to illuminate the pattern of his heroic cycle and ramifications for the maturation of his Hyrulean virtues as a Faërie hero that runs through the entirety of *OoT*.[22] The core elements of the hero's journey identified by Campbell, departure, initiation, and return, manifest in the initial sequence of the game to incorporate the player into Link's transformational development of intentionality as a courageous, wise, and powerful hero of Faërie.[23]

Link's departure begins with a call to adventure that requires him to courageously forsake ordinary expectations. Concerning "The Call to Adventure," Campbell writes, "Typical of the circumstances of the call are the dark forest, the great tree, the babbling spring, and the loathly, underestimated appearance of the carrier of the power of destiny"[24]. Navi announces authoritative summons to the journey, while Link's portentous dreams have already heralded his responsibility. Navi provides the player-avatar, in Campbellian terms, "an atmosphere of irresistible fascination about the figure that appears suddenly as guide, marking a new period."[25] Because this new period necessitates growth, threshold guardians also appear to ensure Link's proper equipment for the journey: Mido refuses Link entry to see the Deku Tree until the player-avatar obtains sword and shield.[26] Link develops the social component of his heroic identity by acquiring the shield through commercial interaction with the Kokiri society; however, according to Campbell, "his spiritual center of gravity shifts from within the pale of his society to a zone unknown."[27] Thus Link must find his sword alone, in the first of many archetypal labyrinths within the game.

Following the summons, the Departure stage often involves a "Refusal of the Call" and "Supernatural Aid." Because the videogame engages player interaction, gameplay may exhibit little refusal—although the player's decision to have Link go fishing, break pots, or play apparently frivolous target practice games in the face of the impending doom promised by Ganondorf could be interpreted as player-produced refusal. Link himself, however, shows a hint of reluctance at the beginning of the game. Link has been sleeping deeply, apparently, in the middle of the day, deeply enough to have his portentous dreams, suggesting a repressed awareness that he may be afflicted with troubles worse than embarrassment about not having a fairy like his Kokiri friends. Campbell writes "that sometimes the predicament following an obstinate refusal of the call proves to be the occasion of a providential revelation of some unsuspected principle of release."[28] Link might have inferred that if he was having nightmares, he ought to speak to the Deku Tree, and Navi must act to overcome his lack of initiative. She hovers over Link, crying, "The Great Deku Tree wants to talk to you! Link, get up!" When he fails to respond immediately, she says in frustration, "Hey! C'mon! Can Hyrule's destiny really depend on such a lazy boy?" She acts as the "supernatural aid," pushing Link to accept his responsibility. Navi and the Deku Tree thus mirror the mother and the father in their mutual conveyance of the summons to virtue: "Protective and dangerous, motherly and fatherly at the same time, [the] supernatural principle of guardianship and direction unites in itself all the ambiguities of the unconscious."[29] The subconscious power over the imagination thus commits the player to identify with the production of Link's heroic identity. Navi assists Link in accruing the tools necessary for answering the Deku Tree's summons: The Kokiri Sword makes Link appropriately dangerous and the Deku Shield bears the symbol of the Kokiri people—the image of courage. Protected by a manifestation of courage and become a wielder of legitimate (if initiatory) power, Link is guided by the intermediately wise Navi to cross his first threshold.

Approaching the Deku Tree, Link receives affirmation that his dreams were true portents of evil that has already invaded the idyllic forest of the Kokiri and into the depths of the guardian spirit himself. Campbell writes, "With the personifications of his destiny to guide and aid him, the hero goes forward in his adventure until he comes to the 'threshold guardian' at the entrance to the zone of magnified power."[30] The Deku Tree tells Link, "The time has come to test thy courage," giving him passage into his own cursed root system. This test of courage betokens immense trust from the Deku Tree, generating good will between the guardian spirit and the avatar-player dyad as they begin to ascend the scale of Hyrulean virtue in service of protecting an emblematic component of the sub-created world's architecture. Concerning moments of this sort Campbell holds that "the passage of the magical threshold is a transit into a sphere of rebirth."[31] The sacred-tree motif serves as fitting for a descent into the abyss as a type of "tree of life," for "the universe itself grows from this point. It is rooted in the supporting darkness... the umbilical point through which the energies of eternity break into time."[32] Appropriately, therefore, the Deku Tree teaches Link the myth of Hyrule's creation after completion of his first mission.

The player movement through the Deku Tree trial deepens player belief in the sub-creation's urgent narrative intentions. Campbell writes, "Once having traversed the threshold, the hero moves in a dream landscape of curiously fluid, ambiguous forms, where he must survive a succession of trials."[33] A discernable path through the tree and other tools appear to help Link on his mission, including the presence of a Fairy Slingshot, which suggests that other Kokiri have traveled inside of the Deku Tree before; these elements create the impression of "a benign power everywhere supporting him in his superhuman passage."[34] Campbell notes that the abyssal "voyage to the underworld is but one of innumerable such adventures undertaken by the heroes of fairy tale and myth."[35] Having entered into the abyss of his father figure, Link must face the perilous opposites of the values he has been learning; where he met emblems of positive masculinity and femininity in the form of the Deku Tree and Navi, so he meets the male Deku Scrubs who serve the parasitic, spiderlike Queen Gohma, typical of Campbell's characterization of the hero's "journey of darkness, horror, disgust, and phantasmagoric fears."[36] Hence the spider queen, a literal devouring mother, reminds us that the life the Deku Tree symbolizes can also become perverse.[37] As Campbell says of this stage, "No longer can the hero rest in innocence with the goddess of the flesh; for she is become the queen of sin."[38] Queen Gohma's appearance constitutes one of the most chilling openings in dungeon boss fights, where a single, malevolent eye peers at Link in challenge from the shadows, fearfully reminiscent of Tolkien's Shelob.

After the player successfully guides Link to victory, he obtains a glimpse of what Campbell calls apotheosis, "a pattern of the divine state to which the human hero attains who has gone beyond the last terrors of ignorance".[39] Link receives his first Heart Container, increasing his durability, his own life enhanced by succeeding at a fatal encounter with the source of life. Link thus becomes more capable of surviving his quest to stop Ganondorf, and it also empowers the player to overcome more difficult foes. Thus achieving physical edification, Link receives intellectual edification from the Deku Tree through the archetype of the Meeting with the Goddess, or in this case the Three Goddesses, which stage Campbell describes as the "ultimate adventure, when all the barriers and ogres have been overcome" and "is commonly represented as a mystical marriage of the triumphant hero-soul with the Queen Goddess of the World."[40] Link enters into no literal marriage in *OoT*, yet he becomes continually wed to the virtues of Hyrule's creative benefactresses. Din, Farore, and Nayru epitomize Link's heroic adoration of Hyrule's mysteries: "The hero is the one who comes to know. As he progresses in the slow initiation that is life, the form of the goddess undergoes for him a series of transfigurations."[41] The Deku Tree instills in Link a virtuous posture toward the feminine geniuses behind the mystical virtues of the Triforce, virtuous womanhood represented as well by Zelda and the Great Fairies. Moreover, the Deku Tree's peaceful acceptance of his death iterates what Campbell calls the Atonement with the Father.[42] The Deku Tree seals Link's initiation into the first stage of his heroic status with a twofold boon, the gift of the Spiritual Stone of the Forest and his mission to seek out the princess Zelda. Campbell writes that the archetypal boon is "bestowed" in a manner "scaled to [the hero's] stature and to the nature of his dominant desire: the boon is simply a symbol of life energy stepped down to the requirements of a certain specific case."[43] The Kokiri Emerald is the zenith of what the Deku Tree has to offer Link, completing this aspect of his initiation and pushing the player to the next stage of Link's journey.

The third sequence of the hero's journey, the return, occurs in a twofold way for Link. First, he reenters Kokiri, discovering that the world has changed. The threshold guardian, an unnamed Kokiri, no longer bars Link's departure from Kokiri Forest, and the Kokiri's statements shift from superior knowledge to confusion, in contrast with the avatar-player's newly informed resolve. Campbell writes, "When the Hero-Quest has been accomplished, through penetration to the source, or through the grace of some male or female, human or animal personification, the adventurer still must return with his life-transmuting trophy."[44] Although he does not know it yet, Link's departure from Kokiri Forest is actually a return to the wider world of Hyrule—a fact he (as well as the player) will not learn until after clearing the Forest Temple as an adult. While he thought he was being called away from home, Link discovers the calling beckons him to his original home, developing a tension develops between Link's identity as Kokiri and as Hylian. This tension constitutes the drama in the first stage of the return, specifically "The Refusal of the Return" where heroes are "fabled to have taken up residence forever in the blessed isle of the unaging Goddess of Immortal Being."[45] The youthful Kokiri, free of the larger world's obligations, contrast with Link's need to grow up and the player's role in helping him to do so—his is not Peter Pan's fairy tale, nor can it be the player's.

The energy of the hero's potential refusal manifests in Link's encounter with Saria as he meets her on the bridge leading out of Kokiri Forest.[46] Saria's and Link's relationship predated the player's involvement in the story; Thus, player agency momentarily reduces to allow appreciation of the drama. Link's encounter with Saria is one of the most pathos-laden moments, because she, unlike many of the other Kokiri, accepted Link into her community even before he had a fairy companion. Their meeting on the bridge thus signifies Link's need to extricate himself from the most powerful force binding him to the desire to remain a child, and yet she aids him by negating the temptation to refuse his destiny: "I knew...that you would leave the forest...someday, Link... Because you are different from me and my friends..."[47] She also gives Link the Fairy Ocarina, a token of their friendship, with which he learns almost half the songs required to complete the game. Link accepts the ocarina and shares a profound look with Saria before breaking away and running out of the forest. Saria looks on as his footsteps fade.

Link flees in silence from Saria into a new mentor figure, the sagacious great owl Kaepora Gaebora, evoking the motif of the "Magic Flight." A figure of wisdom, the owl provides a segue into Link's quest to find Zelda, and he occasionally will offer Link wisdom and literal flight. Kaepora's eagerly delivered lessons contrast with the pathos of Saria's farewell, making the owl an example of the Campbellian Rescue from Without: "The hero may have to be brought back from his supernatural adventure by assistance from without."[48] This rescue assists the hero with "the paradoxical, supremely difficult threshold-crossing of the hero's return from the mystic realm into the land of common day."[49] Kaepora teaches Link about those regular workings, as when he explains how day and night pass after his life of semi-eternality in Kokiri Forest. As such, the owl prepares Link for the Crossing of the Return Threshold, the sequence of the journey allowing Link to bring the boon he has received from initiation into the general world: "The two worlds, the divine and the human, can be pictured only as distinct from each other—different as life and death, as day and night."[50] Zelda's dream envisions Link as a light from the forest that pierces the dark clouds, holding in his hand a boon: the "green and shining stone."[51] The player's agency returns to Link's character after encountering Kaepora, and so the reunited avatar-player moves from the elfin realm of the woods to the more human world of the Hylians.

The avatar-player's mastery of Kokiri Forest's fairy-tale time and Hyrule Kingdom's human time fulfills Tolkien's notion that the fairy story addresses the human desire to survey the depths of space and time, foreshadowing Link's eventual capacity to master time itself. Link becomes the "Master of the Two Worlds," the status accorded to the hero who passes each stage of Campbell's understanding of the hero's journey: "Freedom to pass back and forth across the world division, from the perspective of the apparitions of time to that of the causal deep and back....is the talent of the master."[52] Link becomes a master of two worlds as the Hero of Time while the player, given the opportunity to master the world of the game, is also reminded of the quest to become a master in the search for meaning. "Freedom to Live" is the power Campbell conceives the individual possessing who has obtained this mastery, "effecting a reconciliation of the individual consciousness with the universal will," which "is effected through a realization of the true relationship of the passing phenomena of time to the imperishable life that lives and dies in all."[53] Zelda, disguised as Sheik, tells Link,

> The flow of time is always cruel... Its speed seems different for each person, but no one can change it... A thing that doesn't change with time is a memory of younger days... In order to come back here again, play the Minuet of Forest.[54]

Through music, Sheik teaches Link how he can move beyond mere reaction, and instead find a stable center of intentionality, a centered identity, which Link can perform only through the player's dedicated play.

Link's intentional indwelling of the spaces of Hyrule, marked by the pursuit of the Hyrulean virtues that enable his Faërie wonderment for the world, makes him the hero of Faërie; likewise, such a heroic identity is forged by those who experience the transformational play afforded by the journey through the gameworld while wearing the garments of Link's intentionality. By enacting Link's heroic journey of Faërie enchantment towards the game's sub-created world, the player can share in the avatar's identification with the Triforce virtues and bring this perspective back to the Primary World. The initial sequence of the Deku Tree's quest thus begins the pattern that will make Link and player the Masters of Two Worlds—yet, in Campbellian terms, further encounters between heroes and their gods will be necessary to fully actualize them both. Those necessary encounters explain archetypally why the series is called *The Legend of Zelda*: while Link becomes a Hero, Zelda embodies the goddess of wisdom for whom he strives to be worthy. Transformational play occurs when the enchantment of sub-creation vivifies the avatar-player's intentional pursuit of virtue, so that the player glimpses in *Ocarina of Time* what it means to be the Hero of Faërie.

Notes

1 Nintendo, *The Legend of Zelda: Ocarina of Time Official Nintendo Player's Guide*, ed. Scott Pelland (Washington: Nintendo of America, 1998), 4.
2 Sasha A. Barab, Melissa Gresalfi, and Adam Ingram-Goble, "Transformational Play: Using Games to Position, Content, and Context," *Educational Researcher* 39, no. 7 (2010): 525.
3 Ibid., 525.

4 Ibid., 526.

5 Ibid.

6 Shigeru Miyamoto, Koji Kondo, Eii Aonuma, et al., *The Legend of Zelda: Ocarina of Time* (Redmond, WA: Nintendo of America, 1998), videogame.

7 See "On Hylian Virtues: Aristotle, Aquinas, and the Hylian Cosmogenesis" by Justus Hunter for a discussion of the Triforce in terms of the virtue ethics. I prefer to term them as "Hyrulean" rather than "Hylian," because the Hylians are a distinct race and the values of the Triforce can be referred to all species in the world.

8 Hunter argues that evil manifestations of power, wisdom, and courage should be seen as distortions of their true nature: "The Hylian virtues (when perfect) are connected... the only possibility for possession of the Triforce without its splintering is in the hands of one with an equal measure of power, wisdom, and courage" (121).

9 Miyamoto et al., *Ocarina of Time*, 1998.

10 Philip Tallon discusses the application of Tolkien's *On Fairy-Stories* to *Zelda* in "The Birth of Gaming from the Spirit of Fantasy: Video Games as Secondary Worlds with Special Reference to The Legend of Zelda and J.R.R. Tolkien." Our essays are complementary: Tallon's emphasis is on applying Tolkien's framework to gameplay experience; my emphasis is on how the *mythopoeia* within *Zelda* itself casts a Faërie glow over the gameplay.

11 J.R.R. Tolkien, "On Fairy-Stories," in *Tree and Leaf* (New York: HarperCollins, 2001), 46.

12 Ibid., 22.

13 Ibid., 47–48.

14 Ibid., 47.

15 Ibid.

16 Ibid., 55.

17 Miyamoto et al., *OoT*, 1998.

18 Ibid.

19 Tolkien, 58. Navi is often maligned by fans. However, I believe her presence is profoundly central to the success of *OoT*'s enchanting quality, as argued here.

20 Tolkien, 60.

21 Barab et al., 526, re: intentionality. I use Campbell for the convenience of his familiarity, although other theorists of the monomyth are certainly valuable. *The Hero with a Thousand Faces*, however, which predates *The Legend of Zelda* significantly, has proved formative in popular manifestations of the hero's journey, and so stands as a natural referent in this context.

22 Of course, I make no claims to originality in seeing the Hero's Journey at work in *Zelda*. Its presence has been more thoroughly underscored by Stephen F. Kuniak, "It's Dangerous to Go Alone: The Hero's Journey in the Legend of Zelda," in *The Psychology of Zelda*, ed. Anthony M Bean (Dallas, TX: BenBella Books, 2019), 23–60. My goal here is to show specifically the psychological utility of the hero's journey for incorporating the player into identification with Link's intentionality, as it intersects with the context of fantasy and content of the virtues of the Triforce.

23 Joseph Campbell, *The Hero with a Thousand Faces* (Novato, CA: New World Library, 2008). Incidentally, Campbell died in 1987, the year *Zelda* was introduced to North America.

24 Campbell, 43.

25 Ibid., 46.

26 Recall that the Deku Shield bears the symbol of the Kokiri people, a stylized representation of the Spiritual Stone of the Forest.

27 Campbell, 48.
28 Ibid., 53.
29 Ibid., 60.
30 Ibid., 64.
31 Ibid., 74.
32 Ibid., 32.
33 Ibid., 81.
34 Ibid.
35 Ibid., 82.
36 Ibid., 101.
37 Of course, such terror can manifest as either masculine or feminine, as seen in the Queen Gohma's adult correspondence, Phantom Ganon.
38 Campbell, 102.
39 Ibid., 127.
40 Ibid., 91.
41 Ibid., 97.
42 Ibid., 105–126.
43 Ibid., 163.
44 Ibid., 167.
45 Ibid.
46 The bridge symbolically cuts through the Lost Woods, the chaotic realm adjacent to his safe home, reminding us that the agents of change surround even the most innocent places.
47 Miyamoto et al., *OoT*, 1998.
48 Campbell, 178.
49 Ibid., 186.
50 Ibid., 188.
51 Miyamoto et al., *OoT*, 1998.
52 Campbell, 196.
53 Ibid., 206.
54 Miyamoto et al., *OoT*, 1998.

5 Twilight and Faërie
The Music of *Twilight Princess* as Tolkienesque Nostalgia

Vincent E. Rone

The fantasies of J.R.R. Tolkien and *The Legend of Zelda* games share a deep connection in their mutual predilection for the past, for nostalgia. In fact, videogame scholars Zach Whalen and Laurie N. Taylor proffer a good working definition of nostalgia, which refers to the "process of looking back to an unattainable past and trying to bring that past into the present," and "the process by which knowledge of the past is brought to bear on the present and the future."[1] Nostalgia, the authors continue, also foregrounds connections between time and space, memory and remembering. Therefore, making sense of nostalgia can become a messy endeavor, which, as one might expect, can run the gamut of good and bad, hope and despair, happiness and grief, as is true in both Middle-earth and Hyrule.

Music especially illuminates the significance of nostalgia Tolkien and *Zelda* share. For instance, *LotR* characters express nostalgia often by recollecting memories through song. Characters in *Zelda* likewise sing and play songs often riddled with intimations of the past. We become familiar with melodies common to several *Zelda* games, which allow characters to recall and even travel to the past. *Zelda* consequently represents genuine Tolkienesque fantasy, *Faërie*. Investigation into the game's nostalgia through the lens of musicology reveals *Zelda* as genuine Tolkienesque fantasy, *The Legend of Zelda: Twilight Princess* (*TP*, 2006) standing as the strongest case.

TP fits particularly well within a Tolkienesque framework because, like the literary reception of *LotR*, reception of the game has proven problematic, divisive even. It ranges from praise for its return to familiar *Zelda* tropes to derision because the game ostensibly prevents the franchise from evolving. Yet reviewers all agree: Nostalgia saturates *TP* down to the levels of design, gameplay, visuals, storyline, and, importantly, music. *TP's* music facilitates nostalgic experiences through complex interactions of diegetic, non-diegetic, and leitmotivic operations

Dedicated to Chris Gleason and especially to the memory of his wife, Dr. Linda Shaver-Gleason—former classmate, colleague, friend, and extraordinary musicologist gone too soon. Namárië, mellon nin.

revealed through a juxtaposition of two narratives, *LotR*'s Lothlórien and *TP*'s Sacred Grove. The mythopoeic power of *TP* thus lies in its music's ability to reveal continuity with *Zelda*'s developing mythology. The music of *TP* cues our personal gaming memories by offering potent moments of bringing the past to bear on the present. We thus can understand *Zelda* in Tolkienesque terms as a mythopoeic work of fantasy elevated, rather than mired by nostalgia.

Faërie and Nostalgic Immersion

Tolkien describes how authors must 'sub-create' a Secondary (fantasy) World, and readers access by practicing "Secondary Belief," thus entering *Faërie*.[2] Plausible Secondary Worlds, however, depend on the Primary (real) World, our world. They should appear, Paul Kocher writes, familiar "but not too familiar; strange but not too strange."[3] *Faërie* therefore *can* contain fantastical creatures like Elves, but it *must* contain recognizable elements for readers to follow and to maintain an inner consistency of reality.[4] Moreover, *Faërie* requires four steps.[5] *Fantasy* engages the imagination and enables our distinguishing what belongs to Primary and Secondary Worlds, which frees us, Tolkien writes, "from the domination of observed 'fact.'"[6] *Escape* refers to our leaving everyday life to enter *Faërie*. *Recovery* allows our return to the Primary World with fresh perspectives so to "remember what we had known but forgotten," according to Stitt.[7] Finally, *Consolation* amounts to the happy ending, what Tolkien calls *eucatastrophe*.

All four steps point toward a return or regaining, which allows nostalgia to resonate so well with Tolkienesque myth, especially given the origin of nostalgia refers to responses to displacement.[8] Indeed, according to R.J. Reilly, *LotR* echoes the dim past and attempts to suggest the depths of time;[9] and characters like Tom Bombadil, Treebeard, and Galadriel represent or attempt to preserve the past. Tolkien himself writes about nostalgia in a letter dated 25 September 1954. He suggests it partly explains the conflicted, bittersweet history of the Elves and their desire to stop the change and growth of Middle-earth, to memorialize the past as they remember it. Upon realizing the futility of that endeavor, the Elves became overburdened with grief and nostalgia.[10]

Faërie and nostalgia thus provide a strong framework for videogames, as players enter gameworlds through similar processes, immersion and intromersion. Scholars Lennart Nacke and Mark Grimshaw describe immersion as a gradual, "progressive experience that includes the suppression of all surroundings... together with attention and involvement in the game."[11] Katie Salen and Eric Zimmerman define immersion as transporting us into a simulated reality "so complete that ideally the frame falls away so that the player truly believes that he or she is part of an imaginary world."[12] Game theorist Jesper Juul argues that play enables interaction "with real rules while imagining a fictional world and a videogame is a set of rules as well as a fictional world."[13] In this volume, Thomas Rowland employs intromersion, a term he coined, as an experience specific to videogames: A virtual space that allows for exploration due to the combination of the videogame's environment and ergodic nature.[14] All definitions require movement from the real to the imaginary, an act of commanding Secondary Belief.

Like *Faërie,* immersion comprises multi-step processes. Andrew Glassner posits three.[15] *Curiosity* refers to a desire to learn about the videogame. *Sympathy/Empathy* suggest we share the perspectives of avatars and form emotional bonds with them, which makes possible communion with Secondary Worlds.[16] *Transportation* suggests our crossing into and out of Secondary Worlds. Laura Ermi and Frans Mäyrä suggest another multi-step process for immersion.[17] First, *Sensory Immersion* denotes the game's audio-visual information overpowering that of the real world. Next, *Imaginative Immersion* enables a range of activities within the gameworld, like forming relationships with characters themselves. Finally, *Challenge-Based Interaction* similarly invites us to participate in activities within the Secondary Worlds. For ease of comparison and contrast, Table 5.1 juxtaposes Tolkien's *Faërie* steps with those of immersion by Glassner, Ermi and Mäyrä.

Immersion can result in powerful nostalgic experiences, which explains in part why game studies are wed to theories of the past. Whalen and Taylor maintain nostalgia figures into the study of videogames because our gaming experiences as players shape our analyses. Moreover, early games and their representative characters quote our shared past and youth.[18] Since *Nintendo* in particular specializes in repackaging

Table 5.1 Multistep Comparison and Contrast between *Faërie* and Immersion

Tolkien's Faërie	Glassner's Immersion	Ermi and Mäyrä's Immersion
Fantasy engages the imagination. *Escape* bids us leave everyday life for the Secondary World. *Recovery* & *Consolation* assist our returning to the Primary World with renewed perspective(s).	*Curiosity* engages our imagination. *Sympathy* & *Empathy* bids us enter the gameworld, typically through our relationship with the avatar. *Transportation* enables our crossing to & from the game and real world (Secondary and Primary World, respectively).	*Sensory Immersion* engages the imagination and begins the crossing from our (Primary) world to the game (Secondary) world. *Imaginative Immersion* & *Challenge-Based Interaction* locate players within the gameworld and encourage them to make choices therein.

classic characters, 8- and 16-bit versions of Mario, Samus Aran, and Donkey Kong appear on modern-day consoles so as to reproduce personal, historical experiences.[19] *Zelda* amplifies this notion through representative titles: *A Link to the Past* (*ALttP*, 1991), *Ocarina of Time* (*OoT*, 1998), and *A Link Between Worlds* (*ALbW*, 2013). Moreover, Anthony G. Cirilla's discussion of *OoT* as a Campbellian Hero's Journey offers an excellent example of nostalgic dialogue typical of the franchise.[20] Sheik teaches Link the "Minuet of Forest:"

> The flow of time is always cruel. Its speed seems different for each person, but no one can change it. A thing that doesn't change with time is a memory of younger days. In order to come back here again, play the Minuet of Forest.[21]

The bittersweet passage of time, memories of younger days, the suggestion of return—so evocative of *Zelda* rhetoric.

Nostalgia in the Reception and Music of *Twilight Princess*

Yet nostalgia has characterized *TP* from inception to reception, so much so that one barely can discuss latter without reference to the former.[22] Game franchises, Natasha Whiteman writes, must have elements of change if constituent installments are to evolve, and developers must temper innovation with established elements of the medium. The balance between the two often becomes the subject of hot debate within reception.[23] Whiteman grounds her study in the theories of Henry Jenkins, who proffers two tenets: Consensus shapes fan reception, and fans evaluate franchise titles against an idealized conception.[24] Such a notion may imply nostalgia, as we often replace past experiences with idealized conceptions to romanticize, memorialize, or forget. For instance, Whiteman discusses the divided opinion on *The Wind Waker* (*WW*, 2003), as cell-shaded graphics became a point of contention among fans.[25] Furthermore, like *Majora's Mask* (*MM*, 2000), *WW* mostly did not occur in Hyrule (above it, rather). Link sailed the Great Sea on the King of Red Lions, rather than riding Epona through Hyrule. Such changes amounted to the absence of established *Zelda* tropes and made fans nostalgic for an idealized *Zelda*.

Nintendo producers consequently planned for a game to return to its *OoT*-esque roots. Then came *TP*, a game with nostalgia virtually encoded into its DNA. Reviewer Casey Covel reflects on *Nintendo's* preview of *TP* at the 2004 Electronic Entertainment Expo (E3), which "showed it to be nothing short of a return to *Ocarina of Time's* graphic style, [and] fans went berserk."[26] Jonathan Metts writes how *TP* fills a gap apparently left by *WW*. He believes *WW* felt differently from a true *Zelda* game, and *TP* brings the series back to its roots.[27]

Finally, Dan Ryckert states no other launch title comes close to the excellence of *TP*, which assumes the role as spiritual heir to *OoT*.[28]

Not all reviewers consider *TP* favorably, however. Matthew Rickert believes *TP* feels dated, an unoriginal recycling that ultimately traps *Zelda* in the past.[29] According to Gene Park, *TP's* predilection for the past became its biggest disappointment, failing to deliver on those grounds and discourages adherence to the traditionalism the franchise embodies.[30] Mark Serrels judges the *TP* 2016 HD remake for the *Nintendo WiiU* most damningly as obtuse, strange, and nonsensical. He regards *TP* as unenjoyable outside a purely nostalgic framework by virtue—or vice—of its mimicking *OoT*.[31] Finally, *Zelda* creator Shigeru Miyamoto himself admits *TP* feels like something is missing.[32] *TP* received meteoric acclaim upon its launch but problematic reception in the long term.

Regarding *TP's* music, critics focused on synthesized sound technology and familiar tunes. Covel and Kristian Reed call *TP's* sound and music 'old school' and endearing, as "if the designers are playing as much on people's associations with past *Zeldas* as anything."[33] Rickert suggests *Nintendo* developers preoccupy themselves too much with nostalgia at the expense of innovation, respectively, synthesized and orchestrated music.[34] Although some authors suggest *Nintendo* retained synthesized sound for nostalgic purposes, Koji Kondo himself states it was a logistic, budgetary decision to do so.[35] Yet *TP* became the last *Zelda* game for a major *Nintendo* home console to use entirely synthesized sound, which situates it with *WW, MM, WW,* and *OoT* before it. *TP's* nostalgia consequently increases because we have opportunities to rehear sounds similar among four previous games.[36]

Reviewers also lauded the return of familiar tunes but did not discuss *how* it manifests nostalgia. According to Timothy Summers, music factors into games projecting their "world into the player's understanding of its universe and plot."[37] A signature feature of the *Zelda* franchise constituted music performance as a ludic tool through the game controller. Ludic music making, Summers writes, enhances our understanding of games in ways deeper than other communicative layers and constitutes part of the game experience.[38] Music also has a special relationship to themes of time and the past in *Zelda*, as ludo-musical performance facilitates time travel. This notion rings true when music making assumes leitmotivic properties.

The Leitmotifs of *Twilight Princess*

Leitmotifs play a critical role in developing the mythology and nostalgia of *Zelda*. In Western art music, leitmotif loosely refers to a theme used to represent a person, place/location, thing, or idea.[39] They depend on associativity, the forging of connections between two ideas such that one may evoke or recall the other. Matthew Bribitzer-Stull suggests we can understand associativity best when leitmotifs connect musical themes to dramatic contexts, which happens all the time in *Zelda*.[40] Stephanie Lind explains how their ludic properties can deepen our emotional investment.[41] According to Lind, Kondo attempted to integrate music into *Zelda* and aimed, "for a more developmental use of thematic recurrence, a true leitmotif..."[42] Consequently, she continues, leitmotifs in later games suggest some players will recognize themes from previous installments, which can nuance the experience of the plot.[43]

Sarah Pozderak-Chenevey, too, states the music of *TP* "may invoke feelings of nostalgia, as the player not only links the music to an in-game location but also to the time when he or she played Ocarina [of Time], perhaps summoning memories of childhood, a time irretrievably past."[44] Take Princess Zelda's introduction. Wolf Link and Midna reach Hyrule Castle, where Zelda is imprisoned and cloaked in black. Upon revealing herself, Zelda's familiar lullaby leitmotif plays and provides dramatic context for her identity and plight. The lullaby thus can generate a chain of nostalgic associations. We may remember Princess Zelda and her theme from past games, what mood(s) her Lullaby might suggest, or the relationship we may have formed with each incarnation. Then we might consider the tangential associations to the game—whom we were with, what was going on in our lives, and so on.

Zelda's leitmotifs also involve diegetic and non-diegetic functions. Diegetic music originates in the game; characters hear, perform, and respond to it. Non-diegetic music refers to the score outside the narrative space. As Lind writes, the leitmotifs of *OoT* engage us deeply because they blur diegetic and non-diegetic functions.[45] For example, we advance the plot within the game (Secondary) world by controlling within our (Primary) world virtual instruments: *Oot* and *MM's* ocarina; the wind-waker for the eponymous title; and the Goddess Harp for *Skyward Sword* (*SS*, 2011). For *TP*, Wolf Link howls melodies into "Howling Stones." Instances of these diegetic/non-diegetic blurrings can deepen nostalgic potential and can move us into *Faërie*. When we tap into music with leitmotivic properties, it can remind us of our gaming past(s), as well as that of the *Zelda* mythology—an irretrievable pasts of Primary and Secondary Worlds.

TP includes 25 leitmotifs from five previous titles: *The Legend of Zelda* (*LoZ*, 1986), *ALttP*, *OoT*, *MM*, and *WW*.[46] Table 5.2 surveys these leitmotifs, a *tour de force* of self-reference. In it I list the earliest game, alphabetize the theme within that game, and juxtaposes each theme's original dramatic contexts with those of *TP*.

Pozderac-Chenevey argues the music of *TP* suggests nostalgia *inside* and *outside* the gaming universe—Primary and Secondary Worlds—and manipulates our nostalgia so as to mirror what the protagonist feels.[47] *TP's* leitmotif repository can our summon experiences of five previous games, even more so due to the ludic functions of the Howling Stones and the leitmotifs associated with familiar places, narrative themes, or

Table 5.2 The Leitmotifs of Zelda from LoZ to TP

Theme/leitmotif	Original presentation	Twilight Princess (2006)
Item Catch	**Legend of Zelda (LoZ, 1987)** • *Gameplay:* Link discovers, retrieves, or captures an item.	• *Gameplay:* Same function as in previous games.
Main/Overworld Theme	LoZ, 1987 • *Gameplay:* Plays at the Title Screen & wall-to-wall music for the Overworld.	• *Cut Scene:* Title Screen • *Cut Scene:* Spirit Faron restores Wolf Link to his Hylian form, clothes him in the green tunic, and imbues him with the power of the Hero of Time. • *Cut Scene:* Link attempts to rescue the children from the Bulbins in Kakariko Village. • *Cut Scene:* Link obtains the Master Sword in Sacred Grove. • *Cut Scene:* Denouement. • *Cut Scene:* End credits.
Ganon/Ganondorf's Theme	**A Link to the Past (ALttP, 1991)** • *Cut Scene/Gameplay:* Original theme for sorcerer Agahnim. • *Cut Scene:* Attributed to Ganon when he is revealed as the alter ego of Agahnim. • *Cut Scene:* Link tracks Ganon to the Dark World, and Ganon speaks to Link.	• *Cut Scene:* The Sages at the Mirror Chamber tell Link about Ganondorf's failed execution. • *Gameplay:* In counterpoint with the Hyrule Castle leitmotif as Link searches for Ganondorf. • *Gameplay:* Final Battle with Ganondorf
Hyrule Castle	ALttP, 1991 • *Cut Scene/Gameplay:* Link enters Hyrule Castle and rescues Princess Zelda from Agahnim.	• *Cut Scene:* Zelda recounts Zant's siege of Hyrule Castle. • *Gameplay:* Link searches for Ganondorf in the castle. Three instances increase the complexity of the music to parallel Link's drawing closer to his foe: 1. Monophonic texture that dissolves into the second phrase of Ganondorf's theme; 2. March-like and homophonic texture. Statement segues into the Ganondorf theme; 3. Ganondorf and Castle themes in counterpoint.

(*Continued*)

Theme/leitmotif	Original presentation	Twilight Princess (2006)
Kakariko Village	ALttP, 1991 • *Gameplay:* Theme for the village.	• *Gameplay:* New theme whose theme quotes the opening six-notes of the original.
Master Sword	ALttP, 1991 • *Cut Scene:* Theme for Master Sword discovery, retrieval, and/or return.	• *Cut Scene/Gameplay:* Same context as *ALttP*.
Select Screen/ Fairy/Great Fairy	ALttP, 1991 • Institutionalizing the music for the Select Screen. • Theme for Fairy domains. • *Gameplay:* Link throws money in the Pond of Happiness.	• Select Screen music; • *Cut Scene:* Link's encounter with the spirit of Eldin; • *Cut Scene/Gameplay:* Link meets the Great Fairy in the Cave of Ordeals.
Zelda's Lullaby	ALttP, 1991 • *Cut Scene:* Zelda's rescue from Hyrule Castle; She and Link flee to the Sanctuary. • *Cut Scene:* Link rescues one of the Seven Maidens.	• *Cut Scene:* Wolf Link and Midna meet Zelda in Hyrule Castle. • *Cut Scene:* Zelda's sacrifice to save Midna. • *Diegetic/Gameplay:* Howling Stone melody in Sacred Grove. • *Gameplay:* Ganondorf possesses Zelda and battles Link.
Boss Music	*Ocarina of Time (OoT, 1998)* • *Gameplay:* Boss music for King Dodongo in Dodongo's Cave, as well as Volvagia in the Fire Temple.	• *Gameplay:* Boss music for Stallord in the Arbiter's Grounds.
Epona's Song (also known as "Lon Ranch")	OoT, 1998 • *Gameplay:* Lon Lon Ranch theme. • *Diegetic/Gameplay:* Ocarina Melody to summon Link's horse, Epona.	• *Cut Scene/Gameplay:* Link's first encounter with Epona in Kakariko Village after its terrorization by the Bulbins. • *Diegetic/Gameplay:* Link summons Epona by blowing through grass; Wolf Link also howls to summon Epona.

Escape from Ganondorf	*OoT*, 1998	• *Cut Scene:* Ganondorf's failed execution and banishment to the Twilight Realm.
	• *Gameplay:* Escape from Hyrule Castle after Ganondorf's defeat.	
Goron City	*OoT*, 1998	• *Gameplay:* Identical context and music from *OoT*.
	• *Gameplay:* Goron and Death Mountain leitmotif.	
Legend of Hyrule/ Chamber of Sages	*OoT*, 1998	• *Cut Scene:* Spirit Lanayru tells Link where to find the Fused Shadow.
	• *Cut Scene:* The history/mythology of Hyrule and scenes in the Chamber of Sages:	
	1. The Deku Tree tells Link and Navi about the three goddesses, the creation of Hyrule, and the Triforce;	
	2. Zelda tells Link about the Sacred Realm when they meet in Hyrule Castle;	
	3. Link awakens in the Chamber of Sages seven years after obtaining the Master Sword;	
	4. Link awakens each Sage after defeating a Boss;	
	5. Shiek meets Link in the Temple of Time and tells him about the Triforce. Shiek reveals herself to be Princess Zelda in disguise;	
	6. Ganondorf is banished after his defeat;	
	7. The Sages return to Hyrule during the end credits.	

(Continued)

Theme/leitmotif	Original presentation	Twilight Princess (2006)
Link's House	*OoT, 1998* • *Gameplay:* Link's house and the homes of those living in Kokiri Village.	• *Gameplay:* Similar function for the homes in Ordon Village.
Prelude of Light	*OoT, 1998* • *Diegetic/Gameplay:* Ocarina warping melody to the Temple of Time.	• *Diegetic/Gameplay:* Howling Stone melody in Faron Woods. • *Diegetic/Gameplay:* Link blows into Hawk Grass in Ordon Village. • *Diegetic/Gameplay:* Wolf Link tames a Twilit Kargarok near Lake Hylia. • *Gameplay:* Temple of Time dungeon music. The beginning of the music alludes to the rhythmic profile of the "Prelude of Light." *The leitmotif varies the original of *OoT* by way of rhythm, but its pitch content and melodic contour remain the same.
Requiem of Spirit	*OoT, 1998* • *Diegetic/Gameplay:* Ocarina warping melody to the Spirit Temple.	• *Diegetic/Gameplay:* Howling Stone melody in Upper Zora's River.
Saria's Song (also known as "Lost Woods")	*OoT, 1998* • *Gameplay:* Theme for Lost Woods and Sacred Forest Meadow. • *Diegetic/Gameplay:* Ocarina Melody with capabilities: 1. Summon/speak to Link's friend, Saria; • *Goron* leader Darunia gives Link the Goron Bracelets.	• *Gameplay:* music for the Sacred Grove: melody, timbre, and accompaniment adapt to Link's encounters with the Skull Kid. • *Diegetic/Gameplay:* Skull Kid's playing the melody allows Link to navigate the maze of Sacred Grove.

Serenade of Water	OoT, 1998	
	• *Diegetic/Gameplay:* Ocarina warping melody to the Water Temple.	• *Cut Scene:* Theme for the spirit of the murdered Zora Queen, Rutela. The melody features new, extended material.
		• *Gameplay:* Identical context and music from *OoT.*
Song of Time	OoT, 1998	
	• *Gameplay:* Temple of Time theme.	
	• *Diegetic/Gameplay:* Ocarina melody with several capabilities:	
	1. Opens the Door of Time;	
	2. Access to the Master Sword;	
	3. Manipulate blocks with the Symbol of Time on them.	
Zora's Domain	OoT, 1998	
	• *Gameplay:* Theme for the Zora race, Domain, and River.	• *Gameplay:* Identical context and music from *OoT.*
Goron Lullaby	*Majora's Mask (MM, 2000)*	
	• *Diegetic/Gameplay:* Goron Elder and Baby in the Goron Shrine teach Link the music in parts.	• **Diegetic/Gameplay:* Howling Stone melody in Lake Hylia.
	• Puts characters to sleep.	• **Gameplay:* Three note rising motif excerpted in the music of the Goron Mines.
		**Both examples draw from the three-note rising figure of the original theme but without the original accompaniment and continue with different music.

(*Continued*)

Theme/leitmotif	Original presentation	Twilight Princess (2006)
Song of Healing	*MM*, 2000 • *Diegetic/Gameplay:* Taught to Link by the Happy Mask Salesman after recovering the Ocarina of Time. • Abilities: 1. Returns Link to his Hylian form after any mask transformation; 2. Yields masks from others whom Link heals; 3. Repairs broken signs.	• *Diegetic/Gameplay:* Howling Stone melody located in Death Mountain.
Ballad of the Gales	**Wind Waker (WW, 2003)** • *Diegetic/Gameplay:* Taught to Link by the Wind God Cyclos in the Mother and Child Isles. • Abilities: 1. Warp; 2. Obtain Fire and Ice Arrows.	• *Diegetic/Gameplay:* Howling Stone melody located at Snowpeak.
Main Theme	*WW*, 2003 • *Cut Scene:* Introduction.	• *Diegetic/Gameplay:* Melody for the Howling Stone located at Snowpeak. *The percussion following the howling sounds similar to the *WW* main theme.

characters. Pozderac-Chenevey also demonstrates how our nostalgic responses from the music and can heighten our emotional connection to the Secondary World and to Link.[48] Consequently, we in the Primary World form a relationship with the characters through nostalgia summoned through music.

Regarding the Secondary World, the music of *TP* illuminates historical continuity within the *Zelda* universe and allows us to gauge characters and narratives within the mythology's timeline.[49] The *Zelda* mythology detailed in *Hyrule Historia* shows a complex chronology. The original timeline, "The Legend of the Goddesses and The Hero," begins with the earliest recorded events of *SS* and splits into three after Link's time travel in *OoT*: "The Decline of Hyrule and the Last Hero," "The Twilight Realm and the Legacy of the Hero," and "The Hero of Winds and a New World."[50] *TP* belongs to the second, yet its characters perform songs originating from other timelines, which can suggest a shared or collective memory within the *Zelda* Universe. These songs transcend alternate or parallel temporalities, much like Matthew Sautman's discussion of narrative in this volume.[51] *TP* codifies *Zelda's* musical legacy and nuances the game's mythology, which provides a signpost of the past and a point of departure for the future.

Case-Study Comparison

The ability of music to tap into the past within vast mythologies comes to life in no better examples than Lothlórien in *LotR* and Sacred Grove/Temple of Time in *TP*. It punctuates major points of arrival within these larger quests by way of geographic challenges, discovery of hidden places, meetings with guides, and stepping into the past.[52]

Lothlórien

The nostalgia of the Elves becomes virtually palpable in Lothlórien—unchanged and unchanging, immune to the passage of time.[53] Tolkien reveals Lothlórien in stages, like layers of memory, and punctuates important narrative moments with music.[54] As the Fellowship first approaches the river Nimrodel, Legolas sings part of the "Song of Nimrodel" about the eponymous Elf-maiden and her love King Amroth. Legolas echoes the irretrievable past of Lothlórien before it became marked with grief.[55] At the next stage, the Silverlode river, the Fellowship meets a company of Elves led by Haldir. He, too, yearns for Lothlórien's past:

> I do not believe that the world about us will ever again be as it was of old… For the Elves, I fear, it will prove at best a truce, in which they may pass to the Sea unhindered and leave the Middle-earth forever. Alas for Lothlórien that I love![56]

Haldir's words foreshadow the strange feeling Frodo receives upon entering Lothlórien proper. Frodo steps

> over a bridge of time into a corner of the Elder Days, and was now
> walking in a world that was no more. In Rivendell there was mem-
> ory of ancient things; in Lórien the ancient things still lived on in
> the waking world.[57]

Sam feels he wandered into a song; his description recalls Legolas singing as if reliving a memory, whereupon the act of singing or recalling a
song provides the first step through the threshold of the past.

The past becomes manifest most vividly when the Fellowship reaches
Cerin Amroth, the heart of Lothlórien. Frodo receives a sense of wonder
and the perception of things new and ancient as he steps "through a
high window that looked on a vanished world." He feels he has wandered into "a timeless land that did not fade or change or fall into forgetfulness."[58] The revealing of Lothlórien sets nostalgia in full force,
compounded by the great paradox of Elves. They love and are bound
to Middle-earth due to their immortality yet inexorably grow weary
of it due to changes wrought by time. So Elves must choose to depart
Middle-earth forever or remain there and fade. Either choice brings
nostalgia and sorrow.

Twilight Princess: Sacred Grove/Temple of Time

Like in Lothlórien, music reveals Sacred Grove and the Temple of Time
in stages. Before reaching the grove, Wolf Link and Midna approach a
Howling Stone. He performs "Prelude of Light," a century-old melody
originating during the events of *OoT*. The melody summons the Hero's
Shade, who teaches Link a sword technique. After the encounter, Wolf
Link performs "Zelda's Lullaby" at another Howling Stone, which reveals Sacred Grove—a labyrinthine forest leading to a meadow on which
a temple once stood—and the mischievous Skull Kid. Wolf Link and
Midna depend on circuitous guidance; and he frustrates them by disap-
pearing and reappearing at different locations.

The Skull Kid plays a melody from *OoT*, which once characterized
the Lost Woods maze and the friendship between Link and Saria. The
Skull Kid's playing is part of the puzzle as it is part of the solution;
the story cannot continue unless the duo follows the melody through
the Sacred Grove labyrinth. The louder the melody, the closer they
are to the Skull Kid and their goal of locating the Master Sword.
The softer the melody, the further they stray from the Skull Kid and
their path. The Skull Kid eventually reveals a passage leading to the
Master Sword.

Link and Midna must return to the Sacred Grove later in the game. Link speaks with Rusl, an old friend from Ordon Village. Both survey the gorge separating them from Sacred Grove, and Rusl muses nostalgically,

> It's been a while since we took a walk in the forest, huh? Yes, and how our world has changed... Do you know about the far side of this deep gorge? Some say there is an ancient temple deep in the woods that guards a sacred power.

Link and Midna then reenter Sacred Grove, once again encountering the Skull Kid and his antics. Instead of searching for the Master Sword, however, the duo now searches for the past itself. Link and Midna soon discover a door with the Hylian Crest. They cross its threshold and literally step into the past to perceive Sacred Grove as it once was: The Temple of Time. They enter a sanctuary of grey stone and stained glass, through which rays of sunlight peer to illuminate statues and the Master Sword pedestal while a choir chants "The Song of Time" throughout the ancient space. It is exactly as it was 100 years earlier during the events of *OoT*.

Comparison between Lothlórien and Sacred Grove requires examination of nostalgia within Primary and Secondary Worlds. Lothlórien provides a window to view nostalgia in our world. For instance, the story may cause us to think about our first experience of it, or we can personalize details of Lothlórien to a place or time in our lives. We may long to relive a memory, a time in the unattainable past, or we may think of a place we wish to revisit with the hope it remains as we remember it. The plight of Galadriel and her people can mirror these notions: Had we the power to preserve the past the way Galadriel does, would we do it? Would we freeze a time or place of our past into living memory? Such questions invite us to understand "the sorrow of the Elves" as a metaphor for Primary World nostalgia, so richly does Tolkien convey their plight.

Regarding the Primary World and *TP*, the leitmotifs "Prelude of Light," "Zelda's Lullaby," "Saria's Song," and "The Temple of Time" can tap into our gaming histories, associations, and personal relationships with *Zelda* titles. Provided we have played *Zelda* titles before that of *TP*, the leitmotifs can echo our first gaming experiences, whose company we shared, and our first step into "The Lost Woods."[59] If we encounter *Zelda* first by way of *TP*, then the nostalgic potential can occur during our second visit to Sacred Grove.[60] "Saria's Song" in particular can generate a sort of intra- and inter-nostalgic effect. Hearing the song during the second visit to Sacred Grove may take us back to an earlier part of *TP* itself. Yet it also may take us back to *OoT*, the game that originally taught us the melody; the same goes with "Song of Time" in

Temple of Time. Moreover, "Song of Time" connotes Western plain-chant to our ears in the Primary World.[61] The modal pitch content of the melody and wordless male choir can invoke a sense of the ancient, like stepping into a medieval cathedral filled with Gregorian chant.[62]

Nostalgia within in the Secondary Worlds of Middle-earth and Hyrule works similarly, punctuated by musical moments. Here we can look into the nostalgia of Tolkien's characters themselves. Legolas recalls Middle-earth long ago by singing the "Song of Nimrodel," which suggests a degree of enchantment and assists readers in delving into Middle-earth's past. When the Fellowship reaches the Silverlode, Haldir speaks about his longing to experience Middle-earth as it was. Music characterizes much of the narrative space in Lothlórien proper, as Frodo and Sam feel as if they have strayed into a song, and the Fellowship listens to a sung lament for the fallen Gandalf. Most importantly, Galadriel herself punctuates the Fellowship's departure with the epic "Song of the Eldamar."

As in Middle-earth, melodies harken back hundreds to thousands of years within the *Zelda* timeline and facilitate our learning about its history. For example, the "Lost Woods" existed in the original *LoZ* and appeared in several following installments, "Sacred Grove" in *TP*.[63] The Temple of Time, too, has strong associations with *Zelda*, being almost exclusive to the timeline to which *TP* belongs. *TP*'s Howling Stones also channel nostalgia by tapping into *Zelda*'s history through song. The Hero of Time performed both the "Prelude of Light" and "Saria's Song" during the events from it in *OoT* 100 years before *TP*. The lullaby, however, takes on mythological dimensions due to its connection with the goddess Hylia and her incarnations of Princess Zelda; the melody reaches back millennia in the *Zelda* timeline. The past, however, becomes virtually palpable in *TP* by way of "Saria's Song." The music leads Link to the literal past, but it also accompanies Link through several iterations of "The Lost Woods" within the timeline. The song thus functions as an aural representation of a labyrinthine-forest trope within *Zelda*'s mythology. To inhabitants of Hyrule, the song may connote mystery or peril; to others like Link, Saria, and the Kokiri, the forest maze may be a safe haven or secret place.

Concluding Thoughts

TP enjoys a privileged status in the nexus of videogames and Tolkienesque fantasy, which positions *Zelda* writ large favorably as a subject of mythopoeic investigation. The game's rich repository of leitmotifs manifests its mythopoeic potential by facilitating the "consolation" step of Tolkien's *Faërie*. The music collectively gives us a more complex, intimate look into the *Zelda* mythology, one that takes further shape with each installment. While Tolkien admits that fairy-stories never really end—the joy of *eucatastrophe* and the sadness of loss always enacting a cyclical relationship—the nostalgia nested in music of games like *Zelda* functions as a sort of dignified pursuit of similar ends. The nostalgic music of *TP* allows us to feel more intensely the joy of happy endings and the bitterness of grief, which demonstrates to us how powerful the relationship of fantasy and music can be.

Notes

1 "Playing the Past: An Introduction," in *Playing the Past: History and in Video Games* (Nashville, TN: Vanderbilt Press, 2008), 3.

2 Verlyn Flieger defines *Faërie* as "a literary construct, an imaginal exercise, a make believe world, a place to go to, and an altered state of being—a series of ideas easier to picture than to explain," in "When is a Fairy Story a *Faërie* Story? Smith of Wootton Major," *Green Suns and Faërie: Essays on J.R.R. Tolkien* (Kent, Ohio: Kent State University Press, 2012), 67.

3 *The Fiction of J. R. R. Tolkien: Master of Middle Earth* (New York: Random House, 1972), 2.

4 J.R.R. Tolkien, "On Fairy-Stories," *The Tolkien Reader* (New York, NY: Ballantine Books, 1966), 38, 60.

5 The original order is Fantasy, Recovery, Escape, and Consolation. For purposes of comparison, I have reordered it to Fantasy, Escape, Recovery, and Consolation.

6 Tolkien, "On Fairy-Stories," 69.

7 J. Michael Stitt, "Tolkien's *On Fairy-Stories*," *Tolkien Fantasy and Literature*, accessed 1 March 2018, https://faculty.unlv.edu/jmstitt/Eng477/ofs.html.

8 Svetlana Boym, *The Future of Nostalgia* (New York, NY: Persius Book Group, 2001).

9 R.J. Reilly, "Tolkien and the Fairy Story," in *Understanding the Lord of the Rings: The Best of Tolkien Criticism*, eds. Rose A. Zimbardo and Neil D. Isaacs (Boston, MA and New York: Houghton Mifflin Company, 2004), 94.

10 J.R.R. Tolkien, *The Letters of J.R.R. Tolkien*, ed. Humphrey Carpenter (Boston, MA: Houghton Mifflin Harcourt, 2000), 197.

11 Lennart E. Nacke and Mark Grimshaw, "Player-Game Interaction through Affective Sound," in *Game Sound Technology and Player Interaction: Concepts and Developments*, ed. Mark Grimshaw (Hershey, NY: Information Science Reference, 2011), 270; c.f. Oliver Grau, *Visual Art: From Illusion to Immersion* (Cambridge, MA: The MIT Press, 2003), 13; Karen Collins, *Playing With Sounds: A Theory of Interacting with Sound and Music in Video Games* (Cambridge, MA: The MIT Press, 2013), 133–135; and Timothy Summers, *Understanding Video Game Music* (Cambridge, UK: Cambridge University Press, 2016), 58–60 and Chapter 3.

12 Katie Salen and Eric Zimmerman, *Rules of Play: Game Design Fundamentals* (Cambridge, MA: The MIT Press, 2003), 450; see Collins, 134.

13 Jesper Juul, *Half-Real: Video Games Between Real Rules and Fictional Worlds* (Cambridge, MA: The MIT Press, 2011), 1.

14 Thomas Rowland, "Extrapolated Silence in Mythopoeic Spectacle, or, Why Does Link Look so Bored?" in this volume.

15 Andrew Glassner, *Interactive Storytelling: Techniques for 21st Century Fiction* (Wellesley, MA: AK Peters, 2004), 81–82.

16 Ibid., 133; qtd. in Summers, 85.

17 Laura Ermi and Frans Mäyrä, "Fundamental Components of the Gameplay Experience: Analyzing Immersion." I reorganize the order from Sensory Immersion, Challenge-Based Interaction, and Imaginative Immersion. Paper presented at the Digital Research Association conference, 2005; c.f. Collins, 134.
18 Zach Whalen and Laurie N. Taylor, "Playing the Past: an Introduction," in *Playing the Past: History and Nostalgia in Video Games*, eds. Zach Whalen and Laurie N. Taylor. (Nashville, TN: Vanderbilt Press, 2008), 4, 6.
19 Ibid., 2.
20 Anthony G. Cirilla, "The Hero of *Faërie*," in this volume.
21 Shigeru Miyamoto, Koji Kondo, Eii Aonuma, et al., *The Legend of Zelda: Ocarina of Time* (Redmond, WA: Nintendo of America, 1998), videogame.
22 Salehuddin Husin, "*The Legend of Zelda: Twilight Princess*," *GameAxis Unwired* 42 (February, 2007), 43.
23 Natasha Whiteman, "Homesick for Silent Hill: Modalities of Nostalgia in Fan Responses to *Silent Hill 4: The Room*," in *Playing the Past: History and Nostalgia in Video Games*, eds. Zach Whalen and Laurie N. Taylor (Nashville, TN: Vanderbilt Press, 2008), 32.
24 Henry Jenkins, *Textual Poachers: Television Fans and Participatory Culture* (London: Routledge, 2004), 95–97.
25 Whiteman, 35–36.
26 Casey Covel, "Review, The Legend of Zelda: Twilight Princess (Wii)," *Geeks Under Grace*, 8 August 2014, accessed 16 January 2018, www.geeksunder grace.com/gaming/review-the-legend-of-zelda-twilight-princess/.
27 Jonathan Metts, "The Legend of Zelda: Twilight Princess," Nintendo World Report, 18 November 2006, accessed 17 January 2018, www.nintendo worldreport.com/review/12434/the-legend-of-zelda-twilight-princess-wii.
28 Dan Ryckert, "Review: Legend of Zelda: Twilight Princess (Wii)," *Lawrence*, 14 November 2006, accessed 17 January 2018, www.lawrence.com/ news/2006/nov/14/review_legend_zelda_twilight_princess_wii/.
29 Matthew Rickert, "The Legend of Zelda: Twilight Princess," *RPGFan*, 4 April 2007, accessed 18 January 2018, www.rpgfan.com/reviews/zeldatp-wii/index.html.
30 Gene Park, "The Legend of Zelda: Twilight Princess Review," *Gamecritics*, 23 February 2007, accessed 22 September 2019, https://gamecritics.com/ gene-park/the-legend-of-zelda-twilight-princess-review/.
31 Mark Serrels, "Twilight Princess Is A Game Out Of Time," *Kotaku*, 7 March 2016, accessed 13 September 2019, www.kotaku.com.au/2016/03/ twilight-princess-is-a-game-out-of-time/.
32 Stephen Totilo, "Shigeru Miyamoto Interviews Me about Hardcore Games, Also Talks 'Punch-Out' and 'Mario,' 'Zelda' Shortcomings," *MTV News*, 29 October 2008, accessed 13 September 2019, www.mtv.com/news/2457976/ shigeru-miyamoto-punchout-mario-zelda-portal/.
33 Covel, "Review: The Legend of Zelda: Twilight Princess (Wii)," accessed 22 February 2018; Kristian Reed, "The Legend of Zelda: Twilight Princess Deserves a Spotlight," *Eurogamer*, 3 April 2008, accessed 21 September 2019, www.eurogamer.net/articles/r_zeldatp_wii.
34 Rickert, "The Legend of Zelda: Twilight Princess," 18 January 2018.
35 Chris Kohler, "VGL: Koji Kondo Interview," *Wired*, 11 March 2007, accessed February 2018, www.wired.com/2007/03/vgl-koji-kondo-/. Koji Kondo took a supervisorial role for *TP*; c.f. Bozon, "Koji Kondo: An Interview with a Legend," *IGN*, 12 March 2007, accessed 22 February 2018, www.ign.com/articles/2007/03/12/koji-kondo-an-interview-with-a-legend.

36 Sean Fenty, "Why Old School is "Cool:" A Brief Analysis of Classic Video Game Nostalgia," in *Playing the Past: History and Nostalgia in Video Games*, eds. Zach Whalen and Laurie N. Taylor (Nashville, TN: Vanderbilt Press, 2008), 21–23.
37 Summers, 59, 86–87.
38 Ibid., 72, 80.
39 Richard Wagner (1813–1883) developed the leitmotif in his music dramas. Later, film and videogame composers adopted the technique. Tim Summers demonstrates how game music has taken on the cinematic features of film scores in *Understanding Video Game Music*, 143–177.
40 Matthew Bribitzer-Stull, *Understanding the Leitmotif: From Wagner to Hollywood Film Music* (Cambridge, UK: Cambridge University Press, 2015), 92, 95–101.
41 Stephanie Lind, "Active Interfaces and Thematic Events in *The Legend of Zelda: Ocarina of Time*," in *Music Video Games: Performance, Politics, and Play*, ed. Michael Austin (New York: Bloomsbury Publishing Inc., 2016), 85; see Collins, 55–62.
42 Lind, 95.
43 Ibid., 97.
44 Sarah Pozderak-Chenevey, "A Direct Link to the Past: Nostalgia and Semiotics in Video Game Music," *Divergencepress.net*, 2 June 2014, accessed 17 September 2019, http://divergencepress.net/articles/2016/11/3/a-direct-link-to-the-past-nostalgia-and-semiotics-in-video-game-music.
45 Lind, 83.
46 Vincent E. Rone, "A Case for Twilight Princess: the Music," Part 1, *Zelda Dungeon*, 2 January 2015, accessed 21 September 2019, www.zeldadungeon.net/a-case-for-twilight-princess-the-music/.
47 Pozderak-Chenevey, "A Direct Link to the Past," accessed 20 September 2019.
48 Ibid.
49 Ibid.; See also SWE3tMadness, "More than just noise: Nostalgia and homecoming," *Destructoid*, 9 September 2010, accessed 21 September 2019, www.destructoid.com/more-than-just-noise-nostalgia-and-homecoming-183290.phtml.
50 Patrick Thorpe, ed., *The Legend of Zelda: Hyrule Historia*, trans. Michael Gombos, Takahiro Moriki, Heidi Plechl, Kumar Sivasubramanian, Aria Tanner, and John Thomas (Milwaukie, OR: Dark Horse Books, 2013), 69.
51 "A Link Across Adventures: the Mythic Nature of Queer Time in The Legend of Zelda Series," in this volume.
52 Pozderak-Chenevey, "A Direct Link to the Past..." accessed 20 February 2018.
53 David K. O'Connor, "Tolkien and Nostalgia," *Thomas International Center*, accessed 1 March 2018 www.ticenter.net/tolkien-and-nostalgia/. He calls Lothlórien a dead, unchanging world.
54 Wayne G. Hammond and Christina Scull, *The Lord of the Rings: A Reader's Companion* (Boston, MA and New York: Houghton Mifflin Company, 2005), 308.
55 J.R.R. Tolkien, *The Lord of the Rings: The Fellowship of the Ring* (Boston, MA: Houghton and Mifflin Co., 1994), 329–332.
56 Ibid., 340.
57 Ibid.
58 Ibid., 341–342.
59 Bribitzer-Stull, 93–94.

60 See Isabella van Elferen, "¡Un Forastero! Issues of Virtuality and Diegesis in Videogame Music," *Music and the Moving Image* 4, no. 2 (Summer, 2011), 31.
61 Lind, 96.
62 Bribitzer-Stull, 92–93, 115. The "Song of Time" bears verisimilitude to chant, which summons the topical construct of "old" and "ancient."
63 *ALttP, Link's Awakening* (1993, "Mysterious Woods"), *OoT, MM* ("Woods of Mystery"), *Oracle of Seasons* (2001), *Oracle of Ages* (2001, "Fairie's Woods"), *Four Swords Adventures* (2004), *The Minish Cap* (2004), *Spirit Tracks* (2009), *ALbW* (2013), and *BotW* (2017).

6 The Domestic Champion in *The Wind Waker*

Michael David Elam

The Wind Waker's seascape looms as the most unique navigable territory in *The Legend of Zelda* series.[1] Indeed, *Wind Waker* buries the large landscapes of previous games under a literally inundating sea.[2] As with other flood myths, the overpowering sea not only destroys civilizations but also preserves life and hope for its flourishing. Initially life-depriving water stifles regeneration but later becomes paradoxically life-giving. Moreover, floods separate and isolate, destroying established connections. Such is the case with *Wind Waker*'s Great Sea, highlighting isolation over integration despite occasional contact among inhabitants of the gameworld. The setting also presents a view of small, localized communities characterized by closeness. Such community reveals the importance of the domestic, the family household. No grand castle figures in *Wind Waker*'s initial hero's journey. And though the end of the game's narrative suggests the possibility of expansion, players fulfill the hero's journey in a remarkably domestic, albeit dangerous, world.[3]

Indeed, *Wind Waker* reinforces domesticity by the very elements of fantasy and adventure that characterize it. As J.R.R. Tolkien points out in "On Fairy-Stories," a function of fantasy is to reveal more clearly the importance of the Primary World, what Tolkien describes as "regaining a clear view.... 'seeing things as we are... meant to see them.'"[4] As gamers in the Primary World witness the story unfold, then, they guide Link through the Secondary World on the hero's path of recovery. Gamers help Link complete the cycle of the hero's journey, securing safety for domestic spaces and unveiling the possibility for society's enlargement to its pre-flood scale. They see that such safety and enlargement ought to characterize their own world.

In its domestic context, Link's journey also iterates the monomyth, the hero's quest described by Joseph Campbell in *The Hero with a Thousand Faces*: "the formula represented in the rites of passage: *separation – initiation – return*."[5] Campbell's paradigm, however, does not account for the primarily physical value of the hero's success, discussed near the end of this essay. In fact, when one examines details of *Wind Waker*'s quest in light of Campbell's paradigm, preservation of the family unit, the basic creative force for society, rises as one of the most important elements of the hero's goal.

In a mythic context, the importance of Hyrule needing to be a generative, domestic society should not be surprising. Establishing, protecting, and maintaining domesticity characterize other mythic heroes' sea-faring journeys. For example, the *Aeneid* and *Odyssey* each emphasize the importance of domesticity, both featuring the sea as a major narrative element. In the *Aeneid*, the sea is the road by which Aeneas makes his way to Latium to fulfill his mandate for a new, fruitful nation. The sea becomes a weapon the gods used against him, a way to test the hero-founder. In the *Odyssey* also, Odysseus ultimately quests for home, peaceful and nurturing its inhabitants—not exploited by disturbers of domestic tranquility. And the sea also threatens his success. So in *Wind Waker*, though Link starts at home instead of seeking it, the hero must confront a threat that undermines the stability of households. Link must also navigate a dangerous sea, at once path and barrier to establishing peaceful homes. Campbell categorizes such a hero's journey as deluge, characterized by destructive flood, and points out the "deluge hero is a symbol of the germinal vitality of man surviving even the worst tides of catastrophe and sin."[6] Link, the boy, symbolizes a domestic seed to be sown, cultivated, and protected; and players help Link accomplish what he symbolizes: the guarantee of restored fruitfulness for an inundation Hyrule, the hope of domesticity.

Other flood narratives, such as those of Noah, Utnapishtim, or the sinking of Atlantis, also have an element of human failure provoking divine wrath. Indeed, in modern fantasy writing, J.R.R. Tolkien's own mythology reiterates the deluge-narrative as a divine punishment that effectively resets society, with the refugees from Numenor establishing new cities in Arnor and Gondor in Middle-earth.[7] Such floods destroy to restart with a domestic unit at the narrative core. Not merely a seed to plant or a relic to preserve, the hero of the saved household renews households in a cleansed earth.[8] Floods purge threats to domestic peace. Unlike the dismissal of rebels by Aeneas or the killing of suitors by Odysseus, which purge on smaller scales, floods purge worlds.[9] Flood narratives reveal households worthy of preservation, the heads of which undertake the hero's journey. Details may vary, but saving a household, a domestic remnant, in flood narratives underscores the need for peace and protection from disturbers of household order.

Preservation of domestic remnants in deluge stories also emphasizes the household as society's basic unit. In the story of Noah, for example, the only divinely protected survivors are Noah and his immediate family. Similarly, though not as massive as the biblical account of the Noahic flood, the inundation around which the quest of *Wind Waker* occurs demonstrates significant judgment on Hyrule.[10] Unlike the Noahic flood, however, the Hyrulean flood does not recede. Link must travel a sea made permanent by judgment.

Domestic Markers

Before looking more closely at how Link's quest in *Wind Waker* conforms to Campbell's overall hero's journey, one should understand what elements of the journey in *Wind Waker* emphasize domesticity, fruitfulness, and familial harmony as important ends served by Link's quest. In his quest to restore domestic order, Link symbolizes potential generativity. Indeed, the breaking of his household drives Link into the hero's journey.[11] Parental absence, moreover, strongly suggests broken domestic continuity. Outset Island, still a domestic space, preserves cultural memory needed for symbolizing the journey from childhood to adulthood. But when the Helmaroc King kidnaps Aryl, Link's sister, the community-sanctioned symbol becomes a literal journey to save the community.

Link's journey places the domestic firmly at the center of societal order and flourishing. Seemingly an accident at first, Link undertakes his quest only to save his sister from a kidnapping.[12] In previous games, Link seems to accept adventure from the start for the sake of matters other than merely his home. For example, after Link attempts to break the curse upon the Deku Tree in *The Ocarina of Time*, the Deku Tree directs Link to find the Princess of Destiny (Zelda) and establishes early Link's journey to stop Ganon. By contrast, throughout much of the journey in *Wind Waker*, Link progresses along the hero's path to rescue his sister, his ultimate goal. Saving Hyrule from Ganon comes later, through Link defending his household. Later, Tetra's rescuing Link leads into the larger world-saving quest. After confronting the force that kidnapped his sister, Link returns to Outset Island, but the restoration of his family at this stage in *Wind Waker* is temporary.[13] The threat against his family's flourishing still exists on a larger scale. Link must defeat it to make the restoration permanent. *Wind Waker*'s narrative effectively pauses the reblooming of the household so Link can complete the hero's journey. Indeed, the pausing itself indicates the journey's parenthetical nature compared with the more important matter of the household's peace and longevity.

The Hero's Journey

To see Link's journey in *Wind Waker* more fully as myth, Joseph Campbell's *The Hero with a Thousand Faces* provides a helpful framework. Indeed, *Wind Waker* and other myths present variations, sometimes drastic, on the hero's journey.[14] Nevertheless, Campbell's scheme identifies mythical features that situate Link's journey in *Wind Waker* in the same category as journeys told by Homer, Virgil, Dante, and others. Indeed, the major points that characterize Campbell's understanding of the hero's journey are worth noting: Something causes the hero to depart on an important journey; the initial threshold draws the hero into an unusual experience; within the strange experience the hero reaches the culmination of the journey; the hero returns with his gain, a gift for himself and his society.[15]

Crossing Thresholds

The call to the hero's journey in *Wind Waker* comes by way of a chance sighting of the kidnapped pirate captain, Miss Tetra, drawing Link to the threshold of adventure. Link's willingness to search for Tetra, though he may see himself merely aiding a stranger, indicates his worthiness to undertake the mythic path of the hero. The usual features of the call to adventure take the stage here: The high wood of Outset Island serves as the dark forest, while Tetra struggles in a great tree, dropped by a loathly beast whose unexpected appearance foreshadows the narrative's first threshold moment.[16] In going after Tetra, however, Link absents himself from his sister, who is taken from the home, the place of generativity and vitality. And other iterations of the family occupy Outset Island: Link and his sister, by their very role in the framework of the hero's journey, represent future potential for domestic flourishing. The particular arrangement of the call in *Wind Waker*, though, underscores the sacrificial nature of the journey to restore the world's flourishing. In this case, Link undertakes a personal journey, but his sacrifice for his own household leads to global renewal and societal growth. His initially altruistic act of seeking Tetra validates his subsequent seeking his kidnapped sister, Aryll. The dark force sequestering her both symbolizes and causes barrenness.

Link's new motivation, recovering Aryll, connects to Campbell's discussion of the hero's need to go within and battle that which disrupts his psychic well-being. As Campbell puts it,

> the first work of the hero is to retreat from the world scene of secondary effects to those causal zones of the psyche where the difficulties really reside, and... eradicate them in his own case (i.e., give battle to the nursery demons of his local culture) and break through to the undistorted, direct experience and assimilation of what C.G. Jung has called 'the archetypal images.'[17]

But in the case of Link, the nursery demons of his own world become literal disruptions that take Aryll—the most recent occupant of the nursery, where the family protects its vulnerable members—leaving Link's household not just incomplete, but broken. Psychic health should be found in households, where families are safe. Recovery of Link's sister, then, is recovery of the family unit and restoration of household safety.

Recovery, though, includes aid from supernatural helpers, most often an old figure who comes to the hero at the time he accepts the call to adventure.[18] In *Wind Waker* Link's grandmother initially stands for the figure of such supernatural aid. Although Campbell's examples show figures often unrelated to the hero, Link's grandmother first grants him special aid by way of ritual passage into adulthood.[19] The absence of Link's immediate parents further suggests loss of the fruitfulness and knowledge that perpetuate society. To bridge the gap between the generation of youth represented by Link, and the passing generation of Link's grandmother (and Orca and Sturgeon), Link first receives help from his grandmother to defeat Ganon. Her help highlights the family unit and its flourishing as the center of Link's journey in *Wind Waker*.

As for the timing of Link's undertaking his quest, starting the quest on his birthday symbolizes Link's birth into hero, and his subsequent journey enacts stages of development as hero. On the day celebrating Link's birth, the villain's work of iniquity plays a kind of zero-sum game: The birth of the hero marks the loss of his sister. But Link, the domestic hero, abolishes the villain's game. Link's birth is addition, growth, and his recovering Aryll shows the importance of domestic thriving. "Only birth," Campbell writes,

> can conquer death—the birth, not of the old thing again, but of something new. Within the soul, within the body social, there must be—if we are to experience long survival—a continuous 'recurrence of birth' (*palingenesia*) to nullify the unremitting recurrences of death.[20]

Link's self-sacrifice for the sake of his sibling embodies the mythos of such birth.

Such apparently tragic self-sacrifice facilitates redemption beyond mere self-awareness.[21] But the inwardly turning quality of Link's quest also has external salvific results. Link's journey of the individual, which players witness and facilitate, paradoxically serves to affirm society too. Later, Campbell continues his discussion of the external ramifications of the inward quality of the hero's journey having value for the hero's world: "The passage of the mythological hero may be over-ground, incidentally; fundamentally it is inward—into the depths where obscure resistances are overcome, and long lost, forgotten powers are revivified, to be made available for the transfiguration of the world."[22] Link's journey through various physical locales in flooded Hyrule, then, may be seen as an inward journey that benefits others beyond himself.

Still, Link's journey is not entirely self-isolation after which he brings a gift to the world; he remains in and part of his world, questing in it initially, not for it. And, paradoxically, Link's going out to save Aryll also helps bring himself, the boy, to age. Link does not quest initially for his world's sake; he wants to recover his sister, a part of his home now missing. And though a family without a sister is not necessarily an evil (as players know at some level), a family that has a sister seized out of it is: Link steps out of his home in order to retrieve its missing piece. So among *Wind Waker*'s multiple thresholds, the doorway of home stands out most.

Link's quest opens before him with Aryl's kidnapping on his birthday, tying him to the reality Outset Island's coming-of-age rites symbolizes.[23] As Campbell demonstrates, each quester, whether taking an adventurous or mundane route, is saved "by virtue of the inherited symbolic aids of society, the rites of passage."[24] Therefore, Link's symbolic coming-of-age converts to the very journey the domestic custom symbolizes, his singular journey preserving the importance of the household's less adventurous ways. He quests for his sister, not a hero's status—though he gains that too by virtue of his resolve. In his case, the exceptional serves the mundane.

Link crosses two minor thresholds between his departure from Outset Island and his arrival at the Forsaken Fortress, the primary first threshold of Link's journey.[25] One is the literal crossing of the threshold of the sea to the Forsaken Fortress in Tetra's ship. The other is the crossing of the platforms below decks of Tetra's ship. The platform crossing, part of the player-tutorial, foreshadows the hero's journey to restore the household and affirms desire to undertake the quest. Certainly Niko, a diminutive member of Tetra's pirate crew, is not quite the dangerous figure one would expect in a hero's crossing a primary threshold, but he does enforce the boundary keeping Link from undertaking his quest in earnest. Link must pass the test for the ship to reach the Forsaken Fortress, a small test affirming capacity to complete challenges ahead. Crossing the first threshold, however, only initiates Link as worthy to be called across a greater threshold. He is not yet the consummate hero. When Link emerges, he only moves one degree closer to the kind of hero who, as Campbell puts it, "passes back and forth across the horizons of the world."[26] For now, the enclosed location of the platform-crossing inside Tetra's ship foreshadows the greater infernal journey associated with the whale's belly.

This may be, however, too august a view of Link at any stage of his journey. Lawrence Coupe, underscoring the hero's comedic potential, says the hero

> has the centrality of a reviving god, but he has the sense of absurdity of a laughing animal. For above all, his universe will be 'humorous'; and he himself will emerge from the ranks of 'clowns' or 'loons.' He is, then, a force for endlessly productive imperfection rather than for arid and static perfection.[27]

Coupe's later discussion of the shaman-type hero shows Link's additional connection to a comedic kind of the myth-hero. In contrast to the priest—the individual versed in dogma to gain power—the shaman "acquires his own power. There is no *logos*, no fixed scheme or formula, for him to hold onto: he has to trust to the *mythos*, the narrative process of spiritual exploration."[28] In this sense, gamers recite the hero's journey in the act of playing the videogame.[29] The usual barrier between narrative and audience becomes an interface establishing the reciprocal relationship between story and hearer; players facilitate the hero's journey as they witness it. Indeed, Coupe points out, "Orthodox beliefs and systems have to be left behind, and one must proceed by the sheer force of imagination."[30] And though Coupe does not refer to the act of playing videogames, his point about the imagination as a driver of action applies. Gamers are analogous to audiences, but they also direct, in part, the hero's journey. Still, the story is Link's, though it testifies that gamers may have such stories of their own.[31]

In *Wind Waker*, then, the average person completing the hero's journey serves primarily to protect domestic flourishing. Coupe, again, reveals the importance of such flourishing and describes frameworks strikingly similar to *Wind Waker*'s mythical paradigm. He shows that extraordinary heroes maintain the cycle of life by standing against ever-threatening chaos.[32] And the power Link acquires through *Wind Waker* restores and secures the home.

The Road Beyond the Threshold

Once Link crosses the complex threshold from the forest-rescue of Tetra to his first foray into the Forsaken Fortress, the series of quests (even side quests) fits into the stage Campbell describes as the "Road of Trials." Interestingly, the seascape and the various points of Link's adventure literally manifest Campbell's description of this road: "the hero moves in a dream landscape of curiously fluid, ambiguous forms, where he must survive a succession of trials."[33] In fact, the very metaphorical quality of fluidity Campbell sees in the archetypal hero's journey coalesces into the literal realm of *Wind Waker*. Any landscape where the hero faces trials offers fluid experiences, but the *Wind Waker*'s Great Sea physically emphasizes this state of flux. The seascape also isolates the hero throughout his trials, even submerging Link in a hidden past, abandoned and ambiguous.

Additionally, at the Forsaken Fortress Link must embark on what Campbell might describe as "the perilous journey into the darkness... into the crooked lanes of his own spiritual labyrinth."[34] Here, the hero's encounters purify him by "dissolving, transcending, or transmuting the infantile images of our personal past" and help him to achieve salvific knowledge.[35] In the case of *Wind Waker*, however, Link's personal journey serves mainly to reorder a fruitful cycle whereby society's members may journey from infancy to adulthood in the household, the domestic garden by which society flourishes.

Still, Campbell, recounting Inanna's journey into the nether realm, emphasizes the hero's need to die to self.[36] Link's journey, though, even if self-sacrificial, is not necessarily self-death. In *Wind Waker*, a kind of dying characterizes Link's descent early on, with his initial failure to rescue Aryl from the Forsaken Fortress. Death happens early for Link. Indeed, one might see him as dead already. For Link discovery and self-building, not death, follow on the hero's road. The journey fulfills, as Tolkien puts it, desire to "Escape from Death."[37] In fact, one might see Link as initially a dead self, steeped in perfunctory ritual, no matter how meaningful the thing it symbolizes. The experience of and powerlessness to stop loss shows the self already dead, empty of vital power to stand against threat. Link must reconstruct himself and be reborn. The various items Link finds along the way then become tools by which to accomplish such rebirth. They enable Link to exercise his will to undertake trials—and succeed. He resurrects the ego, the previously dead thing inhabiting the boy on Outset Island. He does not die to self. His dead self becomes alive.[38]

To that end, Link's journey into the Tower of the Gods combines elements of Campbell's "Meeting with the Goddess," the point of overcoming major obstacles, and "Atonement with the Father," which tests the hero's resolve.[39] The Temple of the Gods offers such obstacles and tests, revealing Link's worth to serve as the Hero of Winds.[40] This central point acts as a kind of baptism or anointing, serving as a narrative hub for Link's journey, a base of operations, launching Link into the stages that build his resurrected self.

Returning Across the Threshold

Link's subsequent journeys into the Temples of Earth and Wind also function as the initiation rites that, as Campbell puts it, reconcile hero with father-figure and enable his return to the world. Link must restore the power of the Hero's sword by descending deep into the bowels of these temples, becoming more and more alive, to resurrect the power that will put death itself to death. Throughout the game, Link's multiple immersions—into the Tower of the Gods, the submerged Hyrule Castle, and Temples of Earth and Wind—echo the descent of Gilgamesh into the waters to find the plant of eternal life.[41] And though the hero's Sword is of different, even opposite, quality from that of the plant of life, it remains the means by which the hero brings blessing to his own world.[42]

Still, *Wind Waker* emphasizes not establishing a kingdom's power but the lowly household's flourishing. Indeed, Campbell's illustration of the restoration of Job emphasizes such domestic prosperity, the result of reconciliation between the tested hero and father figure. Just as Job is questioned by God concerning his inability to capture the primordial Leviathan, Link similarly is tested by Jabun, who holds Nayru's Pearl.[43] Link must find Jabun, analogous to Leviathan, in his hiding place guarded by a whirlpool in the sea. While each account contains significant differences, both show the need for reconciliation with primordial forces and beings whose power contextualizes each hero's journey. Job's journey omits physical travel for mental exploration, while Link's relies on movement. The results for each hero are similar though. Job's restoration does not merely provide reparations for Satan's afflicting him with pain and loss. Job also sees the continuance of his household into its fourth generation, revealing the value in being tested by and yielding to the divine.[44] Job must encounter wisdom to return to fruitfulness, wisdom the Satan's afflictions obscure. Similarly, Link, by successfully contending with the forces that hide Jabun, ultimately sees the restoration of both his home and his larger world.

Moreover, Link's actual journey includes encountering wisdom directly, namely in the Triforce of Wisdom, possessed by Tetra/Zelda. The game's story shows that obtaining and benefitting from wisdom also requires shrewdness. Sequestering Tetra/Zelda in the inundated Hyrule castle hides wisdom from the prying eyes of Ganon, whose possession of the Triforce of Power seduces him to take wisdom. Unopposed, Ganon eventually will possess the Triforces of Wisdom and Courage, unless wielders of Wisdom and Courage oppose him.[45] Ganon counts on ignorance and apathy—related to lacking wisdom and courage—to guarantee none will wield either wisdom or courage against him.[46] But Ganon attempts nevertheless to guarantee his victory by cowing any that might take up a Triforce against him. He intimidates the hero, whose victory is unsure. Yes, Link inevitably must fulfill his quest, but inevitable fulfillment emerges only in hindsight. In the case of defeat, the thwarted "hero's journey" paradoxically becomes the backdrop against which the true hero's journey occurs, for the true hero's journey must succeed.[47] Returning then to hiding Zelda, *Wind Waker* demonstrates courage hiding wisdom from power, and wisdom combining with courage to overcome blind power.

The movement here matches much of Campbell's "Meeting the Goddess," which tests the hero's resolve.[48] For Campbell, the goddess must challenge the hero consciously. In *Wind Waker*, however, Tetra, though in the goddess role, does not test Link consciously as goddess. Tetra instead tests Link indirectly by taking him to the Forsaken Fortress, then validates the hero's early resolve by returning to save him, though his first attempt to confront Ganon fails. Domestic Link successfully meets the goddess. Indeed, the foreshadowed union between Zelda/Tetra and Link indicates a divine sanction to preserve and cultivate domesticity.

So the domestic nobody in rising to free his sister secures domestic fruitfulness for him and his world. But Ganon's ambition grasps for self-glory in stasis, like a king ruling for the sake of being seen, subject always to his own whims. Indeed, Campbell instructively contrasts hero against tyrants. He points out that "becoming" characterizes the hero, whereas the tyrant seeks to possess power.[49] The tyrant's ambition subjugates and stagnates the household; the hero frees it.

So Ganondorf seeks power not merely to wield but to possess. He emerges from the past as a reversal of growth, caring little for time so long as he possesses its matter. As Campbell puts it, the tyrant "is Holdfast not because he keeps the *past* but because he *keeps*."[50] Campbell points out that pride undermines the tyrant: "He is proud because he thinks of his strength as his own; thus he is in the clown role, as a mistaker of shadow for substance; it is his destiny to be tricked"—or defeated outright.[51] So Campbell's tyrant, faced by the hero, helps clarify the nature of Ganondorf in *Wind Waker*. But the hero requires a boon.

The boon Link gains is the power to become the Hero of Winds and imprison evil so the mundane may continue. What Campbell describes— namely the hero seeking the sustaining substance (grace) of the gods and goddesses—applies to Link's successful navigation through the Earth and Air temples, leading to his apotheosis.[52] With the fully restored Hero's Sword, Link will defeat Ganon and banish his life-limiting ambitions.[53] But a final leg on the road of the hero's initiation remains: to find the fragments of the broken Triforce of Courage. Link gathers courage for his confrontation with power, becoming the courageous warrior aligned with wisdom to confront isolated power. Ganon's power is not guided by wisdom and courage but by the folly of self-ambition—the desire to possess without sharing distinguishes hero from tyrant.[54]

The hero, then, must include himself in the community of others, something players witness in directing Link on his journey. Link's apotheosis depends on fellowship. Failure of apotheosis stems from desire to withdraw into the self or limit community.[55] Link's journey initially sets him to rescue his sister, the member of his immediate family. Only later must he suppress forces seeking to oppress a world made up of communities like his own. Far from being an abstract realization of hidden mystery, Link's apotheosis is mundane.[56] Link becomes the champion of the hearth, the household. His success also redeems the royal house to become smaller and participate in the better institute of the domestic, even as it safeguards society's members—its actual members, not merely society as abstraction. Such is the boon Link brings to his world.

The Hero's Gift

After the recovery of Aryll and the sequestering of Zelda/Tetra, Link must defeat Ganon, a quest involving self-sacrifice. But Link's resolve should appear more exemplary than didactic. Didacticism indeed has a place in paradigms of the hero's journey, and Link's example teaches virtue. Yet Link's act is his own, because one, not many, must undertake it. His lesson is not, as Campbell implies, a private revelation of abstractions. Rather, Link shows the husbandman fulfilling his responsibility, to do the work that allows his household to flourish.[57] And as the husbandman works alongside a helper fitting for such tasks, so Link works with Zelda/Tetra to tend their land. It is the mythos of Chapter 2 of Genesis, where the divinely formed community reflects the ideal state in which differentiated individuals live. Rather than seeing male-female union primarily as erotic, the mythos emphasizes its procreative nature, procreation in service of flourishing community.

Though Campbell emphasizes a kind of amalgam of dualities in the hero's achievement, *Wind Waker* celebrates distinction among real individuals in community with others.[58] Procreation begets diversity, and even though union of individuals leads to regeneration, one individual is not subsumed into the other, nor, as Campbell suggests, are either negated into something else. Indeed, companionship offers the potential for the intensification of individuals and strengthening each one's contribution to community.[59]

Campbell's discussion, however, tends to marginalize threats on the outside of the hero in favor of seeing the hero's journey as revealing the appalling nature of the hero's self. Campbell, for instance, presents the Transfiguration of Christ as a kind of physical disguise of the psyche being undone, where "Flesh had dissolved... to reveal the Word."[60] Nevertheless, flesh remained, showing the Disciples that the Word was part of the world, participating in it with them, showing even that fishermen had status in it.[61] The revelation is not an immersion into profound depths but an emerging from the isolated depths into the reality of spiritual and physical integration. That is the mythos operating in the culmination of *Wind Waker.* If the hero's journey merely symbolizes the individual finding wholeness—itself a metaphor for universal wholeness—such a hero's journey cannot sufficiently account for external realities. Yes, the journey in *Wind Waker* arguably reorganizes Link's psyche for the sake of organizing societal psyche, but Link's journey is significantly physical.

The union of Link to Tetra/Zelda after their defeating Ganon evinces integrated renewal. This accords with Campbell's paradigm of return as a kind of union between Primary and Secondary experience, but *Wind Waker* presents a paradigm that challenges Campbell's emphasis on the separation of hero from his world. Though Hyrule Castle will not rise again, a new chance for propagation, fruitfulness, and peace stands before Link and Zelda in the ordinary world. The sacred, represented by Zelda, informs Primary experience, represented by Link, the avatar of the common, so that there is no taboo to avoid or touch from which to refrain.[62] Neither Link nor Zelda are sacred in the sense they require insulation from the world they occupy. On the contrary, the resolution of the hero's journey in *Wind Waker* suggests they, mundane and sacred, become integral parts of the redeemed world. The hero's insight is not, as Campbell suggests, a burden to bear in a world that cannot or will not understand his gained experience. He is not the world's totality or a mere microcosmic signpost to some other reality. Rather the hero's insight enables him to be small in the world, a part of it.

Again, although Link's reintegration into the world he saves does not negate Campbell's vision, Campbell's vision recedes before Link's perspective, which emphasizes a limited hero preserving the world's commonplace quality. Thus, non-heroes, audiences, may connect more nearly to Link and his journey and better understand the myth encountered in *Wind Waker*. Link champions the reality of the mundane, of households occupied with duties, family members moving among the members of others, interacting with each other. Link's journey quells power's blind ambition. Courage and wisdom temper power so that it perpetuates peace for the flourishing of the household, itself a paradox of sameness and newness. The routine—perhaps getting up, eating, tilling—serves as a tapestry through which the unique is woven: The variety is as endless as the sameness in which it occurs. This is the life Link anticipates at the beginning of *Wind Waker*, and the life to which gamers return him. Link offers the insight that the fabric of the mundane is the essence of life. One rightly hopes for peace and for a hero whose deeds are for the sake of the everyday.

Notes

1 Mitsuhiro Takano, Hajime Takahashi, and Eiji Aonuma, *The Legend of Zelda: The Wind Waker HD* (referred to throughout as *Wind Waker*, with the series referred to as *Zelda*).

2 See *The Legend of Zelda: Hyrule Historia* (*Hyrule Historia*), 123; *The Legend of Zelda: Encyclopedia* (*Encyclopedia*), 256.

3 This essay addresses *Wind Waker* primarily as narrative controlling players' experience of the game, a matter discussed in this volume by Nathan Schmidt, though he focuses mainly on the ways gaming environment shapes players' experience of the gameworld. See also J.R.R. Tolkien, "On Fairy-Stories," in *Tree and Leaf*, in *The Tolkien Reader* (New York, NY: Dell Rey, 1966), 72–73, and his category "Faërian Drama." Similarly, *The Legend of Zelda and Philosophy: I Link Therefore I Am*, ed. Luke Cuddy, Popular Culture and Philosophy 36 (Chicago, IL: Open Court, 2016), contains essays exploring the relationship between gamers and games: see, for instance, Jonathan Frome, "Why Do We Care Whether Link Saves the Princess?," in *The Legend of Zelda and Philosophy: I Link Therefore I Am*, ed. Luke Cuddy (Chicago, IL: Open Court, 2013), 3–15; Kristina Drzaic and Peter Rauch, "Slave Morality and Master Swords: Ludus and Paidia in *Zelda*," in *The Legend of Zelda and Philosophy: I Link, Therefore I Am*, ed. Luke Cuddy, (Chicago, IL: Open Court, 2008), 65–74, and Luke Cuddy, "Zelda

as Art," in *The Legend of Zelda and Philosophy: I Link, Therefore I Am,* ed. Luke Cuddy (Chicago, IL: Open Court, 2008), 153–164.

4 Tolkien, "On Fairy-Stories," 77.

5 Joseph Campbell, *The Hero with a Thousand Faces,* 2nd ed., Bollingen Series 17, (Princeton, NJ: Princeton University Press, 1973), 30. Mark Hayse, "The Mediation of Transcendence within the Legend of Zelda: The Wind Waker," in *The Legend of Zelda and Theology,* ed. Jonathan L. Walls (Los Angeles, CA: Gray Matter Books, 2011), 83–96, also discusses *Wind Waker* in light of Campbell's *The Hero with a Thousand Faces* and Tolkien's "On Fairy-Stories." Hayse, however, confesses not completing the game (see note 31 below). While not necessarily bad, abandoning the game thwarts seeing the story's recovery, leaving players' experience of the narrative incomplete.

6 Campbell, 37, n. 42.

7 See *Akallabêth,* recounting the drowning of Númenor, and *Of the Rings of Power and the Third Age,* in *The Silmarillion* (Boston, MA: Mariner Books, 2001), 259–304.

8 In Indian mythology, for instance, Shraddhadeva Manu, warned of a great flood, preserves nine seeds. *Mahabharata* 3.186.

9 *Aeneid* 5.774–834 and *Odyssey* 22.

10 King of Red Lions recounts this (Takano, Takahashi, and Aonuma).

11 Link is not an adult in most *Zelda* games, so the inundated Hyrule should contextualize the symbolism of Link-as-youth in *Wind Waker.*

12 The Helmaroc King seizes Aryll because she, like Zelda/Tetra, has pointed ears.

13 Cf. Campbell, 20.

14 See Campbell, vii–viii, 245–246. One should not think Campbell's diagram catalogues all mythic frames.

15 See Campbell, 245–246.

16 Campbell, 51–52: "Typical of the circumstances of the call are the dark forest, the great tree, the babbling spring, and the loathly, underestimated appearance of the carrier of the power of destiny."

17 Campbell, 17–18. Tolkien, "On Fairy-Stories," 33–90 (esp. 57–68), offers finer understanding of what may entail Campbell's "nursery demons."

18 Cf. Campbell, 71–74. Later, King of Red Lions fills this role.

19 Cf. Campbell, 69–77.

20 Campbell, 16–17.

21 Presenting a Pandora's-box motif from a dream, Campbell emphasizes the individual as the primary beneficiary of the hero's journey in that the "dangerous task of self-discovery and self-development [transports one] across the ocean of life" (23).

22 Campbell, 29.

23 "The green clothes ... symbolize the hope that the boys will grow up to be courageous" (*Hyrule Historia,* 125).

24 Campbell, 23.

25 Campbell alludes to the possibility of multiple threshold crossings, 131, n. 48.

26 Campbell, 93.

27 Coupe, *Myth,* 40. Indeed, *Wind Waker*'s extensive use of humor reveals comedy in its mythic paradigm.

28 Coupe, 45.

29 See Dario S. Compagno, "I Am Link's Transcendental Will: Freedom from Hyrule to Earth" in Cuddy, 179–189.

30 Coupe, 45.

31 Though confessing not to have finished games in the series, Toni Fellela, "Link's Search for Meaning," in *The Legend of Zelda and Philosophy: I Link Therefore I Am*, ed. Luke Cuddy (Chicago, IL: Open Court, 2013), 45–54, argues that the game's main purpose is to give Link, and players, meaningful experiences. However, abandoning a game before its conclusion, sadly, thwarts experiencing its complete narrative body.
32 Coupe, 48.
33 Campbell, 97.
34 Ibid., 101.
35 Campbell, 101. Vincent E. Rone points out to me similar periods of purification and strengthening the Master Sword in *Skyward Sword*.
36 Campbell, 105–109.
37 Tolkien, "On Fairy-Stories," 85.
38 See Tolkien's "On Fairy-Stories," particularly his section "Recovery, Escape, Consolation" and the epilogue, 75–90.
39 Campbell, 109, 131–33.
40 *Hyrule Historia*, 128.
41 D.M. Burke, "The Necessity of the Triforce in the Defeat of Ganon," in *The Legend of Zelda and Theology*, ed. Jonathan L. Walls (Los Angeles, CA: Gray Matter Books, 2011), 155–170, also references the *Epic of Gilgamesh*, showing Ganon as "chaos and disorder …. that must be defeated or brought under control," 166.
42 See Campbell's discussion of Gilgamesh's journey, 185–88.
43 One of three pearls Link must find to enter the Tower of the Gods. Job, chapter 41.
44 Job 42.
45 Cf. *Encyclopedia*, 13; *Hyrule Historia*, 128.
46 The Triforce of Wisdom is itself split, half held by Tetra, the other by her ancestor, King Daphnes Nohansen Hyrule, King of Red Lions.
47 Josh and Rachel Rasmussen, "Freedom versus Destiny: A Hero's Call," in *The Legend of Zelda and Theology*, ed. Jonathan L. Walls (Los Angeles, CA: Gray Matter Books, 2011), 71–82, discussing the Triforce goddesses' omniscience, offer models for understanding Link's actions as a fully actualized hero of monomyth.
48 Campbell, 116.
49 Ibid., 337.
50 Ibid. For a connection between possessing and productivity, see Ruth Scodel, "Odysseus' Dog and the Productive Household," *Hermes* 133, no. 4 (2005): 401–408. Scodel argues that Homer's account of Odysseus' short-lived reunion with Argus, his dog, functions to highlight the difference between the mere possession of wealth and the proper use of wealth for the flourishing of the household, what she terms, "productive economic activity" (401).
51 Campbell, 337.
52 Ibid., 181.
53 For a theological argument of Ganon's evil, see Burke, "The Necessity of the Triforce," 155–170.
54 Tolkien, "On Fairy-Stories," 78, offers a similarly helpful view in his discussion of creative fantasy (arguably what gamers participate in): it "may open your hoard and let all the locked things fly away like cage-birds. The gems all turn into flowers or flames, and you will be warned that all you had (or knew) was dangerous and potent, not really effectively chained, free and wild; no more yours than they were you."
55 Campbell, 149–171.

56 Campbell emphasizes abstraction as the apex of the hero's development: e.g. "the androgynous character of the presence," 162; or "annihilation of the distinction between life and release-from-life," 163.
57 An account of Cincinnatus seems particularly instructive, found in Livy, *History of Rome*, 3.26–29.
58 Campbell often emphasizes the dissolving of biological-sexual differences and disintegrating of physical and spiritual distinction. *Wind Waker*, on the other hand, seems to rejoice in the diversity of its characters—a veritable *commedia dell'arte* of stock characters, whose generic qualities emphasize diversity rather than coalesce into unity, integration of parts rather than their disintegration.
59 Although Campbell's scheme does not deny value in the concept of male and female working in companionship, his discussion favors more the transcendent experience of religious discipline that generates intellectual revelation more than day-to-day experiences that offer a different perspective on such revelation—namely, that looking after the domestic restores and protects society. For an examination of *Zelda* narrative using a heteronormative-queer dichotomy, see Tison Pugh, "The Queer Narrativity of the Hero's Journey in Nintendo's *The Legend of Zelda* Video Games," *Journal of Narrative Theory* 48, no. 2 (2018): 225–251, whose study often privileges the eroticism over the procreation of sexuality and also points out important homosexual elements of samurai culture that may color readings of *Zelda* narratives (cf. esp. 239); Pugh also refers to Campbell's paradigm as a major model of the hero's journey in her study.
60 Campbell, 230.
61 Gospel accounts of the Transfiguration are found in Matthew 17:1–13, Mark 9:2–13, and Luke 9:28–36.
62 Cf. Campbell, 224–228.

There's Something Mything Here

Problems of Counter-Structure or Contra-Structure in *Zelda's* Mythopoeic Methods

7 "You Played the Ocarina Again, Didn't You!!"

Catastrophe and the Aesthetics of Evil in *Ocarina of Time*

Nathan Schmidt

In a 1999 interview with IGN, *Legend of Zelda* mastermind Shigeru Miyamoto spoke at length about *The Legend of Zelda: Ocarina of Time*, which premiered the year before. Much of the interview focuses on the differences between *Ocarina* and *Super Mario 64*, the two Nintendo games for the console that radically explored the possibility of three-dimensional spaces. Discussing the choice to make the game's camera react to the character's surroundings instead of giving the player the relative level of control over the camera experienced in *Super Mario 64*, Miyamoto said,

> The center of the game is not Link, but rather the world which he lives in is a base for making the total world, the total gaming world, and the camera work has been designed in a way to reflect that concept.[1]

The Ocarina of Time, in other words, is fundamentally an environment-driven text down to its core mechanics, as the game's camera focuses not simply on the individual "hero" of the story but always points beyond him into the surrounding world. As a writer for 1Up.com noted about the game's use of the A button as an "action icon:"

> That is to say, its [the A button's] function differed depending on where Link was and what was near him. Rather than load the controller up with button functionalities that were only used at certain times, every action that depended on Link's surroundings was mapped to A.[2]

Rather than creating a complicated system of discrete button combinations that players would have to memorize to make the game's central protagonist perform the complex sets of tasks required throughout gameplay, the development team ingeniously devised a system by which a single button on the controller would respond to various situations in the character's environment. When standing next to something that could be climbed, the A button would make Link climb. When Link was rather than is swimming in water, A would make him dive. When Link was next to NPCs (non-player characters), A allowed him to interact with them. *Ocarina of Time* is a game wherein the ludic, or play-related, structure makes no sense outside of the immediate context of the environment in which the players find themselves.

Of course, however innovative such a place-based ludology may have been for its time, a simple attention to immediate surroundings does not adequately express the breadth and depth to which *Ocarina of Time* is fundamentally focused on matters of environmental concern. These preliminary observations provide an important starting point for thinking about *Ocarina of Time* as a game primarily driven by the environment—a videogame in which the environment, in the playspace between rules and fiction Jesper Juul calls the "half-real," figures both as a key ludic and narratological element.[3] *Ocarina of Time* does not simply focus on the player's immediate surroundings within the game; it also foregrounds ecological relationships as a part of its narrative, especially issues related to ecological catastrophe. These themes play out most tellingly in the aesthetic register, where the game's puzzles and narrative structure meet. *Ocarina's* world of Hyrule constantly faces the brink of environmental devastation, and the aesthetics of catastrophe dominate the game in such a way that they become central to the world players learn to inhabit through the avatar Link on the screen. The aesthetics of catastrophe are consistently employed to suggest the presence of evil in the gameworld. Consider, for example, the scene of devastation that first greets adult Link outside the Temple of Time once the evil Ganondorf has taken over Hyrule Castle Town, or the impending eruption of the Death Mountain volcano, or the freezing over of Hyrule's watershed in Zora's Domain. At each of these key moments in the game, environmental catastrophe functions as the aesthetic placeholder according to which players know something has gone wrong and requires remediation.

This handful of moments in the game suggests the aesthetics of catastrophe should occupy a key place in the game's mythopoeic structure. It is necessary, however, not to conflate aesthetics and semiotics in such a reading: environmental catastrophe does not *represent* evil in the game. Environmental catastrophe does not serve a purely semiotic function. Rather, following Jacques Rancière, the term "aesthetics" here indicates a break or rupture in the neat signifying system of *poiesis* (making) and *aisthesis* (the experience of art) that representational or mimetic structures attempt to force into a unity.[4] The appearance of environmental catastrophe on the screen expresses something immanent to the world of Hyrule intended to reach players on an affective rather than a signifying level. In the same way Middle-earth features hobbits living in holes with round doors and wizards carrying staffs that allow them to perform inexplicable feats of magic, Hyrule features children called Kokiri who never grow up, vaguely humanoid creatures called Gorons subsisting on a diet of rocks, and the presence of evil plunging the world into environmental crisis. Because Hyrule exists in the medium of videogames, it is not necessary to make this element of the world explicit in the narrative through dialogue or narration. Indeed, one of the most striking things about *Ocarina* that distinguishes it from other games of its kind and era is the way it tells a coherent story without the (over)use of on-screen explanation and dialogue, focusing on a non-speaking/silent protagonist. The game's aesthetics express this mythopoeic relationship between evil and catastrophe, which defines an intense zone of interlocution between the "fact of the matter"—what the player sees displayed on the screen; the "heart of the matter"—the affective registers evoked or cultivated by what is on the screen; and "the matter itself"—which in the case of a videogame is the phenomenal simplicity of the state of play.[5] Rather, the mythopoeic world of Hyrule *is the kind of world* in which evil and environmental catastrophe are inextricably intertwined.

Consider this brief and dense beginning as a kind of "dungeon map" for the paths ahead—perhaps useful to glance at before diving in to the real puzzles that await, but hardly sufficient to display the complexity of the labyrinth exposed before us. A number of questions follow, as well, from this initial juncture: What about *Ocarina of Time* makes it ecologically important, and why does it matter? Does the conflation of environmental catastrophe with mythical evil in the gameworld not simply reproduce anthropocentric mythologies that conflate natural disasters with agential malevolence? What is all this about aesthetics as a split between sense and representation? And what does any of it have to do with a videogame? To lock on to these questions and grapple with them, a reader traversing the "dungeon" that follows will encounter three "rooms," the first being an overview of *Ocarina of Time* as an environmental text, focusing in particular on the eco-cosmology suggested in one of the earliest cutscenes of the game. The next room puzzles over the relevance of videogame aesthetics more broadly, considering the specific aesthetics of evil as catastrophe inscribes it in *Ocarina*, and addresses the question of anthropocentrism in the apparent conflation of environmental catastrophe with evil. The third room ties these tenuous and winding strands together into a knot of purpose: allowing oneself to become immersed in a story that one loves, even in a videogame, need not impede thinking about dire and devastating real-world environmental concerns. It may instead be the case that to lose oneself in mythopoeia with an ecologically attentive eye is to find oneself confronted face to face the cultivation of a more fruitful, hopeful present in the face of devastating forces too large to face alone. After all, Tolkien the world-builder counts "the desire of men to hold communion with other living things" among "one of the primal desires that lie near the heart of Faërie."[6]

Hyrulean Eco-cosmology

In his groundbreaking work *The Environmental Imagination*, Lawrence Buell identified four key elements that define what he calls an "environmental text." They do not capture every possibility for what form such a text might take or what content it might pursue, but they do serve as a useful heuristic for an opening discussion such as this one. He lists these four criteria in his introduction:

1 The nonhuman environment is present not merely as a framing device but as a presence that begins to suggest that human history is implicated in natural history.
2 The human interest is not understood to be the only legitimate interest.
3 Human accountability to the environment is part of the text's ethical orientation.
4 Some sense of the environment as process rather than as a constant or a given is implicit in the text.[7]

At the time when Buell articulated these four definitions, the discipline now known as "ecocriticism" was in its relatively early stages, and the field now has moved well beyond the simplicity of matching these four criteria to the various elements of the text, game, or object in question. They do not function here as a schematic; rather, they hover over the following discussion of Hyrule as a mythopoeic world with an environmentally driven cosmology, intervening at moments when further guidance is necessary.[8] All four elements feature prominently in *Ocarina* and other games in the *Legend of Zelda* franchise, but they emerge organically as they appear in context, rather than attempt to force the game to follow them in a linear and straightforward way.

Like most other mythopoeic games and texts, the world of *Ocarina of Time* has a creation narrative explaining the origins of the world, not unlike the *Ainulindalë* that opens Tolkien's *Silmarillion*. In one of *Ocarina's* earliest cutscenes, when young Link is living in Kokiri forest, a guardian known as the Great Deku Tree tells Link the story of Hyrule and its creation: Before the beginning of time, three goddesses fly through the void of space and create a world together. Each goddess has a particular attribute that defines her essential character: Din, the goddess of power, Nayru, the goddess of wisdom, and Farore, the goddess of courage. As the text narrating the cutscene states at the bottom of the screen, Din "cultivated the land and created the red earth."[9] Nayru gives the world "the spirit of law," and Farore creates living beings "who would uphold the law." As Kyle Blanchette points out in his essay for *The Legend of Zelda and Theology*, certain similarities exist between the Hyrule and Christian creation narratives, especially the institution of order in a chaotic void.[10] The cosmology of Hyrule also differs from the Christian one in important ways. The elements of Christian cosmology that Hyrulean cosmology changes or omits are essentially consonant with the ones Lynn White suggests are responsible for the bulk of the ecological problems the earth faces today. "Man named all the animals," White states,

> thus establishing his dominance over them. God planned all of this explicitly for man's benefit and rule: no item in the physical creation had any purpose save to serve man's purposes. And, although man's body is made of clay, he is not simply part of nature: he is made in God's image.[11]

This is not the only available reading of the Christian narrative, and White himself looks toward a more Franciscan model of faith in his attempt to think his way out of the crisis he defines. However, it is important here to note that there is no hierarchy of beings within the created order of Hyrule—in a world populated by multiple species, in which it is even implied that sexual intimacy is possible across species,[12] there is no "great chain of being" worked into the game's *mythos*—it is not even implied. Farore creates all living beings at the same time, sharing a common purpose and a common law. Indeed, Ganondorf's true crime may be his attempt to enforce an order that makes him a higher form of being.[13] The creatures that attack Link throughout the game could even be attributed to Ganondorf's perversion of a prior, more longstanding harmony.

Really, though, even compared to something like Tolkien's *Ainulindalë*, another relatively recent cosmology with a creation myth, the narrative offered at this point in *Ocarina* leaves much to speculation and is relatively simple.[14] It occurs during that most-maligned element of the videogame-as-genre: the cutscene. But as a cutscene it actually makes its most important gesture toward an environment-centered cosmology. When Din first makes the earth, players sees a storm of rocks surrounded by lightning that finally settle into a reddish-brown landscape devoid of life. The text of the cutscene next states that Nayru only "poured her wisdom into the earth" to create the law, but the screen actually shows the appearance of a blue, cloud-studded sky over a gray, misty desert space. Farore appears in a space already sprinkled with grass and fills it with fireflies. This is important because, by showing the creation narrative in this way, the cutscene articulates the three most important elements of the story of Hyrule: power, wisdom, and courage. At the same time, each element is articulated in a direct relationship to some part of the environment—power with the earth, wisdom with the atmosphere, and courage with life, growth, and verdance. The moral and juridical backbone of this mythopoeic world could have been articulated in any number of other conceivable ways, but it is expressed, both in its visuals and its narrative, in terms explicitly connected to Hyrule's environment. Those inclined to find inspiration in something as bound to the complex morass of commercial interests and culture industry as a videogame might be especially compelled by the relationship between life and courage. In Hyrule, the state Paul Tillich calls "the courage to be" that resists anxiety and despair is entirely divorced from any anthropocentric definition of courage and spread out evenly across the simple fact of life-as-*zoe*[15] for all things.[16]

The triptych of power, wisdom, and courage structures the entire story of *Ocarina*—a crucial component to the mythology of the Triforce running across the entire narrative trajectory of the *Legend of Zelda* series. Without these three elements, and the three characters who embody them—Ganondorf, Zelda, and Link, respectively—no *Zelda* mythos exists: no Triforce, no creation of Hyrule, no story, and no game. Here the cutscene aesthetically equates power with earth, wisdom with atmosphere, and courage with animate life. These are not accidents but important elements of the game and its world that happen to occur in a part of the game where players tend to suspend their attention. In this sense, *Ocarina of Time* moves beyond Buell—it is not simply the case that "human" (in a loose sense here, since Hyrule is a world with several different humanoid species) history and natural history are implicated in one another, but they *are* one another. The two histories make each other in the same way Karen Barad describes the state of a subatomic particle not properly existing in place or velocity outside the context in which it is measured[17]—or, to take an example closer to home in this context, the way a videogame does not properly exist without the concatenation of controls and interface. In Barad's terms, narrative history and natural history co-constitute each other. One does not simply depend upon the other, because the two make each other possible. Hyrulean cosmology thus is truly an eco-cosmology, because its "rules" preclude ways of accounting for the properties of power, wisdom, and courage—essential to the story—without also encountering the earth, the atmosphere, and the biological life of the world's inhabitants. This analysis may appear to make overmuch of a two-minute cutscene, but it comes at a pivotal point in the game and describes precisely the kind of worldbuilding details that distinguish *Ocarina of Time* from its predecessors and competitors. A pithy and direct creation myth constitutes an important foundational story. Furthermore, many subsequent games build on this eco-cosmological base, from the power over the wind Link receives from the Wind Waker, a conductor's baton passed down by the Hyrulean Royal Family, to the way that Link (associated with courage), in *Twilight Princess*, *Wind Waker*, and *Skyward Sword*, comes from a background that emphasizes agriculture or husbandry, or both.

Even beyond this initial tale-telling, there are a number of other important ways that the environment becomes a point of central concern in the game's story. When Miyamoto and his team created *Ocarina*, it was the only game to deliberately craft a world with a watershed: Zora's Domain. A watershed is a key defining point for spheres of environmental relationality, where waters divide from one another and from which they flow. The National Oceanic and Atmospheric Administration (NOAA) describes it as "a place that channels rainfall and snowmelt to creeks, streams, and rivers, eventually to outflow points such as reservoirs, bays, and the ocean."[18] Environmental activists and scholars working in the ecocritical vein take the watershed as a place of particularly intense convergence of ecological issues, especially those who, like Peter Berg, consider bioregionalism as an alternative to state-based, capitalistic structures of geopolitical gathering. Berg describes bioregionalism as "a geographic terrain and a terrain of consciousness" that "restore[s] and maintain[s] local natural systems; ...practice[s] sustainable ways to satisfy basic human needs such as food, water, energy, housing, and materials; and...support[s] the work of reinhabitation."[19] In other words, bioregionalism is a kind of affiliation with one's particular local ecosystem, in which matters relating to that ecosystem supersede matters of state and national governance.

Watersheds are often the best points of reference for such forms of ecological collectivity. The fact that Hyrule contains a watershed like Zora's Domain, and that an important element of the game involves the freezing over of this watershed due to uncharacteristic and extreme climatological activity, does not explicitly align the game with bioregionalism as a political project in itself. Precious few games since have imbricated watershed ecology into the story in such a vital way, to the degree that, as Buell would put it, "Human accountability to the environment is part of the text's ethical orientation."[20] The game does not set out to be a moralistic ecological fable—nevertheless, the centrality of the Hyrule's watershed to the story and to the gameplay suggests an unusually high emphasis on environmental issues for a game of its time.[21]

None of this makes *Ocarina* a perfect or ideal environmental game, of course. No games are. Link slaughters hundreds of creatures in this game, and the game portrays these creatures as threatening and hostile. There also is valuable insight in Alenda Y. Chang's criticism that describes

> the abstract, ever-receding pastoral ideal that Raymond Williams once derisively called 'a babble of green fields,' which lurks in all the medieval and pre- or alter-industrial lands of games like...the Legend of Zelda series....[22]

The game's narrative and puzzles do frequently skip past opportunities to foreground ecological problems. However, later games foreground these themes even more specifically. Consider the sequel, *Majora's Mask*, where Link is tasked with bringing ecological restoration to four specific ecological zones, or *Twilight Princess*, in which Link actually becomes an animal. Also, straightforward ecological didacticism need not lead popular media platforms to engage with environmental ethics most effectively. The environmental issues in *Ocarina* may not be placed directly front and center, as they are in games like Chen and Clark's *Flower* (2009), for example. Yet the environment matters significantly in *Ocarina* when the concerns of players coincide with those of the game's broader "ecosystem," precisely because of the game's mythopoeia. This is clearest in the aesthetics of catastrophe, which haunt the game from beginning to end, especially after Link has grown into an adult and Ganon has used the Triforce to plunge Hyrule into nightmare.

Videogame Aesthetics and Ecological Catastrophe

Everyone who grew up playing *Ocarina* will remember the moment when adult Link first stepped out of the Temple of Time into Hyrule Castle Town, now under Ganondorf's rule. When all players have known is a bright and cheerful town full of garrulous NPCs with cats roaming the streets at night, the "new" gothic Castle Town represents the players' first step into a foreboding and dangerous new world, populated with shrieking ReDead monsters, ghost salesmen, and other dangers. In 1998, this was the moment when players, who until now had moved through a relatively playful world in the avatar of a child, were not proverbially in Kansas anymore. One quick look at the background of the scene shows Death Mountain surrounded by a ring of fire. It, with the barren grounds at the Temple of Time, indicates to players that the ecology of Hyrule has run amok. Trees have withered and grounds once covered in quiet vegetation are now riddled with invasive, carnivorous foliage. Volcanoes are on the brink of eruption and the sky over Castle Town is overcast and forked with lightning. The Zora's Domain watershed has frozen over inexplicably, halting the flow of water into Lake Hylia revealing a dead, polluted lakebed. As Hyrule presents itself in the twin registers of environmental and moral balance, an imbalance in the game's narrative world results in an ecological imbalance.

This is best understood on the more complex level of aesthetics, where images need not represent a specific "thing" directly, not any kind of direct mimetic representation. As Simon Estok defines it, "ecophobia" occurs in "[r]epresentations of nature as an opponent that hurts, hinders, threatens, or kills us—regardless of the philosophical value or disvalue of the ecosystemic functions of the dynamics being represented."[23] Estok's concept and his methodology have faced a certain level of scrutiny within the broader ecocriticism community.[24] Nevertheless, his argument captures *Ocarina*'s representation of nature. So far, Hyrule has presented itself as a world where nature is supposed to be balanced and uniform, and the weather is supposed to be nice. Bad things happen; then bad weather follows. This is exactly the kind of anthropocentric layering that ecocriticism interrogates—the expectation that, when something happens in the environment that is detrimental to humans, the environment becomes the enemy to be tamed and defeated because only humans really matter. Now, one would need to revise Estok's "us" for his critique to hold in the case of *Ocarina*, since no "us" exists in the game per se, although some kind of subjective "we" does intervene via the avatar of Link. In addition, Link shares Hyrule with other beings. Still, the simple conflation of bad weather with moral evil does the game no favors as a meaningful representation of environmental crises and concerns.

Žižek suggests a potential critique of this kind of representation in an extended interview for the Dutch broadcaster VPRO in 2010. He states:

> The image of nature that we spontaneously accept: nature as a balanced, harmonized circulation, which is then destroyed through excessive human agency—that nature doesn't exist. Nature is in itself a series of mega-catastrophes. Nature is crazy. Things go wrong all the time in nature.[25]

Opposed to anthropocentric representations of nature as evil but moving to the extreme in the other direction, this view of "nature" appears frequently enough in the environmental humanities. If something that might be called nature exists at all, a subject itself subject to intense scrutiny,[26] then it is chaos. Potentially devastating and destructive crises have no particular "meaning." Could a game like *Ocarina of Time* that uses environmental crisis to suggest the presence of evil have something to say about ontological entanglement with the environment that resists either of these extremes?

Ecological crisis in the gameworld does not *mean* anything any more than ecological crisis in the real world has *meaning*. It feels meaning*ful*, which is part of the game's affective and aesthetic appeal, but while it suggests things have gone awry in the world of the game's narrative, it does not stand in for evil specifically as a signifier. The halo of fire around Death Mountain does not signify evil in the world, at least not on a semiotic register. Rather than a simple representation of evil, ecological crisis in *Ocarina* foregrounds the presence of an aesthetics of evil, which simply exists immanently. The crises in the game present players with an a-signifying affective experience, as simple as the incipience by which adult Link steps out of the Temple of Time into a moment where players know nothing except that the world has changed, and something has gone terribly wrong.

Therefore, unless we briefly pause and take stock of the meaning of "aesthetics" in relation to videogames—especially to *Ocarina*—it will be difficult to proceed further. The postulate that will be taken *a priori* for the time being is that videogames have a visual appearance, and therefore there is something to be said about their aesthetic qualities.[27] Scholars like Graeme Kirkpatrick and David Myers have considered this notion in detail, mostly focusing on the relationship between play in games as an aspect of their aesthetic appeal and possibility, taking the concept of aesthetic play from Kant and Schiller and reading it through theorists like Theodor Adorno and Espen Aarseth. Kirkpatrick suggests that games cannot be formally understood, only ludologically—rather that "the kind of play we engage in with it [the game] is best understood as an embodiment of the subjective experience of play associated with art objects and reflected in the philosophical discourse of aesthetics."[28] Similarly, David Myers writes that videogames inhabit a liminal aesthetic space he terms the "anti-form," in which what *"seems to be* becomes, in the videogame, *what is*; and the psychophysical is therein asserted and confirmed as the physical."[29] The aesthetics of videogames rely on play, as a matter of course. However, buried within this question of aesthetic play lies another question of aesthetics: What does it look like? What kind of experience do players have, and why? Without dismissing the question of play as irrelevant, the next step requires inquiry into these more fundamental questions of visual aesthetics.

According to Jacques Rancière, we may think we have gone beyond a model of aesthetics in which the "stage, the audience and the world are taken in one and the same continuum."[30] Yet a common assumption remains that a direct and possibly even correlative relationship between art and (radical) politics can exist. Rancière notes, however, this simple and apparently intuitive connection has faced scrutiny since Rousseau and Schiller, and it appears in various forms that can be traced to ancient Greek and Latin thought. A critical point for Rancière is that aesthetics must forsake the question of signification altogether, which is tantamount a complete rupture between sign or symbol and its apparent referent. To study aesthetics is to study a "collapse...between the texture of the work and its efficiency."[31] Rancière equates the "texture of the work" and its "efficiency" earlier in the essay with *poiesis*, that which is produced in the process of making art, and *aisthesis*, from which the word "aesthetics" derives etymologically, but which means something more like "the complex of the forms of perception and emotion through which it is felt and understood."[32] Put together in classical aesthetics, these two would become mimesis.

However, this straightforward unification simply does not happen. No such direct and perfect mimesis is possible. Instead, viewers are left with an asignifying rupture in which they cannot divorce the heart of the matter and the fact of the matter from one another in any meaningful way. Asking, "What does the game look like?" therefore does is not the same as asking what players should see or do. Aesthetics neither show nor represent—they play, and feel. If environmental catastrophe simply signified or symbolized evil in the game, then Estok's concept of ecophobia would figure into the present analysis thus:

> Even though the game begins with a strong focus on ecological concerns in its play, its cosmology, and its landscape, *Ocarina of Time* is a mostly ecophobic game that puts the forces of nature in league with evil because of anthropocentric bias.

Even after re-reading evil and catastrophe in the game as an aesthetic, asignifying rupture rather than a symbolizing movement, one might still be inclined toward an Estok-style reading, and such a critique could lead to fruitful possibilities. Other possible readings come to light, however, beyond the signifying gesture of semiotics and into the strange space of asignifying play and aesthetics.

Put simply, aesthetics, which does not signify, stands for the incipient moment in which the game works to create a particular affect. Mythopoeic videogames suit this notion in particular because players subvert and overwhelm their subjectivity until it is melded into a space of forgetfulness between the hand, eye, and screen. Environmental catastrophe in *Ocarina of Time* creates a shock or rupture within the player's own comfortable experience of the gameworld, which explains why most of the catastrophic moments happen after Link has grown into an adult—players return to previously familiar spaces. What does the game look like? Well, the aesthetics of evil and catastrophe give rise to impressions that something is off-kilter about a frozen Zora's Domain. A space once open and welcoming before is now *unheimlich* and forbidding (albeit with a kind of polygonal sublimity). In a space one knows, the unfamiliar intrudes. The lack, or subsumption, of signification into affective incipience redeems what could have appeared as ecophobia into something more complicated and interesting: a world where creators Miyamoto and his team considered their options for showing players how and when things went awry in the game's narrative. They consequently decided to build a concern with environmental catastrophe right into the mythopoeic world itself—because Hyrule *is a world* in which environmental devastation accompanies the presence of evil, not signifying it, emanating it in a vibratory incipience. In *The Three Ecologies*, Felix Guattari calls this kind of emanation *pour-soi* [for-itself] instead of *en-soi* [in-itself].[33] As Link walks over the broken drawbridge into a Hyrule field now under the rule of evil forces, the overcast sky compels players to feel the beating heart of a world predicated upon ecological balance, in which the asignifying aesthetics of catastrophe create shock, displacement, and the possibility for an ethic of care, even in such a hopelessly small and half-real space as a videogame.

Into the Ecology of Mythopoeia: The Song of Storms

A new kind of mental ecology that resists the chthonic tentacles of Integrated World Capitalism becomes possible in an imaginative space that plays instead of signifying. Guattari writes, "At the heart of all ecological praxes there is an a-signifying rupture, in which the catalysts of existential change are close at hand, but lack expressive support from the assemblage of enunciation."[34] Through complex verbiage in which Guattari both critiques Freudian psychoanalysis and suggests a new framework to view subjectivity with ecology, he arrives at a straightforward destination: "In short, no one is exempt from playing the game of the ecology of the imaginary!"[35] It is not accidental that Guattari turns, however briefly, to the language of aesthetics here. An asignifying framework of rupture, like a moment of ecological crisis, opens the space of possibility for a new way of thinking and being toward an environmentally conscious present.

As opposed to a simple conflating of bad weather and mythic evil, the aesthetics of evil in *Ocarina* suggest a fully constructed world containing within itself asignifying moments that tell players something has gone horribly amiss. Hyrule is a world where the balance of power, wisdom, and courage—founded upon the balance of the environmental factors within the world—falters in favor of power and becomes a world of environmental devastation. This unbalanced state describes the conditions of real-world environmental crisis as much as it describes Hyrule's downfall. Videogames and mythopoeia also bear some responsibility for this crisis. Both can distract from the pressing and exigent problems facing humanity on a planetary level. *Ocarina* combines the two in an especially seductive way by presenting the fantasy of a Hero and a Princess who put power back in its place and restore a ruined world. Losing oneself entirely in such distractions without an eye on the pressing issues of a devastating reality would be dangerous indeed.

This is why it is precisely so "dangerous to go alone" into the landscape that opens up before us now. That games, stories, films, and so forth attract many followers does not imply an unavoidable mass seduction into the soporific morass of neo-Romantic distraction. One of the most-played and most-loved videogames in history has environmental issues both at its heart and on its surface. Players must be willing to engage in an "ecological bias," which denotes direct and careful attentiveness to the presence or absence of environmental issues in places one is not used to looking. Such a bias may yield fruitful readings of other kinds of cultural productions that attain similar statuses of common love over time. Many are mythopoeic, after all. Awareness of the ecological in the mythological may garner broader attention for a pressing issue that empirical, scientific observation and sincere activism so far have failed to generate on a scale as massive as necessary.

The title for this chapter comes from a brief comical sequence in *Ocarina*. Inside a mill, an organ-grinding character named Guru-Guru teaches Link the Song of Storms, which allows him to summon a thunderstorm at will. There are a handful of instances in which the song is useful for securing an item or entering a dungeon, as a part of the game's famous puzzles. For the most part, though, the song is just... there. The player can make Link get out his ocarina and perform it at any particular time, for no particular reason. Incidentally, Guru-Guru gets very upset when Link plays the song in front of him inside the mill. Reference to the Song of Storms makes for an appropriate chapter title because it forces the questioning of the preceding content thus far. If *Ocarina* is an intrinsically environmentally connected game, and the aesthetics of environmental catastrophe contribute to the making of this mythos in such a way as to call for a stronger sense of environmental ethics in players, then why would the game's central protagonist receive the power to summon a minor catastrophe any time he wishes? Aesthetically, the sequence displayed on the screen during the Song of Storms appears nearly identical to rainstorm in Kakariko Graveyard or the thunderclouds that block the sun above Hyrule Castle Town.

The presence of the song further counters the reading of *Ocarina* as ecophobic by demonstrating bad weather is not *always* or *necessarily* conflated with evil in the game. Furthermore, earlier in the game, princess Zelda receives a vision in which Link is himself described as a force of nature that counters the "dark clouds" of evil spread by Ganondorf—Link learns to summon these "dark clouds" himself.[36] The song also hearkens back to Buell's statement that environmentally conscious texts should include "some sense of the environment as process."[37] Ultimately, a more fruitful reading of the Song of Storms accounts for the way Link can play the song anywhere, at any time, to summon the aesthetics of catastrophe. The song is not limited to any narrative instance or sequence of puzzles, although many players probably limit its use in such a way. But what if Link walked through Hyrule, summoning thunderstorms as he pleases, simply to recall that one of the possible responses to a catastrophe caused by an imbalance of power is to create one's own small moments of incipience, to summon up a storm just to splash in it and take courage? Such free play suggests that certain crises in Hyrule can be translated into *eu*catastrophe, Tolkien's neologism for an end that barely skirts destruction, "not essentially 'escapist,' nor fugitive.' In its fairy-tale—or otherworld—setting, it is a sudden and miraculous grace: never to be counted on to recur."[38] Mythopoeia gives us permission to lose ourselves in a world we love. To wander. One might call it wandering practice.

In an important section of his essay "On Fairy-Stories," Tolkien quotes a poem he wrote to an inquirer who asked if mythopoeia was not simply, as the interlocutor put it, "Breathing lies through silver."[39] In the poem, Tolkien famously wrote back, "[W]e make still by the law in which we're made."[40] The devout Tolkien likely had a certain way in which "we" are "made" in mind. As White suggested earlier, a number of ways exist in which assumptions about humanity's supposedly divine origins can create problems, as well as a worthwhile number of ways in which a more environmentally inflected and humbler attitude toward religious belief can solve them. But what if Tolkien's words were transposed into something a little different, more earthy? The eco-cosmology Ocarina offers need not be connected to the beings Donna Haraway calls the "sky gods," who come with "civilizing agents" to "set up chief Singletons and their tame committees of multiples or subgods, the One and the Many."[41] Instead, the powers attributed to Nayru, Farore, and Din are more like those powers Haraway attributes to the "Chthonic ones:" "monsters in the best sense; they demonstrate and perform the material meaningfulness of earth processes and critters."[42] What if to make by the law in which we are made were to recognize that we are finally earthy beings, developed across the eons of deep time into this blip of the earth's long history? And what if an immersive experience, like a mythopoeic videogame, were precisely the phenomenal and aesthetic register in which to discover such an earthy entanglement?

Haraway draws on Ursula Le Guin's "carrier bag theory of fiction," which suggests the origins of storytelling belong not with swords and hunters but with containers like gourds and rucksacks, which allow the worker (and the storyteller) to move things from place to place with an earthy generosity, rather than a thirst for epic and bloody vengeance. Le Guin writes: "I now propose the bottle as hero. Not just the bottle of gin or wine, but bottle in its older sense of container in general, a thing that holds something else."[43] As a mythopoeic videogame, *Ocarina* certainly deals in the tropes of the sword-swinging hero and all the anthropocentric baggage that comes with them. But one of the most valuable items in the game, frequently offered as an unexpected reward for helping non-player characters, is the bottle. The bottle functions as a carrier for water, potions, and fairies, for digging into the meat of the story, the earth of Hyrule; a catcher of bugs and fish; a transporter of precious items from one place to another. "How did a sling, a pot, a bottle suddenly get in the story?" Haraway asks. "How do such lowly things keep the story going? ...With a shell and a net becoming human, becoming humus, becoming terran, has another shape—that is, the side-winding, snaky shape of becoming-with."[44] In *Ocarina's* complex narrative, and in its aesthetics, Link trucks with both modalities: the hero triumphant *and* the carrier of water, the restorer of ecosystems. With an ecologically minded view of the game as an aesthetic object oriented toward environmental catastrophe, Link and players may learn to "become-with" one another, into an earthier Hyrule and a kinder inclination toward our own large Earth.

Notes

1 IGN, "Sensei Speaks: IGN64 Talks to Zelda Creator Shigeru Miyamoto. The Full Interview." January 29, 1999. Archived by the Internet Archive Wayback Machine, https://web.archive.org/web/20130820235938; www. ign.com/articles/1999/01/30/sensei-speaks, accessed 26 June 2018.

2 1Up.com, "Classic.1Up.com's Essential 50: 40. *The Legend of Zelda: Ocarina of Time*." https://archive.is/20120718054136; www.1up.com/features/ essential-50-ocarina-time.

3 See Jesper Juul, *Half-Real: Videogames between Real Rules and Fictional Worlds*, Cambridge, MA: MIT Press, 2005: "The entire theory can therefore be described as the intersection between games and rules and games as fiction, and the relation between the game, the player, and the world" (197).

4 See Jacques Rancière, "Aesthetic Separation, Aesthetic Community: Scenes from the Aesthetic Regime of Art," *Art and Research* 2, no. 1 (2006): "Aesthetic efficiency means a paradoxical kind of efficiency that is produced by the very break of any determined link between cause and effect."

5 To talk about aesthetics without play would be, not simply to dismiss Kant, Schiller, and all who have followed in their wake (like Huizinga and Eugen Fink), but to miss the most important and innovative difference that the critical study of videogames makes available.

6 J. R. R. Tolkien, "On Fairy-Stories," in *The Tolkien Reader* (New York, NY: Ballantine Books, 1966), 43.

7 Lawrence Buell, *The Environmental Imagination: Thoreau, Nature Writing, and the Formation of American Culture* (Cambridge: Belknap Press, 1995), 7–8.

8 Buell is, in this sense, the Kaepora Gaebora of Zelda and ecocriticism.

9 Shigeru Miyamoto, *The Legend of Zelda: Ocarina of Time* (Kyoto: Nintendo, 1998), videogame.

10 See Kyle Blanchette, "Linking the Landscapes of Twilight Princess and Christian Theology," in *The Legend of Zelda and Theology*, ed. Jonathan L. Walls (Los Angeles, CA: Gray Matter Books, 2011).

11 Lynn White, "The Historical Roots of Our Ecologic Crisis," *Science* 155, no. 3767 (1967): 1205.

12 Although, in Link's case at least, the relationship is not necessarily desired—I am thinking here of his engagement to the amphibious Zora princess Ruto, who, although the player first encounters her as a child, even as an adult sees no species-related barriers to a relationship with Link.

13 There is unquestionably a social hierarchy in Hyrule, a place that has kings and princesses—the main point here is that the creation myth does not set up an *ontological* hierarchy such as that suggested by the Christian mythos, in which "man" is made to rule over the "beasts."

14 To be fair to the game's creators, it is worth noting that a certain speculative simplicity can be a reasonable starting place for a myth, even a necessary one. As Tatiana Chernyshova has it, "Mythology as a unitary, albeit contradictory, image of the world naturally did not come into being all at once; but empirical myths strive to coalesce into a system—their cyclical character attests to this." See Chernyshova, "Science Fiction and Myth Creation in Our Age," *Science Fiction Studies* 31, no. 3 (November 2004), 346.

15 I am borrowing the distinction here between *zoe*, as the physical state of aliveness, and *bios*, as a particular state of being alive, from Hannah Arendt's and Giorgio Agamben's re-readings of these concepts articulated by Aristotle. See Aristotle's *Politics* (Oxford: Oxford World Classics, 2009), Arendt's *The Human Condition* (Chicago, IL: University of Chicago Press,

1998), and Agamben's *Omnibus Homo Sacer* (Redwood City, CA: Stanford University Press, 2015) for more on the complex and variegated shades of this distinction.

16 Paul Tillich, *The Courage to Be* (New Haven, CT: Yale University Press, 1980). Tillich himself suggests that courage need not be a property only of humans in or other presumably "rational" beings in his chapter on vitality and courage: "The right courage therefore must, like the right fear, be understood as the expression of perfect vitality. The courage to be is a function of vitality.... To strengthen vitality means to strengthen the courage to be." (79).

17 See Karen Barad, *Meeting the Universe Halfway* (Durham, NC: Duke University Press, 2007).

18 NOAA, "What Is a Watershed," National Ocean Service, https://oceanservice.noaa.gov/facts/watershed.html, accessed 30 June 2018.

19 Peter Berg, "What Is Bioregionalism." Cascadianow.org, 2002, www.cascadianow.org/about-cascadia/cascadia-bioregionalism/what-is-bioregionalism/, accessed 30 June 2018.

20 Buell, 8.

21 The frozen Zora's Domain includes the Ice Cavern sub-dungeon, the passageway to the Water Temple, and plays a major part in the Biggoron Sword sidequest.

22 Alenda Y. Chang, "Games as Environmental Texts," *Qui Parle* 19, no. 2 (2011): 59.

23 Simon Estok, "Theorizing in a Space of Ambivalent Openness: Ecocriticism and Ecophobia," *Interdisciplinary Studies in Literature and Environment* 16, no. 2 (Spring 2009): 209.

24 See Louisa Mackenzie and Stephanie Posthumus, "Reading Latour Outside: A Response to the Estok—Robisch Controversy," *Interdisciplinary Studies in Literature and Environment* 20, no. 4 (December 2013), 757–777.

25 VPRO and Slavoj Žižek, *Lecture: Living in the End Times with Slavoj Žižek*. YouTube, www.youtube.com/watch?v=Gw8LPn4irao, accessed July 1, 2018.

26 See Timothy Morton, *Ecology without Nature* (Cambridge, MA: Harvard University Press, 2009).

27 It should not go unnoted that this presumption indicates a strong current of ocular-centric ableism that runs through videogames more broadly. Significant exceptions to this include the highly successful audio-only game *BlindSide*, released in 2012 by Aaron Rasmussen and Michael T. Astolfi, and other audio-only games like Somethin' Else's *Papa Sangre* (2010, re-released 2013) and *The Nightjar* (2011), although none of Somethin' Else's titles appear to be available on the app store at this time (July 1, 2018).

28 Graeme Kirkpatrick, "Between Art and Gameness: Critical Theory and Computer Game Aesthetics," *Thesis Eleven* 89 (May 2007): 75.

29 David Myers, "The Video Game Aesthetic: Play as Form," in *The Video Game Theory Reader 2*, eds. Bernard Perron and Mark J. P. Wolf (New York, NY: Routledge, 2009), 59.

30 Rancière, "Aesthetic Separation, Aesthetic Community."

31 Ibid.

32 Ibid.

33 Felix Guattari, *The Three Ecologies*, trans. Ian Pindar and Paul Sutton (New Brunswick: The Athlone Press, 2000), 53.

34 Ibid., 45.

35 Ibid., 57.

36 Zelda describes this dream when Link first meets her in Hyrule Castle. After Link affirms that he has the Kokiri's Emerald, Zelda says,

> I had a dream...In the dream, dark storm clouds were billowing over the land of Hyrule...But suddenly, a ray of light shot out of the forest, parted the clouds and lit up the ground...The light turned into a figure holding a green and shining stone, followed by a fairy....
>
> (Miyamoto 1998)

In this volume, Elam also states that Link symbolizes a "seed to be sown, cultivated, and protected."

37 Buell, 7.
38 Tolkien, "On Fairy-Stories," 86.
39 Tolkien, 74.
40 Tolkien, 74.
41 Donna Haraway, *Staying with the Trouble: Making Kin in the Chthulucene* (Durham, NC: Duke University Press, 2016), 31.
42 Haraway, 2.
43 Ursula K. Le Guin, "The Carrier-Bag Theory of Fiction," in *The Eco-criticism Reader*, eds. Cheryll Glotfelty and Harold Fromm (Athens, GA: University of Georgia Press, 1996), 150.
44 Haraway, 40.

8 A Link Across Adventures

Literacy's Relevance to Time in *The Legend of Zelda* Series' Mythopoeia

Matthew Sautman

Miyamoto's *The Legend of Zelda* series—henceforth referred to as *Zelda*—utilizes mythopoeia by expanding *Zelda*'s mythos across each canonical *Zelda* game. Mythopoeia is the word Tolkien uses to describe the creation of fantasy worlds that do not "destroy or even insult Reason [sic]" nor "blunt the appetite for, nor obscure the perception of scientific verity."[1] In other words, mythopoeia describes detailed, consistently believable fantasy worlds that reward those who invest their attention in these worlds' aesthetics, lore, customs, languages, music, and other non-plot elements. Verlyn Flieger and Douglas Anderson note that Tolkien developed mythopoeia in response to linguist Sapir-Worf's and Inkling Owen Barfield's theories "that humankind comes to perceive and relate to its world" by "naming things—establishing them with words."[2] Philip Tallon is amongst the earliest *Zelda* scholars to link *Zelda* with mythopoeia, noticing resonances in *Zelda*'s aesthetic design to Tolkien's Faërie—"a kind of parallel world" that "overlaps with our own from time to time."[3] That is, the events that take place across *Zelda*'s continuity are not intended to take place on a version of our earth. *Zelda*'s mythos takes place in a world that resembles ours but possesses a history separate from our own.

Tallon's foundational work in *Zelda* studies, though significant, is flawed. Tallon dismisses the possibility that the mythopoeia Miyamoto and subsequent developers use to shape *Zelda* resembles Tolkien's crafting, asserting "[*Zelda*] shows nothing in its design to indicate a Tolkienian level of consistency and planning."[4] While Tallon is not wrong to distinguish these creators' works—Tolkien's work relies on language and often can be far more esoteric than *Zelda*—Tallon does not consider the process Tolkien used to "plan" a consistent world.

The mythopoeias present in these series are not synonymous, but the story-structures present in both series resonate with one another. Tolkien's approach to mythopoeia establishes continuity across Middle-earth's mythos through repeated acts of non-linear storytelling. While more mainstream fans of Tolkien primarily encounter Middle-earth through *The Hobbit* and the *Lord of the Rings* trilogy, the world informing these novels did not manifest without precedent. Christopher Tolkien notes, the earliest versions of Middle-earth emerge "in battered notebooks extending back to 1917,"[5] meaning J.R.R. Tolkien developed his mythos for almost 20 years by the time he first published *The Hobbit* in 1937-17 years before he published *The Fellowship of the Ring* in 1954. Christopher Tolkien emphasizes "Middle-earth and its history was built up gradually and delicately... a long series of small shifts or combinations would often lead to the emergence of new and unforeseen structures."[6] That Tolkien's Middle-earth emerged through excursions across continuity—not only through linear exploration of plot and subsequent revision—resembles the mythopoeia explored further on in this chapter that Miyamoto and subsequent developers use to expand *Zelda*'s continuity not just into the future, but also into the past and across multiple timelines that possess aesthetic continuity. This structural similarity bodes well for *Zelda* scholars who wish to explore the linkages between Tolkien's *and* Miyamoto's and subsequent *Zelda* developers' approaches to mythopoeia, as well as their contrasts.

This chapter considers a contrast between the mythopoeias of Middle-earth and *Zelda*. Tolkien's mythopoeia and the approach used by Miyamoto and other developers both produce richly imagined fantasy worlds, but these worlds are not as equally accessible to their audiences. For example, *The Hobbit* and *The Lord of the Rings* trilogy retain popularity into the 21st century, but the majority of texts dedicated to Middle-earth's mythos—e.g., *The Silmarillion, Unfinished Tales, Lost Tales, The Shaping of Middle-Earth*—do not share this popularity arguably due to these texts' dense storytelling. Consider the opening paragraph from "Ainulindalë," the first section of *The Silmarillion*, a book that caused me to stop exploring Tolkien's larger mythos when I was in middle school:

> There was Eru, the One, who in Arda is called Ilúvatar; and he made first the Ainur, the Holy Ones, that were the offspring of his thought, and they were with him before aught else was made. And he spoke to them, propounding to them themes of music; and they sang before him, and he was glad. But for a long while they sang only each alone, or but few together, while the rest hearkened; for each comprehended only that part of the mind of Ilúvatar from which he came, and in the understanding of their brethren they grew but slowly. Yet ever as they listened they came to deeper understanding, and increased in unison and harmony.[7]

This passage details the creation story of Tolkien's mythos, but for readers who encounter *The Silmarillion* after only reading Tolkien's most popular novels will find themselves confronted with lore that commands slow-reading, note-taking, and patience. Furthermore, many of the names such a reader would likely find familiar—e.g., Gandalf, Sauron,

Isidur, Gollum, Galadriel, and Saruman—are altogether absent in this opening section, concealing the continuity present here and elsewhere in Tolkien's mythos. Consequently, as Christopher Tolkien notes, a

> complete consistency (either within the compass of *The Silmarillion* itself or between *The Silmarillion* and [Tolkien's] other published writings...) is not to be looked for, and could only be achieved, if at all, at a heavy and needless cost.[8]

Tolkien Studies mere existence proves that this exploration is worthwhile, yet texts like *The Silmarillion* serve as barriers that complicate ability of readers to immerse themselves in Middle-earth's mythos. *Zelda*'s continuity, as this chapter explores in further detail, is also complex. *Zelda*'s mythos is not always readily apparent to all players. Yet *Zelda* immerses players in a Faërie world similar to Tolkien without alienating those players who have not invested themselves in the mythos of every canonical videogame. This chapter aims to understand how *Zelda*'s mythopoeia creates a mythos similar in complexity to Tolkien's without alienating players.

Methodology

This chapter explores *Zelda*'s rhetorical situation. Lloyd Bitzer's original conceptualization of rhetorical situations consists of three core components: *exigence* (i.e. "a defect, an obstacle, something waiting to be done, a thing other than it should be"), an *audience* (who is "constrained in decision and action), and *constraints* (that "influence the rhetor and can be brought to bear upon the audience").[9] The exigence in *Zelda*'s rhetorical situation I explore emerges through a single question—how does a series with a continuity as complex as *Zelda* remain accessible to players who have not played every game in the *Zelda* series? While *Zelda*'s audience also includes gamers who play (if not beat/complete) every canonical *Zelda* videogame, this audience subset comprised of both casual fans and players new to the series reveals constraints present in *Zelda*'s design. These constraints pertain to videogame design (how can the videogame be designed to welcome new, casual, and seasoned players?) and worldbuilding (how can the videogame's world have meaning independently and simultaneously extend the world of other canonical videogames?). The exigence of *Zelda*'s accessibility suggests Miyamoto and subsequent developers utilize specific techniques across *Zelda* releases to overcome these constraints. This chapter's exploration of players' literacy, plot expansion, and temporality in relation to constraints based on videogame design and worldbuilding reveals that at least three of the techniques *Zelda*'s developers use to expand *Zelda*'s continuity imbue *Zelda* with a queer temporality that enables *Zelda* to be intricate and accessible simultaneously.

Literature Review

Past scholarship on *Zelda* provides limited insight into how *Zelda* reaches an audience of players less familiar with the series' overarching continuity. Oversight in this scholarship likely is a byproduct of these authors underestimating constraints that affect a player's videogaming experience with *Zelda*, an example being a player's knowledge of *Zelda* prior to playing. Jonathan Frome notes audience immersion in *Zelda* results from "some aspect of our minds" treating *Zelda*'s characters as "real," even though "we know the characters are not real."[10] Frome does not specify what role developers play in ensuring each *Zelda* videogame achieves this psychological effect. Toni Fellela argues *Zelda*'s audience immersion emerges from players' "need to face challenges," the emphasis *Zelda* places "on growth, development and responsibility," and the "levity written into the game that softens the seriousness [of the game's existential stakes]."[11] Fellela's claim implicitly suggests *Zelda* possesses a narrative structure across its entries akin to Campbell's "hero's journey," wherein "A hero ventures forth… into a region of supernatural wonder" where that hero encounters "fabulous forces" and wins "a decisive victory" that gives the hero "the power to bestow boons."[12] Although Fellela's work calls attention to a consistent narrative strategy developers use when designing new *Zelda* videogames, Fellela does not clarify how this strategy establishes a meaningful continuity with a complex overarching plot. Kristina Drzaic and Peter Rauch suggest that *Zelda* immerses players by appealing to multiple play styles. This design allows players either to "play the game 'start to finish' in a straightforward fashion… save Zelda, defeat Ganon" or "to design [their] own goals within the gamespace, goals outside of the expected game design," e.g., utilizing the Fierce Deity glitch in *Majora's Mask* to make Link the protagonist "run about the land as a powerful giant… killing every monster in sight, getting stuck in doorways, and acting like a lumbering troll" until the "game invariably crashes."[13] Drzaic and Rauch do not specify whether or how *Zelda*'s developers achieve this effect in a unique way, nor do they clarify the effects this kind of videogame design has on continuity. No work in *Zelda* studies concerned with audience immersion has considered the role literacy plays in the process until the publication of this anthology.

Defining Literacy

This chapter considers literacy as a significant constraint affecting *Zelda*'s rhetorical situation. Literary specialist James Paul Gee originally defines literacy as "control of the secondary uses of language," i.e. the language skills necessary to navigate contexts like "school, workplaces, stores, government, offices, businesses, or churches."[14] Gee's later work refines this definition to describe an epistemology grounded in reading, wherein literacy refers to a person's "abilities to 'read' texts… in certain ways or to certain levels."[15] Per Gee's definition(s), *Zelda*'s relationship to literacy references players' abilities to navigate the world of each *Zelda* videogame *and* to read the events that occur in this world in reference to *Zelda*'s larger continuity. This first form of literacy centers on a player's capacity to control Link as an avatar through digital space and emerges through a player's content with a single videogame. This second form of literacy centers around what Gee calls "the principles and patterns" that allows players to "recognize what is and is not acceptable content" in a videogame and its genre.[16] Shannon Carter expounds on Gee's work regarding this second kind of literacy, noting that it describes a capacity of players "to develop the ability to effectively read, understand, manipulate, and negotiate the cultural and linguistic codes of a new community… based on a relatively accurate assessment of another familiar one."[17] While Carter primarily envisions communities in reference to groups of people who practice a particular skill, the word just as easily applies to development teams that craft the videogames players play. Subsequently, each experience players have with videogaming is a literacy event. Building upon Shirley Brice Heath's *Ways with Words*, Perry Dantzler defines literacy events as "situations in which people engage with reading or writing for any usage at any level."[18] In other words, any moment a person encounters an interpretable text, e.g., a *Zelda* videogame, is a literacy event.

That every playthrough of any *Zelda* videogame is a literacy event suggests player immersion depends on the ability of players to understand the signifiers present in each game. Even if, as Anna B. Janssen notes, every *Zelda* videogame is designed to provide players "with certain tools and skills that will assist [them] with later challenges,"[19] i.e. to teach players *Zelda* literacy; their initial *Zelda* literacy impacts their ability to acquire these tools and learn these skills from the game. *Zelda* literacy is a term this chapter uses to describe a player's knowledge of the *Zelda* canon they possess *prior* to and learn over the course of playing any given canonical *Zelda* videogame. This knowledge subsequently affects how players play.

Literacy's Impact on *Zelda*'s Audience

As a literacy event, each *Zelda* game has a potential to alienate players. When players start playing the original *Zelda* on the Nintendo Entertainment System (NES), for example, they are placed into a digital space without any inventory and any context for their adventure—unless players read the instruction booklet prior or allowed the game to remain on screen long enough for the prologue to appear. The avatar (Link) is placed into a pathway that splits in three directions near what appears to be an entrance to a cave. Should Link travel in any of these three directions, players will notice they are surrounded by monstrous creatures. Should players read these monsters' presence as evidence Link should not travel in these directions until players arms themselves, they ideally will make their way to the cave and receive their first sword—if players did not already enter this cave out of curiosity. However, there is no guarantee the players will enter the cave before they grow frustrated with the game and subsequently quit. Their videogame literacy, specifically their *Zelda* literacy, enables them actually to play, and subsequently enjoy, the game.

As a literacy event, *Zelda*'s mythos may appear irrelevant to the literacies players need to enjoy *Zelda* as a videogaming experience. The capacity of players to move Link, use items, fight enemies, and solve puzzles—the literacies necessary to beat/complete any game in *Zelda*—are not inherently dependent on their capacity to comprehend the significance of Link's actions in the larger *Zelda* continuity. Such a conclusion, however, discounts how *Zelda* is structured to teach players the mythos across each game. For example, if players only have played the *Zelda* Gameboy Color titles—*Oracle of Ages* (OoA), and *Oracle of Seasons* (OoS)—then they gains some knowledge of Link's adventures without encountering the complexity of the *Zelda* timeline. OoA and OoS take place in the realms of Labrynna and Holodrum, respectively. As Link develops control over the power of time in OoA and seasons in OoS, he works to free the oracles Din and Nayru in these separate videogames. Yet if players complete one of the *Oracle* games, then they are presented with a passcode that allows them to transfer their data to the other title, unlocking an additional storyline where the witches known as Twinrova resurrect Ganon by kidnapping Princess Zelda. In this specific case, playing multiple *Zelda* videogames enables players literally to access aspects of the mythos that makes the overall gameplay a richer experience. However, this is the only case in the *Zelda* series where continuity is unlocked through a passcode system that links multiple videogames together.

Zelda's rich mythos does not rely primarily on players establishing physical links between game files as we witness with the *Oracle* videogames. This mythos instead accumulates through repetitions the players encounter that signal continuity amongst storylines. For example, if players who have played only the *Oracle* games start playing *Ocarina of Time* (OoT), then they likely will notice OoT contains similar characters and situations present in the *Oracle* games. The first of these similarities emerges in a secret opening cutscene players can access if they allow the entire opening title screen to play without hitting any buttons. In this secret cutscene, players witness Twinrova attacking a red-headed female character players with limited *Zelda* literacy will not recognize—Nabooru, the Spirit Sage. The presence of Twinrova signals to these players that continuity exists between OoT and the *Oracle* games, but equally as important, Twinrova's presence suggests Nabooru's moral orientation long before players encounter her. Should players not access the secret sequence, however, the first similarity they should notice between *OoT* and the *Oracle* games begins with *OoT*'s opening cutscene. *OoT* opens with a talking tree, the Deku Tree, who provides players the exposition necessary to understand *OoT*'s gameworld. The Deku Tree's presence resembles two talking trees both called the Maku Tree from the *Oracle* games that serve as mentors to Link. The Deku Tree calls attention to the Maku Trees' larger significance and consequently their significance in the *Oracle* games attributes further significance unto the Deku Tree during the first playthrough of players.

The mythos that emerges through repetition in the *Zelda* series may not always appear readily apparent to players and may even lead them to misunderstand the mythos should they not dedicate enough time to each *Zelda* videogame they play. For example, during the Deku Tree's exposition in *OoT*, players witness the "kidnapping" of Princess Zelda. A mysterious woman (Impa) on horseback holds Zelda as they are followed by a green-skinned man (Ganondorf) riding a black horse out of Hyrule Castle. Since *OoT*'s opening resembles events in the *Oracle* games that lead to Twinrova resurrecting Ganon, attentive players may infer from this cutscene the mysterious woman and Ganondorf are associated with Twinrova and Ganon. But when players play through *OoT* and meet Impa in Hyrule Castle for the first time, *OoT* teaches them to "reread" this opening cutscene by introducing the mysterious woman from the cutscene as Zelda's bodyguard, suggesting instead the event players witnessed depicts Impa saving Zelda from Ganondorf. This interpretation is reinforced by the conversation Zelda has with Link before Impa appears. Zelda remarks, "What Ganondorf is after must be nothing less than the Triforce of the Sacred Realm... he wants to conquer Hyrule... no, the entire world!" While players playing through *OoT* for the first time may not possess the *Zelda* literacy necessary to interpret *OoT*'s opening cutscene correctly, the game gradually provides players the necessary information to interpret this scene more accurately as they make their way through Kokiri Forest and into Hyrule Castle. Players need only play the game long enough for the game to teach them its contribution to *Zelda*'s mythos.

Zelda Literacy and Continuity

Zelda appears intentionally designed to reach multiple audiences' literacy levels simultaneously. Game design that gradually immerses players in *Zelda*'s mythos helps explain how *Zelda* can be an easily accessible game series and yet possess a complicated continuity across the entire canon. As Dantzler suggests, an audience's capacity to make "connections that require sophisticated criticism and close reading of [a] visual text" can serve as "a reward for paying such close attention."[20] This certainly appears to be the case in *Zelda*. In the previous example from *OoT*, players who associate Twinrova and Ganon with Impa and Ganondorf do not need to conduct additional research to arrive at this conclusion. Their *Zelda* literacy allows them to make this inference. Yet videogaming serves also to correct potential misreading of this scene, allowing players to overcome gaps in their *Zelda* literacy, so they have a stronger overall comprehension of the mythos. This design is especially noteworthy since players initially may not recognize that this gap in their *Zelda* literacy exists and that this gap serves as a constraint that interferes with their ability to access the series' overall mythos fully. *A priori* reasoning thus suggests continuity literacy is a reward players accumulate through prolonged exposure to *Zelda*'s canon videogames. But since other sources can also teach players *Zelda* literacy, such as Nintendo-authorized publications, for example, the book *Hyrule Historia (HH)* and online fan communities,[21] continuity literacy is not unique to the videogames alone.

Recognizing that *Zelda*'s game design gradually teaches players the *Zelda* literacy necessary to complete the game provides *Zelda* scholars a limited understanding of how *Zelda*'s continuity remains accessible to players regardless of their pre-existing experiences with *Zelda*'s canon. This does not mean that particular prior *Zelda* literacies will not enhance certain player's gameplay experiences with some titles more than others. Vincent E. Rone's work on leitmotifs elsewhere in this volume provides one such example of how playing *Zelda* videogames in the chronology of their original release date rewards players with musical callbacks that players could miss should they play the games in a different order. However, even though Miyamoto's original approach to continuity in *Zelda* treats continuity literacy as a reward granted to seasoned players for playing canon *Zelda* videogames in particular chronologies, videogame design based on continuity literacy alone does not reveal how each canon *Zelda* videogames is crafted to have a meaningful continuity. For continuity to be present, plot must also be present.

Defining Plot

The presence of what we in the West would recognize as an overall plot structure in *Zelda*'s continuity implies each entry in the series cannot tell its narratives based on repeated aesthetics alone. As a Westerner with limited knowledge of Japanese storytelling traditions, I am uncomfortable asserting the Western tradition applies to how Miyamoto—or other non-Western videogame developers who have worked on *Zelda*— understand the plot structure of the series, but the Western tradition remains relevant to any analysis of *Zelda*'s rhetorical situation that concerns itself with how an audience that includes Westerners perceives this plot structure. A prevailing attitude in the Western literary tradition establishes a distinction between texts that reiterates the same cast of characters across multiple titles and texts that possess a plot. This distinction emerges from Aristotle's *Poetics*. Aristotle notes, "An indeterminately large number of things happen to any one person, not all of which constitutes a unity... the plot, as the imitation of an action, should imitate a single, unified action."[22] Modern fiction writing guides preserve this attitude into the 21st century. David Jauss observes, "teachers and students of writing," as well as writers of fiction writing guides, "almost universally use the word *plot* to refer to a single, monolithic organizing principle, one characterized by a focus on causality and character change."[23] Jauss emphasizes other plot forms than the causal plot exists—i.e., episodic, juxtapositional, argumentative, expository, associative, lyrical, and hybrid plots—but these other plot forms always rely on "some organizing principle to give it [the plot] form and unity."[24] This chapter approaches plot utilizing Peter Brooks' definition to accommodate for plot forms that Aristotle's definition does not:

> a constant of all written and oral narrative... the principle of interconnectedness and intention... moving through the discrete elements—incidents, episodes, actions—of a narrative.[25]

Plot as a Constraint

Interconnected plot structures in *Zelda* imposes a constraint on every canonical *Zelda* videogame's development—perhaps with the exception of the original *Zelda* on the NES. That is, Zelda's rhetorical situation implicitly requires each canonical *Zelda* videogame to contain a plot that functions independently and interacts with plots present elsewhere in *Zelda*'s canon. Whereas *Zelda* videogames need to immerse novice players gradually into *Zelda*'s mythos and subsequently expand both novice and seasoned players' *Zelda* literacy to make the overall *Zelda* videogaming experience more meaningful and accessible for the maximum amount of players in *Zelda*'s potential audience, the plot of every *Zelda* videogame—excluding remakes/deluxe editions—simply cannot repeat the exact same narrative *ad infinitum* without potentially undermining *Zelda*'s overall narrative stakes. Nor can the plot of every *Zelda* videogame appear so radically different that players cannot envision these games potentially taking place in a same continuity. As Rachel Robinson observes,

> the games are supposed to occur in the same metaphysical world. Some of them may occur in different dimensions or parallel universes, but there's no evidence in the games that the basic laws governing things... are different in these realms.[26]

Without a balance between continuity and narrative innovation in each *Zelda* game, *a priori* reasoning suggests that subsequent entries to *Zelda*'s canon would either be unnecessary—providing players literal reason to play them—or potentially attribute too many different signified meanings for *Zelda* literacy to have any worth. That is, if any recurring character, setting, plot point, has a potential to signify literally anything, the ability of players to apply *Zelda* literacy to enhance gameplay experience could lose its value as the series would gradually become so unpredictable that prior experiences with other *Zelda* videogames would not prepare players for an individual *Zelda* videogame's plot. Each subsequent *Zelda* videogame would exist in an isolated continuity, potentially hindering the overall mythos to expand further. Nathan Schmidt's exploration of *Zelda*'s aesthetics and signification explores this concept further in relation to the signification of natural disasters in *Zelda*.

While the plot of every *Zelda* title seemingly possesses significance in *Zelda*'s overall continuity, the approach to temporality (i.e. time) across the *Zelda* mythos grants developers the capacity to extend continuity in a wide array of directions. *Zelda*'s interrelated plot structures do not force each new *Zelda* videogame to begin exactly from where a previously released *Zelda* videogame concludes or prior to the rest of *Zelda*'s canon as prequels. *Zelda*'s interrelated plots have a malleable relationship with time. The approach to time in *Zelda*'s mythopoeia thus is in line with Tolkien's conceptualization of Faërie, "The magic of Faërie is not an end in itself, its virtue is in its operations: Amongst these are the satisfaction of certain primordial desires. One of these desires is to survey the depths of space and time."[27] New entries appear to enter into *Zelda*'s continuity at any point independent of each game's release date—as evident in Table 8.1. Furthermore, the events of a single game—like *OoT*—is capable of producing multiple branching timelines, introducing alternate canonical dimensions that extend the possible range of *Zelda* plots.[28] *OoT* is currently the only game to produce other timelines, but other *Zelda* titles could expand the mythos's continuity in this way since this precedent has been set. However, since *OoT* branches off into three alternate timelines, further narrative deviations based on time travel plots could render the mythos's overall continuity overly convoluted.

Three kinds of authorial choices appear to influence how interconnected plot structures expand *Zelda*'s continuity in response to previously established narrative constraints present in *Zelda*'s canon. One: *Zelda* games can be plotted across three temporal directions. That is: forward, backwards, or parallel to another videogame in the timeline. Thus far, the *Oracle* games appear to be the only videogames parallel to one another at the same point in the timeline. Two: *Zelda* games can be plotted across varying increments of time present in *Zelda*'s canon. That is, in direct continuation from a previous game—e.g., the *Oracle*

Table 8.1 Game Order in *Hyrule Historia*'s Continuity Versus Release Order

Number in Canon	Name	Number in Release Order
1	*Skyward Sword*	16
2	*The Minish Cap*	12
3	*Four Swords*	9
4	*Ocarina of Time*	5
5 (AT #1)	*A Link to the Past*	3
6 (AT #1)	*Oracle of Ages/ Oracle of Seasons*	7+8
7 (AT #1)	*Link's Awakening*	4
8 (AT #1)	*The Legend of Zelda*	1
9 (AT #1)	*The Adventure of Link*	2
5 (AT #2)	*Majora's Mask*	6
6 (AT #2)	*Twilight Princess*	13
7 (AT #2)	*Four Swords Adventures*	11
5 (AT #3)	*The Wind Waker*	10
6 (AT #3)	*Phantom Hourglass*	14
7 (AT #3)	*Spirit Tracks*	15

[AT= Alternate Timeline]

games' linked content—or after an unspecified period of time between games—e.g., *OoT* and *A Link to the Past*. Three: *Zelda* games can be plotted across multiple dimensions. As of present there are three dimensions in *Zelda* canon, the three timelines *OoT* creates.

These three authorial choices work together to increase the kinds of interconnected plots each *Zelda* game can explore by increasing the range of *when* a plot can take place. In other words, each *Zelda* videogame utilizes temporal space to incorporate new territory into *Zelda*'s preestablished plots. This new territory may pertain to a region players have never been exposed to previously or a previously explored region at a different point in *Zelda*'s continuity—for example a player who explores Hyrule in both the original *Zelda* and *OoT* can subsequently develop the *Zelda* literacy necessary to understand how Hyrule's landscape has been reshaped over eras. *Zelda*'s interconnected plots may limit where in the continuity a new *Zelda* videogame may take place and what the plot of that new *Zelda* videogame may accomplish but *Zelda*'s continuity enables Miyamoto and other developers to discover continuously new ways to extend *Zelda*'s mythos. Consequently, across the decades that have passed since the original *Zelda*'s release, players have not only been able to explore *Zelda*'s mythos through videogames that closely resemble the world present in the original *Zelda*, novel experiences continue to be introduced into the mythos through releases like *The Wind Waker* (where Link travels across a flooded Hyrule by boat), *Spirit Tracks* (where Link travels everywhere in a new Hyrule using the spirit train), *Majora's Mask* (where Link repeatedly travels through time in Termina to prevent the moon from crashing into the region), and *Twilight Princess* (where Link is transformed into a wolf after Ganondorf takes over the Twilight Realm).

How Miyamoto and Other Developers (Re)Shape *Zelda*'s Temporality

Zelda's developers utilize temporal space to overcome possible storytelling-based constraints that emerge through *Zelda*'s interlocking plots, but the continuity Nintendo reestablishes each time they publish a new canonical *Zelda* game effectively revises *Zelda*'s mythos and the *Zelda* literacy needed to access that mythos. Even if particular story and aesthetic elements remain constant across *Zelda*'s canon—e.g., that Link is a heroic protagonist who usually fights his way through dungeons to acquire the tools necessary to defeat supernaturally powerful evil forces, that this evil force usually is—or is associated with Ganon/Ganondorf/the Imprisoned/Demise, that green is a color associated often with the forces of Good—every new videogame added to *Zelda*'s official continuity affects the stakes of previous entries in *Zelda*'s canon that meet one of two observable criteria. Criterion one: The previous entry takes place immediately adjacent to the new canonical videogame. That is, the previous entry takes place either before, after, or alongside the timeframe conveyed in the newly published videogame. Criterion two: The previous entry's plot impacts the plot of the new *Zelda* videogame.

The original Gameboy version of *Link's Awakening* (*LA*) provides one such case study of how a newly published *Zelda* videogame impacts the plots of adjacent videogames in *Zelda*'s canonical continuity. The fourth canonical *Zelda* game, *LA*'s plot is self-contained. *LA* is set after the game that precedes it, *A Link to the Past* (*ALttP*), and before both *Zelda* NES games. *LA* opens with Link riding on a raft in the middle of an ocean before a storm shipwrecks Link on Koholint Island. There Link is revived by a human girl named Marin. The quest that follows leads Link to collect the eight instruments necessary to save a being called the Wind Fish from the influence of the collective entity called Shadow Nightmare. Link's quest culminates in players discovering that the Wind Fish dreamed Koholint Island and everyone who lives there into reality. Waking the Wind Fish up and saving it from Shadow Nightmare destroys the entire world the Wind Fish dreamed. Should a player complete the game without dying, players discover Marin—reincarnated as a seagull—still lives after Link wakes the Wind Fish.

LA's introduction into the continuity has at least three noticeable impacts on *Zelda*'s interconnected plots, and subsequently *Zelda* literacy, when *LA* was originally released. One: The introduction of *LA* into *Zelda*'s canon suggested that the videogames comprising this specific branch of *Zelda*'s continuity are partially interconnected by episodic plots. Even though *LA*'s aesthetics tie into the larger *Zelda* mythos—e.g., Marin's similarity to Malon, shadow form versions of Agahnim and Ganon from *ALttP*, appearances by familiar enemies like Moblins, Octoroks, and Zora—*LA* could be removed from the continuity without drastically impacting the *Zelda* literacy necessary to understand how the plots from the previous three *Zelda* entries connect with each other. Two: Even though *LA* could be removed from this continuity, the impact this *Zelda* videogame has on these interconnected plots implies Link's absence from Hyrule may have allowed Ganon to threaten the region once again. This can—but does not necessarily have to—be read as evidence that *ALttP*'s conclusion is irrelevant and that Link's disappearance enabled Ganon's return. Three: *LA*'s self-contained plot structure reveals that Link is an imperfect hero. The term Nintendo uses to describe his actions in *LA* is annihilation, as in "Though the Link the Hero had once rescued Hyrule, he was also responsible for the annihilation of the dream world."[29] This suggests that Link's return to Hyrule in the original NES *Zelda* could be motivated by Link wanting to redeem himself. *LA* has far more impact on *Zelda* literacy regarding *Zelda*'s overall mythos that is not discussed here.

Skyward Sword (*SS*) provides a case study of a *Zelda* videogame that affects the continuity of any previously published videogame in *Zelda*'s canon with a relevant interconnected plot regardless of that videogame's positionality in *Zelda*'s continuity. *SS* takes place before every *Zelda* game in the continuity with the exception of a few cutscenes from *OoT* that depict the creation of *Zelda*'s universe, even though *SS* was the last *Zelda* videogame released prior to the publication of the official *Zelda* continuity in *HH*. *SS*'s position in *Zelda*'s continuity makes the videogame's impact on *Zelda*'s interconnected plots and *Zelda* literacy readily apparent. *SS* opens with a legend detailing the Goddess Hylia fighting back the demonic hordes of Demise. In this legend, Hylia saves humanity by placing the humans onto an island in the sky—the Isle of the Goddess. These humans eventually settled a series of other flying islands—Skyloft—that serve as *SS*'s initial setting. Link is introduced to players in *SS* as a student at the Knight Academy on the day of the Wing Ceremony, a final exam designed to tests students' abilities to flow large birds called Loftwings skillfully. Following the ceremony, Demise sends the Demon Lord Ghirahim to the Surface and Ghirahim summons a tornado that pulls Zelda down from Skyloft's domain. This initiates a quest that reveals Link, Zelda, and Ganon are consistently reincarnated across time in direct association with the original battle between Demise and Hylia. More work can be done to illuminate the numerous impacts *SS* has on *Zelda*'s interconnected plots, but no other entry into *Zelda*'s canon compares to the stakes and revision *SS* interjects into *Zelda* with the introduction of reincarnation into *Zelda*'s continuity.

Zelda's Temporal Space and Continuity-Based Constraints

This brief exploration of *Zelda*'s continuity suggests that *Zelda*'s temporal space may have more significance regarding player's ability to access *Zelda*'s continuity than simply serving as the means developers use to introduce new entries into *Zelda*'s canon. Additions to *Zelda* like *LA* and *SS* demonstrate that, even if *Zelda* videogames gradually teach players the *Zelda* literacy necessary to complete the game and concurrently understand a given entry's plot structure, the temporal space surrounding the interconnected plots comprising *Zelda*'s official continuity can be explored in any new release. Remakes and deluxe additions also have this capacity, but their capacity is not explored in this chapter. It appears in Miyamoto's best interest—and the best interest of the developers who continue to expand on Miyamoto's original *Zelda* mythos— purposefully never to specify how much time passes between each videogame in *Zelda*'s continuity beyond general temporal markers. Purposefully vague temporality in videogame design subsequently explains how *Zelda*'s continuity employs such an intricate level of interconnected plots when any interconnected plot could be expanded, interrupted, or redefined each time Nintendo expands *Zelda*'s canon. That is, *Zelda*'s accessibility to novice players emerges from Miyamoto's and other developers' usage of temporality to minimize continuity literacy's potential to prevent non-seasoned players from engaging each videogame's individual plot.

Defining Queer Temporality

Temporality provides a tool *Zelda*'s developers use to craft *Zelda*'s continuity. Joan Silber notes that—in narratives—"Time draws the shapes of stories."[30] *Zelda*'s continuity utilizes what queer theorists recognize as "queer temporality" to shape its stories. Queer temporality describes more than just the temporal experiences of non-straight individuals. Queer temporality describes a phenomenology, i.e. a specific orientation in space and time.[31] Working with Merleau-Ponty's *Phenomenology of Perception*, Sara Ahmed remarks, "Queer… is a spatial term" that "comes from the Indo-European word 'twist'" and "then gets translated into a sexual term, a term for a twisted sexuality that does not follow a "straight line."[32] That is, queer in this context means "not normal."[33] The phenomenology queer temporality specifically describes is defined by Elizabeth Freeman' as "time [that] elongates and twists chronology."[34] Rather than progress in a single linear direction, queer time moves indiscernibly, challenging the established order of things by directing our attention to alternate realities and to connections between seemingly disparate moments in time moments. As Jack Halberstam notes, queer temporality allows us to perceive when "different histories… brush up against each other, creating temporal havoc."[35] In other words, queer temporality allows us to see gaps present in narratives—both fictional and historical—calling us into rhetorical situations that complicate the meanings of the texts we encounter by revealing artifices in our daily lives. José Esteban Muñoz articulates queerness as a

> longing that propels us onward... that thing that lets us feel that this world is not enough, that indeed something is missing. Often we can glimpse the worlds proposed and promised by queerness in the realm of the aesthetic... Queerness is essentially about the rejection of a here and now and an insistence on potentiality or concrete possibility for another world.[36]

Queer temporality, as is observable in *Zelda*, thus offers a praxis for interjecting new narratives into a previously established continuity subsequently to revise and expand a mythos.

Queer Temporality's Significance Regarding *Zelda*'s Mythopoeia

Queer temporality's significance in the continual expansion of *Zelda*'s continuity consequently appears intertwined with the series' mythopoeia. Queer temporality's significance in *Zelda*'s mythos is at least threefold. One: The plots of *Zelda* videogames that incorporate time travel—*OoT*, *OoA*, and *SS*—demonstrate that time in *Zelda*'s mythos is manipulatable, open to revision in the same way *Zelda*'s continuity is malleable. The exact effects each of these games portrayals of time travel have on *Zelda*'s queer temporality merits further study. Two: The three timelines that branch off of *OoT* in *Zelda*'s continuity in *HH*'s sanctioned timeline ascribe a queer temporality to the events that take place in each of these timelines. Continuity in each of these three timelines utilizes a combination of aesthetics and interconnected plots, but continuity between videogames in separate timelines emerges through the repetition of characters, locations, events, items, and aesthetics. Three: When the developers interject new videogames between/before/after any previous entries in *Zelda*'s canonical continuity, they utilize queer temporality to open *Zelda*'s mythos to new possibilities and revision. This possibility for expansion and revision pertains most explicitly to *Zelda*'s rhetorical situation and links *Zelda* with Tolkien's model of worldbuilding. Faërie, after all, with its exploration of alternate spaces and times, also signifies a form of queerness. But *Zelda*' queer temporality does more than simply survey space and time; the mythopoeia this temporality informs allows each canonical *Zelda* videogame to teach players the mythos necessary for understanding individual plots in the series without making any singular plot's appeal wholly reliant on its interconnectivity with other videogames in *Zelda*'s continuity.

Notes

1 J.R.R. Tolkien, "On Fairy-Stories," in *On Fairy-Stories*, eds. Verlyn Flieger and Douglas A. Anderson (London: HarperCollins Publishers, 2014), 65.
2 Verlyn Flieger and Douglas A. Anderson, ed., "Editors' Commentary," in *On Fairy-Stories* (London: HarperCollins Publishers, 2014), 113.
3 Philip Tallon, "The Birth of Gaming from the Spirit of Fantasy," in *The Legend of Zelda and Theology*, ed. Jonathan L. Walls (Hollywood: Gray Matter Books, 2011), 47.
4 Ibid., 57.
5 Christopher Tolkien, Foreword to *The Simarillion*, ed. Christopher Tolkien (New York, NY: Ballantine Books, 1977), xi.
6 Christopher Tolkien, Preface to *The Shaping of Middle Earth*, ed. Christopher Tolkien (New York, NY: Ballantine Books, 1986), viii.
7 J.R.R. Tolkien, "Ainulindalë," in *The Silmarillion*, ed. Christopher Tolkien (New York, NY: Ballantine Books, 1977), 3.
8 Tolkien, Foreword to *The Simarillion*, xii.
9 Lloyd Bitzer, "The Rhetorical Situation," *Philosophy and Rhetoric* 1, no. 1 (1968): 6.
10 Jonathan Frome, "Why Do We Care Whether Link Saves the Princess?" in *The Legend of Zelda and Philosophy*, ed. Luke Cuddy (Chicago, IL and La Salle: Open Court, 2013), 14–15.
11 Toni Fellela, "Link's Search for Meaning," in *The Legend of Zelda and Philosophy*, ed. Luke Cuddy (Chicago, IL and La Salle: Open Court, 2013), 53.
12 Joseph Campbell, *The Hero with a Thousand Faces* (Princeton, NJ: Princeton University Press, 1973), 30.
13 Kristina Drzaic and Peter Rauch, "Slave Morality and Master Swords: Ludus and Paidia in *Zelda*," in *The Legend of Zelda and Philosophy*, ed. Luke Cuddy (Chicago, IL and La Salle: Open Court, 2013), 68–69.
14 James Paul Gee, "What Is Literacy?" in *Literacy: A Critical Sourcebook*, eds. Ellen Cushman, Eugene R. Kintgen, Barry M. Kroll, and Mike Rose (Boston, MA and New York, NY: Bedford/St. Martin's, 2001), 542.
15 James Paul Gee, "Literacy Crises and the Significance of Literacy," in *Social Linguistics and Literacies* (London: Routledge, 2007), 44.
16 James Paul Gee, *What Video Games Have to Teach Us about Learning and Literacy* (New York, NY: Palgrave, 2003), 30.
17 Shannon Carter, *The Way Literacy Lives* (New York, NY: State University of New York Press, 2008), 80.
18 Perry Dantzler, "Multiliteracies of the MCU," in *Assembling the Marvel Cinematic Universe*, eds. Julian C. Chambliss, William L. Svitavsky, and Daniel Fandino (Jefferson, NC: McFarland & Company, 2018), 20.
19 Anna B. Janssen, "The Hero with a Thousand Hearts," in *The Legend of Zelda and Philosophy*, ed. Luke Cuddy (Chicago, IL and La Salle: Open Court, 2013), 58.
20 Perry Dantzler, "Multiliteracies of the MCU," 26.
21 For one such example on *Zelda*'s online communities, see: Sean C. Duncan and James Paul Gee, "The Hero of Timelines," in *The Legend of Zelda and Philosophy*, ed. Luke Cuddy (Chicago, IL and La Salle: Open Court, 2013), 85–101.
22 Aristotle, *Poetics*, trans. Malcolm Heath (New York, NY: Penguin, 1996), 15.
23 David Jauss, "'What We See With': Redefining Plot," *Short Fiction in Theory and Practice* 6 no. 2 (2016): 141.
24 Ibid., 156.
25 Peter Brooks, *Reading for the Plot* (New York, NY: Knopf, 1984), 5.

26 Rachel Robinson, "Shape Shifting and Time Traveling," in *The Legend of Zelda and Philosophy*, ed. Luke Cuddy (Chicago, IL and La Salle: Open Court, 2013), 81.

27 J.R.R. Tolkien, "On Fairy-Stories," in *On Fairy-Stories*, eds. Verlyn Flieger and Douglas A. Anderson (London: HarperCollins*Publishers*, 2014), 34–35.

28 Nintendo, *The Legend of Zelda: Hyrule Historia* (Milwaukie, OR: Dark Horse Books, 2013), 69.

29 Ibid., 103.

30 Joan Silber, *The Art of Time in Fiction* (St. Paul, MI: Grey Wolf Press, 2009), 74.

31 Maurice Merleau-Ponty, *Phenomenology of Perception*, trans. Colin Smith (London: Routledge, 1989), xvi–xvii.

32 Sara Ahmed, "Sexual Orientation," in *Queer Phenomenology* (Durham, NC: Duke University Press, 2006), 67.

33 Michael Warner, *The Trouble with Normal* (New York, NY: The Free Press, 1999), 44.

34 Elizabeth Freeman, *Time Binds* (Durham, NC: Duke University Press, 2010), x.

35 Judith (Jack) Halberstam, *In a Queer Time and Place* (New York, NY: New York University Press, 2005), 3.

36 Jose Esteban Muñoz, *Cruising Utopia* (New York, NY: New York University Press, 2009), 1.

9 Haunted by Heroes

Mythology and Hauntology: *Majora's Mask*

Damian Asling

Games regularly task players to save worlds from disaster. Over and over, we play against the clock, enemies, or other players to overcome challenges. These struggles contribute to developing a personal archive that players bring to each game they play motivates them forward. One of the most powerful motivators to beat a game results from the fear of loss that hangs in the back of the mind: the horrifying prospect of losing everything. *The Legend of Zelda: Majora's Mask* (referred to herein as *MM*) presents a mythology centered on this key element against the backdrop of a heroic fairy story. Through these two elements the game unifies the fantasy and horror genres. For example, Termina is characterized in part by oppressive notions of fear, mystery, and anxiety, articulated in the game's instruction booklet as "a kind of parallel world that is similar to and yet different from the land of Hyrule...[where the] people Link meets here may look vaguely familiar at first glance."[1] Though it sits within the wider *Zelda* mythology, its disruptive, uncanny world in need of a hero makes *MM* compelling for study.

Players interact with a world where notions of fear, mystery, and anxiety manifest as ludic elements. These elements act on players from virtual spaces through the hauntological. As interactive media and its consumptive practices shift, we can understand such changes by examining narrative, myth, and memory interaction with audiences. Adrien Robertson describes hauntology, as game communities continuing "to generate specters within gamespace based on game narratives."[2] He examines games that subvert genre and how the specters of genre then influence players and their communities. *MM* takes the idea of the avatar as a ludic tool and combines it with its signature mechanic of using masks to present its mythology. The systematized, frequent ways players also must use time itself as one of these tools also distinguishes this game from other installments—more so than the type of time travel in, say, *Ocarina of Time, Twilight Princess,* and *Skyward Sword.* Through these game mechanics, players explore the mythology of *MM* through regular and repeated actions of control. The contrasting agency these tools then have on players through hauntological elements form the basis for this study.

I argue that *MM* employs hauntological elements of time, moon(s), memory, and masks that culminate in a modern-day myth of apocalyptic fantasy horror. The haunted mythology of the game compels players to take control of the game, save the world, and repeat history. I examine the game through a hauntological lens as the primary method of deconstruction and analysis of the game's associated mythology and urban legends. Then I examine the relationship of form, genre, and history through the studies of Jacques Derrida, Mark Fisher, Christian McCrea, and Lee Sherlock to examine the forces of time, moon(s) and memory, which act as virtual agents. By blending genre, forms of interaction, storytelling, and memories of other media and ludic experiences, the virtual agents act on players through hauntological elements. The next section examines the role of the primary masks in the game that transform the avatar. Through the perspectives of J.R.R Tolkien and Jonathan L. Walls, I investigate how the fairy story is negotiated through masks that demonstrate how *MM's* eucatastrophic elements are linked to a players' hauntological desire for a heroic, mythologized future.[3]

Hauntology and Mythology form complementary concepts that sit both within and beyond the worlds of videogame screens, occupying an ideological area where the ultimate form of control over the virtual space of the game (winning) is juxtaposed by the ultimate loss of control (losing). When we look at storytelling more broadly, the relationship between the hauntological and mythological extends to the communities drawn to stories and the specters they bring with them, where notions of fear manifest by user-generated content, such as ghost-stories, invoke terror by making the game object at the center of these stories completely uncontrollable.

Hauntology: *Time and Falling Moons*

Hauntology, a portmanteau of the words "haunting" and "ontology," refers to ontological states of being, non-being, and notions of place and displacement. Jacques Derrida describes hauntology as "the paradoxical state of the specter, which is neither being nor non-being."[4] Specters are the forces that act on us without a physical or temporal presence and thus transcend past, present, or future. Hauntology helps explain how and why we yearn for what never was or will be, as that which haunts also drives us with memories we have not nor ever will experience. Mark Fisher describes hauntology as "the agency of the virtual, with the specter understood not as anything supernatural, but as that which acts without (physically) existing."[5] In the context of gaming, hauntological forces such as specters comprise of player history, narrative structure, and gameplay. Spectral forces that occupy our temporal space and attention are not specifically "physical;" rather, they occupy space in our minds. Just as Fisher describes, these forces act without physically existing, like a ghost. Content created by players in the form of stories, myths, and urban legends often negotiate with these forces. When the spectral acts, games can influence us in ways beyond play.

Within the spectral is an affinity with 'otherness.' Fisher discusses the concept in reference to the art-pop movement in popular-music culture. The characterization of David Bowie assumed a spectral presence for his creative process. Fisher writes, "identification with the alien meant the possibility of an escape from identity, into other subjectivities, other worlds," whereby an otherworldly presence is made relatable by speaking through the singer who acts as a medium.[6] In this example, Bowie becomes an avatar through which the alien communicates. Avatars within videogames function similarly, as they allow players to identify with 'the alien' and escape their own subjectivity to then travel into other worlds. Affinity with otherness binds the alien with the notion of a spectral presence 'neither being nor non-being.' Players use avatars to escape their existing identity, possessing the avatar to act. Lacking a physical form, the spectral acts through the virtual and speaks through media and audiences to hold agency on the present moment. Identification with the alien avatar represents the significance of 'otherness.' A hauntological lens helps us understand the game and its world as both a narrative device that draws on a history of storytelling and as a functional space where the haunted, memory, and histories of players are negotiated within the game.

An example of this negotiation is the relationship of *MM* to its predecessor, *Ocarina of Time*. Players familiar with both games may be haunted by the mythology constructed in *Ocarina of Time* if they project these experiences onto its immediate sequel. When influenced by the knowledge of the previous game, Termina becomes an 'uncanny' world.[7] If the uncanny refers to what Fisher describes as the 'unhomely,' then *Ocarina of Time* represents the 'homely' and everything familiar. The distortion of so many familiar gameworld's assets, aesthetics, mechanics, and internal principles turned alien creates the uncanny. This distortion facilitates the juxtaposition between the world of Termina as unhomely to the homely world of Hyrule. Players have ventured away from what the game reminds them as their home, Hyrule, and now must save a foreign land from doom. The shift of narrative tone also invokes a sense of the uncanny, considering the central message of *MM* departs from the trope of good vs. evil found in its predecessors. Josh Corman defines two key differences between *MM* and nearly all other *Zelda* titles. First, he describes the tonal shift in narrative, the main antagonist not being an "irredeemable monster like Ganondorf, but simply a lonely kid," and, second, "the message of forgiveness delivered repeatedly throughout the game."[8] The theme of forgiveness subverts straightforward notions of good versus evil, which reinforces Termina as uncanny. Compared to *Ocarina of Time,* where the goal was to defeat the evil Ganondorf, players quest for redemption instead. Players operate outside of Termina's clock, legends, and mythologies rewinding time, rewriting history, and haunted by memories of countless lost futures.

While travelling between the present and past as other games in the series, time in *MM* behaves differently as compared to other games. As Sherlock describes, time in *MM*

> presents the player with a three-day cycle in which a number of heroic missions must be completed to save Termina... To further complicate the matter, these three days are actually not three days; rather, they are three simulated days that take less "real" time to elapse.[9]

Players' notions of temporality take new meaning as the flow of time becomes a key ludic element over which they can exercise some control. Sherlock states, "in the case of *Majora's Mask*, one day of event time takes up about 18 minutes of play time, giving the player roughly 54 minutes to finish the entire game."[10] Although the length of actual, real-world time may only be 54 minutes, the act of constant reallocation of time means, like any other role-playing game, it can be played *ad infinitum*. Players use these 54 minutes, repeat it, and avert disaster by rewinding the clock before the moon crashes.

The looming threat of an apocalyptic lunar collision with Termina propels gameplay forward. Nevertheless, just as Sherlock describes, *Majora's Mask* presents a finite number of spectral forces that shift like the reallocation of time.[11] They become ghosts that cannot move on from their predetermined fate. When players travel back in time, non-playable characters and elements revert to their initial state at the 'Dawn of The First Day' and proceed to act out their predetermined paths until players fail to manage their time correctly and the moon crashes, die in the gameworld, or complete the game by defeating the final boss. As there are a limited number of these non-playable elements in the game, the possibilities of how these elements can act becomes finite and ultimately rests on a singular purpose—to act on players through the virtual, as specters, to motivate the reallocation of time.

The avatar represents as an exception to this rule. Link is not bound by the same rules as the rest of the gameworld. Sherlock identifies Link's identity as bound "to the fragmentation and disruption of time."[12] Time then becomes a simultaneously endless and finite resource. It is always possible to run out of it, but players can replenish it at any point they wish. The caveat is that rewinding time costs immediate progress. For example, a quest line or the progress in a dungeon will be reset. However, by reallocating these finite forces, the player and Link sit outside the common rules of the game, and as such they embody the foreign force able to resist and fight against the predetermined fates shared by the races of Termina.

Time is a haunting force, finite and infinite. Non-playable characters in Termina have no control over it; to them it hangs in the background and is always running out, until reversed. In *MM*, the manipulation of time is a trait unique to Link (the hero). The ability to transcend a pre-determined fate and change it defines the philosophical significance of temporality within the game and, in turn, neither being nor non-being. Sherlock identifies time as holding "amazing power but also threatens an unthinkable loss, of both self-identity and time itself. If time is lost, Termina is lost."[13] The threat of loss haunts the game and players focused through the anxiety of a prospective apocalypse that produces both a sense of horror and a heroic will to fight it. The start of the game sees Link play through all three days, until the final dramatic moments before the moon falls and the prospective apocalypse is made a reality. Players then reclaim the Ocarina of Time from Skull Kid and play the *Song of Time* to rewind the clock. When Link awakens in the clock tower, he learns the *Song of Healing* and uses it to return to his Hylian self and receive the Deku Mask. Time acts as a hauntological element; its agency is virtual as it forces players to embody the heroic will and invoke their unique trait.

The end of the game reflects the beginning, as players must allow time to tick away until just before the moon crashes and summon the four giants who activate the final sequence of events. Through continual re-allocation of time and subsequently, anxiety, the finite resource of time is made infinite for players to reach the final boss, the demon Majora. Once Majora is defeated, anxiety lifts. The clock town carnival and 'The Dawn of a New Day' are free to take place. The flow of time toward a horrible fate has ended.

Hauntology: *Memories and Ghost-Stories*

As players travel through time in *Majora's Mask*, they also travel with memory. Game creators use ghosts of cancelled futures to generate a feeling of horror through the unexpected, which goes hand in hand with the horror genre. Gaming's hauntology, time and time again, has been apparent in its representation of older forms of media to convey horror. For example, Christian McCrea examines how the anachronistic VHS aesthetic of *Siren* (SCE Japan Studio, 2004), the photograph taking in *Dead Rising* (Capcom, 2006), and the frame of the digital video camera in *Michigan: Report from Hell* (Grasshopper Manufacture, 2004) allow games to break themselves down to "form a different kind of suspension of disbelief."[14] Disbelief can become horror when the familiar is made unfamiliar. The hauntology of memory connects the gaming dead with dead media and can horrify us when gaming itself is being hacked and dismembered. Games comprise non-interactive media, such as photography or film, and combine them with interactivity, which then renders these media forms dead. Direct intervention distorts the memory of non-interactive media and the specters of how these anachronisms *should* behave shapes players' experiences.

MM incorporates film, text elements, and the flow of time into its game mechanics to present a "fictive boundary," a hauntological, mechanical force that requires a narrative device to explain its presence as a barrier. An ever-present clock at the bottom of the screen warns the player of impending doom, the countdown to annihilation. In addition, a clock towers over the eponymous town, the center of which begins and ends the game. McCrea notes how hauntology "is one way to come to grips with the muddying of traditions, the ability for figures to permeate across fictive boundaries, and the impact of the audio-visual archive on its ability to remember and forget."[15] Every time we, as players, travel back in time, we bring the time we have already spent in Termina with us. Our own audio-visual archives, built of repeated experiences of the three-day cycle, permeate through the fictive boundaries of *MM*, where we use these now-familiar elements to influence the next three-day cycle.

The game reuses familiar character models, recycled from previous installments; however, these characters are different. New names, histories, and narratives register these characters to players as unfriendly and unfamiliar. Altering the familiar constitutes a key characteristic of *MM*. Dwindling time and the actual appearance of the hero Link are game mechanics that do not advance gameplay in the same way as in other *Zelda* games. *MM* alters these mechanics to contrast presumptions and knowledge players bring from the wider genre of role-playing games.

MM's narrative, graphics, and playing style incorporate elements of horror. Termina suggests an unavoidable apocalypse through its ticking clock and oblivious populace, doomed to repetition. *MM* instills fear by the anxiety resulting from a looming apocalypse. To avoid it, players must forget what they already know about *Zelda's* heroes, characters, mythology, and the genre of role-playing games more broadly. With regard to the act of remembering, Marc Augé writes that, "remembering or forgetting is doing gardener's work, selecting, pruning. Memories are like plants."[16] Like the metaphor of the gardener, players decide when the gameworld needs to forget through the *Song of Time* and by selecting and pruning memory, the relationship between their gaming past, present and future changes. As a result of these memory losses, the anxiety of both running out of time and total amnesia terrifies players; the heroic deeds they accomplish disappear from the collective memory of the gameworld. Anxiety arises from the constant requirement for players to erase their progress and their past to reach the present. Progress is possible only by players accepting their non-belonging to the world; they must simply save it. To move forward, players conditioned to look into their history and knowledge must look away from the past.[17] They become heroes unrecognizable to Termina and thus are forced to rebuild a legendary status analogous to that in Hyrule. The suggestion of running out of time to memorialize Hyrule's legend subsequently haunts the landscape.

Progress becomes possible by reallocating the specter of time that haunts the landscape. In the game, literal clocks represent time; the clock tower and the clock at the bottom of the screen in the user interface. Much like the moon hanging above, ever-present and ever-foreboding time reminds players that they must turn these clocks back to continue. Players simultaneously dwell in the past, present, and future with the looming specter of the clock, native to nowhere (or when). Since time exists both paradoxically everywhere and nowhere, it acts through an existence validated by players having to move the hands of the clock backwards.

Like our understanding of time in general, time in *MM* cannot be killed, nor can it be given new life. Unlike our understanding, however, time in the game repeats itself *ad nauseum*, looping infinitely. The specter (or ghost) of time in *Majora's Mask* therefore is not the same as what we normally define as the temporal. A ghost belongs nowhere and is not the same entity as the person it was in life.[18] Like a poltergeist doomed to re-enact the same moments experienced by a former (living) self over and over, time is stuck. It loops endlessly and ceases to move forward. When time enters this state of infinity it becomes an anachronism, a chronological inconsistency.

Chronological inconsistency allows the specters of dead media to haunt the present. Since the spectral exists in a virtual space that is neither being nor non-being, traces of them can be found as attached to haunted, existing objects. Players navigate the links between the specters of the gameworld through what Christian McCrea calls "traces."[19] In *MM,* traces of the specters of time and memory are attached to clocks and masks. Memory assumes a spectral presence by the loss of the immediate future, loss of control, and loss of the ability to record progress in a linear sense. Through these hauntological artefacts, players interact with chronological inconsistency when they make the sacrifice of immediate progress in one part of Termina for long-term progress in saving the entire world. Link becomes a literal link between the virtual agency of these specters.

Outside the game cartridge, fan-fiction represents an attempt by players to reclaim control of the anachronistic, allowing players to navigate the links between specters beyond the limits of the gameworld. If creating horrifying scenarios exemplifies control over games and players, horror is made real when players lose control. Since the gameworld is currently under the control of Skull Kid and the descending moon, reclaiming control of the world is a priority for players. A *MM* player, known by the internet handle "Jadusable," submitted a fictional ghost-story to forums and gaming discussion boards claiming it as non-fiction.[20] The story traces the yard-sale purchase of a shady cartridge of *MM* by a writer.

As Jadusable continues playing the game, supernatural forces within the game try to communicate with him. The game preys on Jadusable's fears of the supernatural and ultimately reveals it has become haunted by the tortured ghost of the cartridge's former owner, "Ben."

This story is a piece of media where *MM* becomes the haunted object. The story recounts a literal ghost as being attached to the game. However, what haunts the story itself is the reader's memories of playing *MM*. An understanding of play and control is renegotiated in this story, since players ultimately control all games; at any time, they can turn them off and return to real life. The loss of the ability to turn off the machine in Jadusable's story instills fear. It is shocking to hear of other-worldly forces terrorizing players with a message from beyond the grave and infiltrating the untouchable, digital realm, where even removing the power source will not stop the game from seeking interaction.

We access memories of play and generate expectations of what should happen next which are then thwarted by these stories and mythologies. Jadusable's ghost-story, the past legends of *Zelda,* and Hyrule—all these color expectations and pose "what if" questions: What if players lose control of the game? What if time runs out? What if I lose all of my progress? *MM* blends fears of these outcomes with the hero's journey to motivate players to act. The fan-fiction ghost-story exemplifies how virtual agents may act and where specters of memory intersect with our belief of how something should happen. In Jadusable's story, our expectation of buying a game cartridge from a yard-sale is that it does not usually come with the ghosts of the dead attached to it. Expectations of control are grounded in deliberate action; the decisions we take in the game have an effect on the virtual world. The use of time in *MM* as a ludic tool offers an opportunity to erase the effects of these actions on the virtual world. However, despite the reallocation of time players still remember their actions when revisiting a previously explored area, and these memories loom over them just as the clocks and moon(s) of Termina do.

Mythology: *Masks and Heroes*

The avatar, Link, becomes a mask for players to assume the role of the hero. As the hero, they then use this role to interact with the wider mythology of *MM*. In turn, the literal masks of Termina are an integral ludic tool and narrative device in this mythos, as they are key items that survive Link's repeated time-travel. Due to their survival, the masks become intensely haunted objects and facilitate our navigation through the steps of fairy-stories as Tolkien outlines in his essay *On Fairy-Stories*. *MM* players are protagonists who must save a secondary world like that which Tolkien describes. In fairy-stories, secondary (fantasy) worlds exist in contrast to our own primary (real) world. Termina is a secondary world characterized by what Tolkien calls "many things." Like ecosystems in our own primary world, many things such as animals and monsters, endless seas and landscapes, enchanting beauty, and "both joy and sorrow as sharp as swords"[21] all share an internal logic and consistency that can substantiate the events and stories that take place within the secondary world despite how fantastic these events may be.

Fairy-stories and ghost-stories create worlds that suspend our disbelief in the possibility of their fantastic events. As a modern myth of apocalyptic horror, *MM* blends fantasy and horror genres by adding the element of loss as an inextricable part of its secondary world through masks that hold great power. Masks are relics of the future for Termina's populace and relics of the past for Link. Corrupted temporality makes these masks hauntological, as they do not exist in a fixed past, present, or future. They add the sense of loss to *MM's* secondary world through the irregularity of when and where they belong. By deciding when to wear a mask and transform play, players can decide how their story unfolds, making playing with masks a powerful example of Tolkienesque sub-creative processes in *MM*.

To enact these sub-creative processes, players interact with the game they are immersed in. The notions of interactivity and immersion are of considerable significance when coupled with notions of sub-creation and myth-making.[22] Interaction can be interpreted as the agency of the player on the game and their immersion as the agency of the gameworld upon the player. Immersion is the envelopment of the player into the world and their interactions subsequently shape the experience of the game as it unfolds. As the players' own mask, Link facilitates interaction with the game and allows players to immerse themselves in the world by acting out his role as hero. By shaping experience players undertake the process of sub-creating new mythologies through discovering a new way of playing, and in turn, a new interpretation of narrative.

There are four key steps Tolkien outlines as to what makes a traditional narrative identifiably a "fairy-story."[23] The first is fantasy[24]; the second is recovery[25]; the third step is escape[26]; and the fourth is consolation. In particular, consolation provides relationship to the hauntological link among the living, dead, and spectral. According to Tolkien, fairy-stories always have happy endings but at a cost. The joy such an ending brings is both unexpected and unique. Consolation presents the opposite of catastrophe. The joy of saving the day and averting disaster to emerge heroic defines the eucatastrophe.[27] If gaming specters represent the unresolved, then the contrast between the eucatastrophe and the catastrophe of ghost-stories (like Jadusable's fan-fiction) exemplifies the tension between control over the game and the loss of said control, respectively.

As Tolkien notes, if tragedy (that is, catastrophe) is the true form of drama, then consolation (that is, eucatastrophe) is the true form of the fairy-story.[28] I argue that *MM* is a fairy-story with a significant eucatastrophic element as its backdrop. It offers a consolatory approach to its narrative where there is a cost to saving the world. The cost comes when players break Termina out of its infinite loop. Link becomes the only character who has lived countless realities only then to reverse the clock, which erases the memories of his deeds. To reach the end of the game is to lose countless moments in time and memories, and so the idyllic way of playing the game is to lose continuously.

As players relive the same three-day cycle with differing paths, over and over, they develop a detached attitude to gameworld consumables such as arrows and bombs, memories, and even some quest lines. Through following the cycles of loss, players overcome the game as they become increasingly comfortable with sacrificing seemingly immediate progress for long-term gains. The eucatastrophe of *MM* idealizes the ability to accept loss and focus on only the key items. Masks constitute the singular exception to this enforced lesson.

To progress through the game, players must don three masks: The Deku, Goron, and Zora masks allow Link to transform into each of these races and venture into their homelands throughout Termina. Players unlock each mask as they move through the narrative. The main antagonist, Skull Kid, uses the abilities of the stolen Majora's mask to turn Link into a "Deku scrub." Link then later meets The Happy Mask Salesman who teaches the *Song of Healing,* which both transforms Link back into a Hylian and makes the Deku form interchangeable by wearing the requisite mask.

In *MM*, masks of the dead provide Link a way to progress through the parts of the world where he normally cannot go. As players move further through the game, they unlock two subsequent masks by playing the *Song of Healing* to the dying Mikau (Zora) and ghost of Darmani (Goron), whose spirits, which Link heals, transfer into masks that assist him on his quest. Josh Corman describes the relationship Link has with the aiding these dead characters in his work, *The Afterlife and Majora's Mask,* as one of the game's primary tasks outside of saving the world.[29] Assisting living and dead characters augments Link's abilities to allow him access to the four temples that lead him to summoning the four giants. As he travels through Termina, other characters continually mistake Link for Mikau and Darmani, reminding players that they are faceless and foreign, masquerading as natives in a world without a hero. Link assumes the roles of the other, deceased characters that have no future in Termina. Darmani's ghost and Mikau's dying body are stuck in their own infinite loops, repeating their own cycles until Link can free their spirits, who then supply him with a mask as a relic of completion. This is another example of consolation, where the native Zora and Goron of Termina need to pass on to allow Link (and players) to use their abilities to reach a happy ending on their behalf. Subsequently, Link is able to drive the narrative forward due to the loss of Mikau and Darmani's present (and their futures).

The element of loss the masks betoken drives narrative in *MM*. The game's story sets into motion by Link losing his ocarina and Hylian self to Skull Kid's use of Majora's Mask. Link uses the *Song of Healing* so he can lose his seemingly permanent Deku form and return to his Hylian self (and subsequently save the world). The people of Termina potentially lose their future to a perpetually falling moon, and the loss of Termina's peaceful lifestyle to the corruption caused by Majora's Mask itself— both exemplify the relationship between the gameworld's mythos and the element of loss. Aversion to loss and attempts of reclamation bring players through the game to its conclusion. As players are continuously losing something in the pursuit of, or by use of a mask if they are to progress, consolation is a key theme. The game forces players to react to situations rather than act on them. Christian McCrea notes that horror games force players to react to "supernatural forces" in contrast to most action scenarios where players *are* supernatural forces.[30] Only by losing his Hylian form can Link recover it, as one cannot recover what is not missing. Once his Hylian form is recovered, Link is able to progress the story further. Further progression requires losing the Hylian form again (as long as the mask is on) to become a Goron and Zora. Masks and the quests associated with them focus on players averting loss and re-enacting the mythology of the game through reaction to the supernatural, escaping a horrible, crushing fate through the recovery of the self, and consolatory negotiations with the dead (and dying) elements of the gameworld.

In addition to the main questline of preventing the moon from crashing down, players offer consolation to the rest of Termina's populace through side-quests. Successful completion of many of these quests results in obtaining a mask. Not all of these additional masks possess the transformational qualities of the Deku, Zora, and Goron masks, although some give abilities, access to areas, or specific questlines that are not usually accessible when not wearing any mask. The purpose of collecting these masks is never explicitly stated to players through the game's narrative. However, by collecting all 24 (including the default, transformational ones) players may obtain the final, "Fierce Deity Mask."

The Fierce Deity Mask allows an escape from the pressures of the secondary world. Nefarious bosses or the sense of doom no longer threaten players as they make their way to the final stage of the game. When facing Majora, one final act of transformational play turns Link into the Fierce Deity, whose character model is a reused (and slightly altered) asset of "Adult Link" from *The Ocarina of Time*. Anthony G. Cirilla explains that, in *Ocarina of Time*, transformational play activates the sub-creative imagination and offers players insight into the meaning of being the Hero of *Faërie* through "the garments of Link's intentionality."[31] In *MM*, transformational play through the use of masks blends Link with other characters, culminating in a deity modelled on Link's adult self, to offer this insight: an example of how the game unifies the hauntological and mythological to create apocalyptic, fantasy-horror by allowing the non-living (whether ghost or god) to act through the living.

As according to the fantasy of *The Legend of Zelda*, becoming the Hero of *Faërie* is the idyllic form of play. The hauntological element of masks exemplifies the eucatastrophic through the price paid for (and after) their acquisition. When the clock is wound back only the mask itself remains. Only players keep the memory of Link acquiring the mask, while the gameworld forgets. To reinforce this concept, the masks themselves become relics of quests achieved, markers of progress; yet the ultimate prize for players who become problem solvers unbound by time or challenges is a mask that makes them both an adult and a god. The caveat to this mask is that it can only be used in boss battles. The powers and abilities conferred make all of the bosses incredibly easy to overcome, including the embodiment of evil and final boss, Majora.

Link's elevation from fairy boy to adult deity represents Tolkien's consolatory eucatastrophe. Tolkien describes the moment of eucatastrophic consolation as a "turn:"

> however wild its events, however fantastic or terrible the adventures, it can give to child or man that hears it, when the "turn" comes, a catch of the breath, a beat and lifting of the heart, near to (or indeed accompanied by) tears, as keen as that given by any form of literary art, and having a peculiar quality.[32]

When players gain abilities that render the game's greatest challenges impotent, the tension that once existed among impending doom and adversity and resisting it suddenly dissipates. Players can now act as a supernatural force, rather than react. There is no need to race against the clock (or the moon) as they can now save the world when they choose to.

The Fierce Deity Mask renders dark forces all but impotent. McCrea explains that the supernatural haunts us as a threat to human agency with our fear stemming from disembodied forces such as ghosts or gods having influence on the physical world; we are scared when supernatural forces threaten human agency.[33] The Fierce Deity mask shifts the agency of players providing access to the supernatural. Rewinding the clock becomes more or less a chore once the game's many challenges are overcome and the three-days are no longer a limit but an infinite space. The readability of the clock and ultimately the game's narrative logic has changed, as McCrea explains: "it is precisely the image's readability which makes the game, in an important sense, ultimately unreliable."[34] Through the process involved to become the Fierce Deity the player transcends the game's sense of time.

The masks bring players to a moment of total standstill, where the gameworld waits for them to act and is a moment that allows deliberate rejection of one possible future. Termina neither can end nor live on; it is simply stuck in the three-day loop until the player decides to continue. The moon hanging in the sky is just as stuck as players simply can summon the four giants together to hoist it, thereby preventing its collision. McCrea notes,

> we want to feel fear in its absolute, and yet possess everything we need to conquer it. Agency and control well up from the player's history of mastering games, while powerlessness and the monstrous apparitions of horror look to chip away at their confidence.[35]

The Fierce Deity form possesses everything players need to conquer the demon mask Majora. The masks of *MM* take players through its mythos, ushering them from the initial, small-scale struggle between the fairy-boy Link and lonely Skull Kid, into an ultimate, grandiose battle for the future, serving as a reward and final consolation for experiencing all aspects of *MM's* horrifying fairy-tale.

Conclusion

Mythology and hauntology are spectral guides for players in *The Legend of Zelda: Majora's Mask*. Juxtaposition of the two reveals mythology demonstrates to the player *how to act*, while the hauntological constitutes *that which acts on the player*. By playing as Link, we renegotiate our knowledge of how to be a hero based on past experiences with attaining a desired outcome of the game. Robertson notes that videogames are haunted spaces, which can change "ontological certainties" that then call into question our idea of when and where we exist.[36] Time, moon(s), memories, and masks are hauntological elements that stem from a wider *Zelda* mythology and culminate in *MM*. These elements exist in virtual space and subsequently must act through players.

Players reorient themselves outside of the gameworld through shared experiences, creating moments of terror through the renegotiation of their own personal experiences. Robertson contends that "hauntology nevertheless asserts one avenue of play - and therefore action - when attempting to navigate gamespace's systems of controls and dominance: the proliferation and continuation of the game narratives in common spaces online."[37] In these common spaces, players are able to ask questions non-negotiable with the game itself; what if the game started controlling us? What if we do not save the world? Because we can imagine such a future, we resist it.

Players and games share a fear of loss and an idealized version of play. The ultimate form of control over the game (winning) juxtaposed by loss of control (losing) manifest in the tension between mythological and hauntological forces. Becoming a hero who can save the world offers agency to all of us who choose to take up the challenge. Apocalyptic horror plays on our insecurities of everything ending and a complete, final moment of absolute loss, and multimedia mythologies that play in this space are defined by the anxieties of this lost future. Modern stories and myths are told through multiple ways through multiple formats, and with each retelling another group of ghosts begin haunting us.

The Fierce Deity mask is the ultimate prize given to the player in consolation for the loss of multiple futures. Although we may die and rewind the clock many times over, a singular victory over Majora resolves our anxiety. Repeated death and the casting aside of identities toward victory generates specters which haunt players. Like the Hero of *Faërie*, we pay a price for victory, and we experience consolation in the form of complete control after a period of continual loss.

Notes

1 Eiji Aonuma and Yoshiaki Koizumi, *The Legend of Zelda: Majora's Mask. Nintendo 64* (Japan: Nintendo. (Instruction booklet), 2000), 6.
2 Adrien Robertson, *Gaming with Ghosts: Hauntology, Metanarrative, and Gamespace in Video Games*. Master's thesis (Ottawa: Carleton University, 2014), 8.
3 J. R. R. Tolkien, "On Fairy-Stories," in *The Tolkien Reader* (New York, NY: Ballantine Books, 1966), 22.
4 Jacques Derrida, *Specters of Marx*. 1st ed. (New York, NY: Routledge, 2011).
5 Mark Fisher, *Ghosts of My Life* (Alesford, Hampshire: Zero Books, 2011), 18.
6 Ibid., 42.
7 Ibid., 125.
8 Josh Corman, "Take Your Time, Hurry Up, The Choice is Yours: Death and the Afterlife in The Legend of Zelda: Majora's Mask" in The Legend of Zelda and Theology, ed. Jonathan Walls (Hadley, MA: Grey Matter Books, 2011)., 1595.
9 Lee Sherlock in Luke Cuddy, *The Legend of Zelda and Philosophy* (New York, NY: Open Court, 2008).
10 Ibid., 122.
11 Ibid.
12 Ibid., 127–128.
13 Ibid., 130.
14 Christian McCrea, "Gaming's Hauntology: Media Apparitions in Forbidden Siren, Dead Rising and Michigan: Report from Hell," in *Horror Video Games: Essays on The Fusion of Fear and Play*, ed. Bernard Perron (Jefferson, NC: McFarland Press, 2009), 225.
15 Ibid., 221.
16 Marc Augé, *Oblivion* (Minneapolis, MI: University of Minnesota Press, 2004).
17 McCrea, 235.
18 Peter Buse and Andrew Stott, *Ghosts* (Basingtoke: Macmillan Press, 2005). Mark Fisher, "HAUNTOLOGY NOW", Blog, *K-Punk*, 2006, http://k-punk.abstractdynamics.org/archives/007230.html.

19 McCrea, 236.
20 Jadusable, "Youshouldnthavedonethat.Net", *Jadusable Wiki,* 2019, https://jadusable.fandom.com/wiki/Youshouldnthavedonethat.net. Website.
21 Tolkien, 1.
22 Interaction and immersion demonstrate how players and games are the negotiation between primary (real) worlds and virtual, secondary (fantasy) worlds. Immersion (that is, the suspension of disbelief) can only be achieved when there is a logical consistency in the game-world. For further reading see; Gareth Schott and Maria Kambouri, "Moving between the Spectral and Material Plane," *Convergence: The International Journal of Research into New Media Technologies* 9, no. 3 (2003): 41–55.
23 Tolkien, 5–14.
24 Fantasy: Where we use imagination to create a rational world that is consistent, governed by laws of nature and rules that are different from our own.
25 Recovery: We can review our own world through the perspective of another world. Much like the previously discussed affinity for the alien, it allows us to connect our own point of view to that of another world, to reflect on previously unquestioned assumptions and 'recover' our perspective through an examination from the outside.
26 Escape: A space free from the pressures and rules of our own world where the fantastic, legendary, and impossible can take place and teach us lessons that we may not find in our own reality.
27 Tolkien, 22–23.
28 J. R. R. Tolkien, "On Fairy-Stories," in *The Tolkien Reader* (New York, NY: Ballantine Books, 1966), 22.
29 Corman in Walls, 1501.
30 McCrea, 221.
31 See Anthony Cirilla's essay in this volume.
32 Tolkien, 23.
33 Geoff King and Tanya Krzywinska, *Screenplay* (London: Wallflower Press, 2002). McCrea, 221.
34 McCrea, 222.
35 Ibid., 220.
36 Robertson, 89.
37 Ibid.

The Legend of Pedagogy
Theory and Practice

10 The Hero of Time

The Legend of Zelda as Children's Literature

Chamutal Noimann and Elliot H. Serkin

In his famous 1802 letter to Samuel Coleridge, Charles Lamb laments the disappearance of fairy tales and fantasy from children's libraries. The Romantics believed that children should be exposed to as much fantasy and imaginative texts as possible, from *The Tale of Genji* to *One Thousand and One Arabian Nights*, fairy tales to old wives' tales. He complains that children's brains are filled only with facts of the Primary World:

> Knowledge insignificant and vapid as Mrs. Barbauld's books convey, it seems, must come to a child in the shape of knowledge; and his empty noodle must be turned with conceit of his own powers when he has learnt that a horse is an animal, and Billy is better than a horse, and such like; instead of that beautiful interest in wild tales, which made the child a man, while all the time he suspected himself to be no bigger than a child.[1]

For Lamb, books of fantasy and imagination, "wild tales," allow the child reader to see herself as more than a child, and provides her with an image of herself as powerful. This notion is as profound, insightful, and relevant to this discussion about the place of videogames in a child's education and development in our time as it was to Lamb's contemporary focus. Shigeru Miyamoto's *The Legend of Zelda: Ocarina of Time* (1987) exemplifies, particularly via Tolkienesque fantasy, a Neo-Romantic belief in the power of children's literature to mature the imagination of children and renew the childlike imagination of adults.

Action-Adventure videogames, such as *The Legend of Zelda,* are often considered tangentially related to children's literature, mainly because they are narrative-based, often feature child protagonists, and are popular with children. Additionally, these games are predominantly visual in the same way as comic books, graphic novels and picture books and therefore are assumed to be suitable for children. Simultaneously, and, again, much like comic books and graphic novels, their educational value is often dismissed simply because of what they are: videogames. Although there is a growing acceptance that videogames are not as bad as they were once thought to be, narrative-based videogames are associated with digital technology rather than print media, which is still preferred and privileged, especially in education. The prevailing cry against the dominance of screens in children's lives today is rooted in the unawareness of these games' reliance on literary traditions previously established as the fertile soil of children's literature, the same traditions whose loss guardians of education lament.

Children respond passionately to videogames, like *The Legend of Zelda*, precisely because they are grounded in the literary traditions that preceded them. The prevailing themes and features that have attracted children to adventure stories and fantasy are there in action adventure videogames, where they are enhanced and intensified. In *Understanding Children's Literature*, Peter Hunt offers a definition of the genre that is helpful to this discussion. He takes issue with the words "children" and "literature." Hunt explains why the definitions of each word is too vague to encompass or contain everything that children's literature is in our time. Hunt prefers the word "text" to describe a work produced for children. He suggests that "how a story is communicated, then, by spoken word or written word, by picture or symbol, the circumstances of that communication, and the possible effect...have become an integral part of the study of children's literature."[2] By Hunt's definition, Action-Adventure narrative-based videogames, which communicate a story through spoken words, written words, pictures, and symbols, are texts for children and reside comfortably within this genre.

Shigeru Miyamoto's *The Legend of Zelda* series belongs in the canon of children's literature, not simply because it attracts a young audience and offers an escape through narrative featuring young protagonists, but also because *Zelda* is informed by and extends numerous traditions that have been staples of children's literature for centuries. Narrative based role-playing videogames, like *The Legend of Zelda*, continue in the literary traditions of narrative, character development and themes most particularly associated with the Romantic paradigm.[3] *Zelda* builds upon these traditions in a way that allows us to organically include it in the canon of what Peter Hunt calls "texts for children." *Zelda* bears obvious similarities to such classic fantasy adventure stories like *Peter Pan* (1904), *Mopsa the Fairy* (1869) and *The Hobbit* (1937), but it also contains digital elements that help make these similarities become even more compelling. Technology allows the author, Miyamoto, to pioneer new pathways to more fully realize, expand, and extend the classical elements of the genre.

Two established storytelling traditions Miyamoto utilizes in *Zelda* that are useful to consider in connecting the game to its literary canon are Joseph Campbell's Monomyth, as described in *A Hero With a Thousand Faces*, as well as the idea of fantasy as "secondary world" from "On Fairy-Stories" by J.R.R. Tolkien.[4] The narrative theories of Tolkien and

Campbell in tandem provide this discussion with its frame that is based on the solid ground of the Romantics' idealization of childhood. Link's role as the classic hero is fully explored in Stephan F. Kuniak's "It's Dangerous to Go Alone: The Hero's Journey in *The Legend of Zelda*," where he details how closely Miyamoto follows Campbell's 12 stages in every Zelda game with useful charts. He concludes that "the overall pattern of the hero's journey is evident."[5] The hero's journey in children's literature is often inseparable from the *bildungsroman*. From Ruskin's original fairy tale *The King of the Golden River* (1851) to Ursula Le Guin's *Wizard of Earthsea* (1968), coming of age is an important part of the child hero's journey, but the child very rarely matures to full adulthood in the stories. Like most fantasy and fairy tales, Link's journey in the *Legend of Zelda* follows the traditional arc of a hero's journey, but he does not become an adult. Moreover, Link's rebirth in every new version of the story reinforces this arrested development even more than in the Romantic literary tradition.

The Legend of Zelda is also a recent addition to the canon of fairy tales that has only been accepted as a part of childhood in the 19th century. As a genre, fairy tales were first available to children because they were part of a folklore literature created for a mixed audience. By the 17th century, fairy tales started to be viewed as inappropriate and forbidden to children. From the Puritans, who viewed fiction as "telling stories" and therefore lies, to John Locke, who thought they were too scary for children's *Tabula Rasa*, to Sarah Trimmer, who deemed them uneducational and frivolous, fairy tales were banned. The Romantics, who fought to regain the power of imagination that is natural for children, fiercely advocated for their return to the nursery. Charles Lamb was not alone in declaring them essential readings. In his letter to Coleridge, he expresses the general sentiment, "think what you would have been now, if, instead of being fed with tales and old wive's fables, you had been crammed with geography and natural history!"[6] The Romantics' efforts worked all too well and, by the 19th century, fairy tales became a literature almost exclusively created for and read by children.

By 1937, in "On Fairy-Stories," Tolkien rejects the notion that fairy tales and fantasy are literatures exclusively for children. "Children as a class—except in a common lack of experience they are not one—neither like fairy-stories more, nor understand them better than adults do; and no more than they like many other things."[7] Tolkien's complaint essentially seeks to overturn decades of censorship and advocacy to again present fairy tales as a literature that should be read by all regardless of age. This effort is similar to the debate over whether certain videogames are appropriate for adults or children. Following Tolkien's argument, we must conclude that *The Legend of Zelda* as a digital fairy tale suitable for a mixed audience. However, while Tolkien believed that children are not uniquely equipped to understand or enjoy fairy tales, he also admits that they are "a special kind of creature, almost a different race," which is an idea that is Romantic at its core.[8] In *Emile,* J. J. Rousseau writes, "childhood has its own ways of seeing, thinking and feeling, nothing is more foolish than to try to substitute ours [adults] for theirs."[9] So both adults and children should read fairy tales, but each group experiences them differently. This difference in experience is one the Romantics, as well as the Victorians, detected and sought to overcome. At the end of *Alice's Adventures in Wonderland,* for example, Carroll describes Alice waking up and telling her older sister all about her dream. Her sister then closes her eyes and "half believed herself in Wonderland."[10] She tries to recreate her sister's dream, but because she is an adult, she can only half experience it. "She knew she had but to open them again, and all would change to dull reality."[11] This separation between the experience of children and adults was lamented and accepted by the Romantics and Victorians' in their belief of a physical separation of the world of childhood from the world of adulthood. Fairy tales and fantasy belonged to children because they experience them more fully than adults even could.

Narrative-based adventure videogames are children's literature because children are more inclined to experience them fully. Tolkien's "On Fairy-Stories" solidifies the connection between fairy tales and fantasy literature with narrative-based videogames in its discussion of Primary World (Alice's "dull reality") and Secondary World (the world of fantasy). He contends that the Secondary World that fantasy creates is "made out of the Primary World," but is an "unreality" that the reader's mind is fully capable of discerning and accepting as true.[12] Belief in the Secondary World is the suspension of disbelief that allows a reader to immerse herself in the narrative. When adults read fairy tales or fantasy or play games like *The Legend of Zelda,* they are entering the world of childhood, or Secondary world of fairy-tales, the virtual world of Hyrule.

Tolkien's ideas of Primary and Secondary worlds anticipate and predate recent studies that connect fantasy and action adventure videogames with Possible Worlds theory. Suspension of disbelief allows a reader to accept the possible world of the narrative as long as the reader is engaged in the act of reading. For children, as we learned from the Romantics, this process comes naturally. In *Fictional Worlds,* Thomas G. Pavel expands this relationship between the reader's actual and fantasy's possible worlds. "A proposition is possible in our real world if it is true in at least one possible world accessible from ours."[13] In other words, if there exists a link between our real world and the possible fictional world, a proposition can exist that would be true in both. Pavel follows Aristotle in suggesting that a writer's role is not to present facts, but possibilities or "propositions true at least in one alternative to the actual world."[14] Our acceptance of these propositions in the possible world relies on a

connection to the real world of facts and a willing suspension of disbelief, or, alternately, a willingness to play make believe. Pavel draws a
direct line from the link between the actual world and the possible world
of fiction by presenting children at play as a model:

> When a group of children play with mud, they simultaneously touch
> globs of mud – in the really real world – *and* offer one another tasty
> pies in the world of make-believe, which is real within the game.
> Running away from tree stumps in the real world becomes, for
> the same children, a flight from dangerous bears in the world of
> make-believe.[15]

This scenario is familiar; when children pretend play they create a narrative in the real world that relies on their imagination to invent scenarios
that borrow elements from their reality. They transform these elements
in the parallel world of make-believe. The child, then, is the link that
makes the Secondary world possible in the Primary world.

When reading, children use their imagination to accept possible world
scenarios that borrow elements from their own reality and manipulates
them. The child reads about a make-believe story and chooses to accept
its propositions as real within the world of the story, even if it is set in the
same world as the child's own. In *Emile*, Rousseau writes

> As soon as his potential powers of mind begin to function, imagina-
> tion, more powerful than all the rest, awakes, and precedes all the
> rest. It is imagination which enlarges the bounds of possibility for
> us...the world of reality has its bounds, the world of imagination is
> boundless.[16]

This idea has been guiding children's education and their literature ever
since. The Romantics fought to bring back the fairies and fairy tales and
in order to allow children to grow into their imagination rather than into
reality. The Victorians took these ideas even further, creating new fairy
tales and inventing fantasy, wherein children can find reflections of their
imaginative worlds. Narrative-Based adventure videogames, such as *The
Legend of Zelda*, which in itself is influenced by traditional Japanese
ideals similar to those of Romanticism, such as Shintoism and the natural connection humans, especially children, have to nature, continue this
tradition and build on Rousseau's directive even more.[17] "Virtual worlds
differ from fictional worlds in the they become present-for-us through
interactivity, rather than through imaginative and purely subjective operation."[18] Playing videogames gives children the space to grow in a
world of boundless imagination through action.

The Legend of Zelda not only offers children a chance to read about
fairies, but to play with them in a digitally modeled possible world where

they are given rich opportunities for exploration, adding agency to imagination in a way that goes beyond reading. Since *The Legend of Zelda*'s introduction in 1987, over 27 sequels to the game have been released, versions that both simultaneously repeat and expand the mythology and heroic narrative tropes. The basic plot of all the *Zelda* games is the same. The hero is always a boy named Link, who is chosen by the Goddesses of Hyrule to save the world from evil, usually from the chief villain, Ganondorf. While in most games Link is a child of about nine or ten, in *Ocarina of Time* Link is also allowed to grow up temporarily and becomes a 16-year-old young adult. In the later narrative stages of *Ocarina of Time*, the manipulation of time, allowing a player to switch between the child and young adult forms of Link, becomes central. This allows the player to approach puzzles in various ways, as the world and its people change depending on what era of Link's life you play in, but it also presents a central theme of childhood transitioning to adulthood.

Continuing the tradition established in children's literature by the Romantics and Victorians, Miyamoto privileges Link as a child unspoiled, innocent, yet at the same time powerful and inspiring. The child's world is bright and generally carries a lighter tone, and when compared to *Ocarina*'s young adult counterpart is far less dire and consumed by Ganondorf's darkness. NPCs throughout the game remind young adult Link of his childhood. Characters like Maron, a girl living in Lon Lon Ranch, whom Link meets in his childhood, are able to recognize him later on as young adults, but never address him as such. To many NPCs, Link is still the same "Fairy Child" or "Forest Boy" even as a young adult. Link's status as a child leads to his underestimation by some of the characters he meets early on in the game. This occurs both in dialogue between characters, who constantly refer to him as "kid," as well as through the description of items Link encounters in his child stage. Items like the "Hylian Shield" (described as "too big" for Link by Hyrule's Shopkeeper) or the appropriately named "Adult Wallet" (accompanied with the description that "Adults are allowed to carry a lot of money") are inaccessible to Link in his child stage. By contrast, the world of 16-year-old Link's future is grim and dangerous, demanding him to mature and leave his childhood behind, reflected in the way the characters speak to him.

This tension between the world of childhood and the world of adulthood is clearly presented in characters that depend on Link's maturity to survive. Darunia, the Goron leader, belittles Link for his age upon first meeting him as a child and demands Link prove himself to be a "real man." However, as a young adult, Darunia treats Link with as an equal, saying "You turned out to be a real man, just as I thought you would!" and "I want to have a man-to-man talk with you." Sheik engages Link with a unique dialogue that resonates more clearly with a Romantic understanding of the relationship between childhood and adulthood. A mysterious figure in Link's young adult timeline, Sheik is later revealed to be Princess Zelda herself. She does not encourage Link to abandon his childhood out of necessity, but instead encourages him to embrace it, saying "a thing that doesn't change with time is a memory of younger days," and "A childish mind will turn to noble ambition." This central theme is also reflected in the process of buying, planting, and nurturing "Magic Beans," which Link can plant in a wide variety of places in his child stage for them to blossom in his young adult stage, revealing puzzles, treasures, and further adventures. Both Sheik and the planting of the seeds remind Link of his childhood, and how it nurtures and informs him as he grows.

A core portion of the storytelling in *Ocarina of Time* revolves around Link's internal hero's journey as he travels through childhood toward adulthood. At the start of the game, Link meets Navi the fairy and confronts his peer Mido, who bullied him saying "without a fairy, you're not even a real man." Mid-game, Link learns to play the Ocarina's "Song of Time," which allows him to be transported forward in time. From the idyllic environment of his childhood village, Link is thrust into a world deeply entwined with the concepts of masculinity and "growing up." However, as he reflects and relies on the significance of his childhood in his young adult stage, Link connects to his childhood even when facing the world as an adult, perfectly mirroring Miyamoto's belief that "inside every adult is the heart of a child. We just gradually convince ourselves that we have to act more like adults."[19] When creating *The Ocarina of Time*, Miyamoto insisted on including young Link and his transformation into a 16-year-old. His reasons echo the Romantic's appreciation of childhood and the emotional power of childhood nostalgia. In an interview, Miyamoto explains

> the innocent eyes of a child are able to see through to the truth, so Young Link knows instinctively that Ganon is a bad guy. When Adult Link meets him again, and Ganon says he's that boy from years before, it really hits you.[20]

This sentiment could be summed up with William Wordsworth's famous line from "My Heart Leaps Up," a poem in which he hopes to retain and learn from the wonder and imagination of himself as a child when he is older: "The Child is father of the man."[21]

Link is able to transition into a young adult and return to childhood using the ocarina, but his archenemy, Ganon, is an adult throughout. However, being an adult does not automatically make one an enemy of childhood. The Japanese tradition of reverence of old age, in particular, is very much present in *The Legend of Zelda*, especially in the characters of The Deku Tree and Rauru. Link's adult enemies are those connected with those elements that are the Romantics identified as enemies of humanity: the forces of technology, industrialization, greed, power, and spoiled, corrupted nature.[22] Most of the monsters Link fights during his adventure in *Ocarina of Time* represent death, such as Skulltulas, Redead, and Gibdo, or twisted creatures of a corrupt nature, such as Mad Scrub or Deku Baba. Other enemies are products of industry, like blade traps and wallmaster. Link's ability to travel between the world of childhood and adulthood mirrors the child player's ability to transition between the world of the game or fairy tales to the actual world around him. This link reinforces and strengthens the child's commitment to the narrative.

The Legend of Zelda is seeped in an established Romantic premise that contrasts, not only childhood and adulthood, but Nature and imagination versus man-made technology and the destruction of nature. The Romantic saw the natural world as the child's cathedral, the place where childhood exists and finds its inspiration. In "Ode: Intimations of Immortality from Recollections of Early Childhood," Wordsworth called the child "Nature's Priest."[23] Heroes of the children's literature are often between the ages of seven and nine because that age range affords them just enough freedom to rise to the challenges of an independent adventure while still remaining firmly within the realm of childhood innocence. At the age of nine, Link begins his adventure in *Ocarina of Time* at this classic age. The Romantic child is considered superior because he is associated with uncorrupted nature and the world of imagination and creativity. The inspirational connection to nature can be found in Link's main helpers in the game, which are all either connected to the natural world or to the world of fantasy: animals, rocks, fairies. Link's fairy Navi, in fact, is so central to his journey that he is unable to wake up and the game cannot begin until Navi awakens him. She brings with her Campbell's call to action. When Navi leaves Link at the end of the game, it marks both the end of Link's journey through childhood and the start of his natural transition into adulthood, where there are no fairies. In other versions, Navi is substituted with other creatures, but they are always magical and smaller than Link, to emphasize their connection to the natural world and the world of childhood.

Though the Romantics did not produce works of children's literature that are of great or lasting influence, the Victorians took up their mantle and created stories that reflect their ideals and these conflicts. The fight to legitimize fairy tales as suitable for children evolved into the creation of original works of fantasy with the child at the center as the guardian of all that is good. Moreover, the Victorians strengthened children's roles as a mirror to adults in that they reflect and expose adults' depravity. In Wonderland, for example, Alice realizes that adults are "nothing but a pack of cards"[24] who do not scare her anymore. In Oz, Dorothy looks behind the curtain to reveal the Wizard's deception. Significantly, even when he travels seven years into the future, Link is still not fully an adult. As a 16-year-old, he is at just the right age to understand the full power of the world of adulthood and have the physical and moral strength to resist it.

In addition to exhibiting major Romantic and Victorian ideals traditionally present in classic works of children's literature, *The Legend of Zelda* includes other details that we have come to expect in children's stories, especially in classic fantasy. Link's magical ability to travel through time, between the worlds of childhood and adulthood especially, means that the game is firmly rooted in an important tradition invented by the Victorians; it groups Link with other magical travelers such as Alice, Peter Pan, and Dorothy. Although the children in these early fantasies do not themselves transform as Link does, the worlds into which they travel are very obviously worlds populated by adults who are rude, irrational, violent, stupid, and very obviously inferior to the child. Most of the adults throughout *The Legend of Zelda* question Link's abilities and his role as the chosen one. Most adults he encounters are also stupid, violent, incompetent, or corrupt. In fact, the nature of adults causes the conflicts of most *Zelda* games. While most stem from Ganondorf's all-consuming desire for power and sovereignty over Hyrule, conflicts in other *Zelda* games, such as *Minish Cap* and *Majora's Mask,* spawn simply from careless or negligent mistakes that adult characters make; The Happy Mask Salesman losing the powerful item of Majora's Mask at the hands of Skull Kid, for instance, leads to the apocalyptic events that occur in *Majora's Mask*. However, although Link becomes a young adult during his time travel, he does not himself become more violent or corrupt. The fight with Dark Link in the room of illusion in the Water Temple could be seen as Link having an internal struggle to fight the corruption of adulthood and successfully maintain his childlike aspects.

In this insistence on prolonging the period of childhood, Link is modeled after Peter Pan in numerous ways: physical appearance, his ability to travel between worlds (times) at will, and in his devoted fairy friend, Navi, a direct descendent of Tinkerbell. Although Link grows physically, like Peter Pan, he retains his moral superiority and purpose because of his ability to remain a child at heart. Although he insists on never growing up, Peter Pan is the capable, responsible, and trustworthy leader of Neverland, much in the same way Link, though a child, becomes the dependable, brave savior of Hyrule. Both are able to live the Romantic sentimental ideal of the child as a model to imitate, respect, and, when necessary, fear. Whether a fictional literary character or virtual avatar, children's literature remains a powerful medium that allows those who experience it to travel into imaginative worlds where children rule, where adults can be reminded what it was like to possess such power.

Just as when reading, as Tolkien writes in "On Fairy-Stories," the *Zelda* player has the ability to internalize the character and experience the adventure through him in a Secondary World because "the human mind is capable of forming mental images of things not actually present,"[25] which Tolkien relates to imagination, but later also to his idea of Secondary Belief. Playing *Zelda* changes the child player's reality into Tolkien's Secondary Worlds, where he employs his Secondary Belief. But narrative-based adventure games do more than allow children to play pretend in environments that are increasingly scarce in their own reality, such as forests and open fields. They allow them to embody the hero and participate in the narrative construction. In *Tremendous Trifles*, G. K. Chesterton writes,

> Fairy tales do not give the child the idea of the evil or the ugly; that is in the child already, because it is in the world already. Fairy tales do not give the child his first idea of bogey. What fairy tales give the child is his first clear idea of the possible defeat of bogey. The baby has known the dragon intimately ever since he had an imagination. What the fairy tale provides for him is a St. George to kill the dragon.[26]

Miyamoto's *Zelda* also includes dragons and monsters, tells children that they can be beaten, and then gives them the opportunity to actually do so. Narrative-based videogames do not replace or negate literature, they add an empowering, realizing dimension to it by endowing the child reader/player with the power to act upon their emotional investment in the narrative.

The child reader uses her imagination to create a visual representation of the world created in a book, but remains physically passive and does not consider herself to be part of that secondary world; nor can she manipulate it in any way. In a narrative-based adventure game, the player accepts not only the possible world presented to her, she also accepts the possibility of believing herself as being part of that world. In *The Legend of Zelda,* the technology allows for added effects and features that allow agency and mutability, changing the very language the child uses when speaking of the character she identifies with, which raises the level of engagement and flow. The child and hero become one. When playing *Zelda*, for example, the child player is given the option to rename Link. The child can change the name of the hero to her own name, and so for the rest of the adventure, all NPCs will call her by that name. Even if the name is not changed, players usually refer to Link and his actions in the first person (even if the player is a different gender), saying, for example: "I did it!" This self-identification in the first person with Link, a fictional protagonist, allows for a greater psychological and subconscious link that surpasses the kind of intimate relationship the child reader experiences.

Miyamoto named the main character Link precisely because he wanted him to represent a connection between the Primary, actual world of the player and the Secondary, possible world of the game. He wanted to link them all together: The player, child reader, the hero, Link. In "Embodying the Virtual Hero: A Link to the Self," Jonathan Erickson describes the psychological basis for the decision to design the character of Link in this way. He utilizes three psychological principles to explain why the connection between player and character is so successful.

> Psychology has much to say about this experience of the player becoming Link. One promising place to start is the concept of *projection*, whereby an individual projects certain psychological aspects of themselves outward unto something in the world – or in this case, the virtual world of Hyrule. Behavioral research into avatars and identity offers another piece to the puzzle, particularly when considered in tandem with the concept of *theory of mind* from cognitive psychology, which seeks to understand how the mind understands and imagines other minds apart from itself.[27]

One of the most effective ways the game emphasizes projection is that no character speaks a recognizable language in *Zelda*; their speech varies from vocalizations similar to the adults in animated *Peanuts* to more exclamatory sounds. While *Breath of the Wild* is the first of the Zelda games that features characters that speak more than usual, in most of the sequels, dialogue boxes provide the main source of verbal expression. The main form of communication between the characters during gameplay and the player is via written dialogue. Link is the only character who never makes a sound and is never given written lines of dialogue. Link's words belong to the player/reader to imagine, compose, utter, and choose. Characters address Link using the second person, bonding him even more closely with the player/reader. The player may or may not engage verbally while playing, but even if he does not, the necessity of clicking buttons and manipulating joysticks on the controller also advances the dialogue. These actions promote the characters to answer and react, and Link to exhibit physical reactions such as a nod or smile. The player is in control of the pace of the narrative.[28]

> Of course other parts of the brain are quite good at discerning real from fictitious one, but insofar as an individual allows themselves to become absorbed in a fictional world, they begin to experience its characters as if they were real.[29]

The agency provided by these elements means that the player becomes fully, not only a co-author, but a part of the cast of characters existing in the Secondary world, making it a possible world. Digital technology, then, allows for even greater and more intense ways to involve the player actively and emotionally in the narrative.

Good old-fashioned reading and established literary features are required for an action adventure game like *The Legend of Zelda* to succeed, but in turn, digital technology plays an essential role in extending the power of these earlier traditions. Reading in a videogame is not just an action that produces pleasure; it is an action that produces events to occur that would not have otherwise taken place. Reading becomes more powerful. Miyamoto seems to suggest that digital technology and traditional printed storytelling are allies, both fighting the destruction created by industrialization and adults' greed for power. In *Ocarina of Time*, the child uses digital technology to make Link fight these forces represented by industrial technology. In *Breath of the Wild*, Miyamoto takes this idea even further with the Sheikah Slate; a tool Link uses throughout his journey. The Sheikah Slate looks very much like the Nintendo Switch the child player holds in his hands while playing, further enhancing the child's engagement and identification with Link. They are united in narrative and in the technology they utilize.

Other game design features further create an environment that enforces the possibility of this virtual Secondary world and the player's involvement in it, his identification with Link, and the suspension of disbelief. The mechanic of "Z-Targeting," for example, is a way to extend one's presence in the game by heightening the player's focus and accuracy. The inclusion of Navi, Midna, Fi and other permutations of Link's companions and guides extend the player's commitment to the relationship by creating a dialectical interaction and emotional friendships. The companions react to all of his moves and use the second person address to guide and direct. Cutscenes are used for narrative exposition, to reward effort, establish back story, characters, motivation, mood, brief training in skills, and to build up suspense. While the player loses control of the game temporarily, cutscenes are often dialogues between Link and other characters in the world, so the player does not lose engagement.

As it does in film, music plays a central role in *Zelda*. Characters have their own musical themes, each location features unique music that fits its environment and specialized audio cues are attached to actions and items. These features, impossible in traditional literature, enhances player's involvement by providing emotional context.[30] They are part of the language of the game, indicating and anticipating actions, drawing attention, and creating atmosphere where the child player becomes fluent. Music from the Ocarina allows him to control nature, and sometimes even human nature. Link draws the majority of his magical powers from the Ocarina, whose various songs allow him to do things no one else can, validating his and the player's idea that they are special, the chosen one. Manipulating events in the game by plating music, like changing the time from day to night, also affords the child-player power over the flow of the narrative. Mutability is one of the most important features that defines narrative-based action adventure videogames. A book always remains the same. That is part of the pleasure of reading and rereading. We enjoy going back to the same story and to experience it in different times in our lives. Though we change and our ways of reading changes, the book remains the same. This is not true of videogames. In *The Legend of Zelda,* when the player changes, the game changes with him, creating an exciting, new narrative each time. The digital technology of videogames, then, is not inherently contradictory to the literary project. In fact, they are becoming symbiotic. Many children's books are often translated into videogames, like the Harry Potter series, for example. Conversely, videogames are regularly turned into successful books, like Akira Himekawa's *The Legend of Zelda* manga series, making it possible to include the game's narrative in a traditional literature classroom thus diversifying the canon.

Remaining in the classroom, videogames are not only good reading, they teach by utilizing superior principles of learning. In his influential "Good Video Games and Good Learning," James Paul Gee makes use of established rules that govern good literature to demonstrate that they also govern good videogames. The underlying premise in his theory is Romantic in that he emphasizes the way videogames allow players to learn by having their imagination engaged and present them with the possibilities and potential of their abilities. Concentrating on pedagogy, Gee sets 16 basic rules for good video simulation. Three of these rules are of particular interest to this discussion. Gee calls Rule 1 the "Identity Principle" and explains that good videogames, much like good books, demand that the person engaged invest in them part of themselves to form a lasting relationship. "players become committed to the new virtual world where they will live, learn, and act through their commitment to their new identity."[31] While reading, a child might identify with the protagonist. Action adventure videogames allow the player to actually become the protagonist. Rule 2, entitled "Interaction," refers to the difference discussed above between the experience of reading and that of playing a videogame. Gee writes, "Plato in the *Phaedrus* famously complained that books were passive in the sense that you cannot get them to talk back to you in a real dialogue the way a person can in a face-to-face. Games do talk back."[32] Gee's third rule is "Production." We often think of readers as co-writers because they bring their own perspective into the text and add to it. According to Gee, this is also true for videogames: "players are producers, not just consumers; they are 'writers' not just 'readers'...Players help 'write' the worlds in which they live."[33] In a good videogame, words and deeds are all placed in the context of an interactive relationship between the player and the Secondary or possible world. In fact, nothing happens until a player acts and makes decisions. Gee's rules recognize a fundamental connection between digital technology and the old technology of books, between playing and reading.

Shigeru Miyamoto created a medium that is dependent upon active
reader participation to create a simulation that takes the experience of
reading to new levels by infusing the conventional experience of reading with the possibilities of digital technology without treading over tradition. The Romantic antagonism toward technology exhibited in the
game, even as the child player uses Nintendo's latest iterations to engage
with it, places the game in the realm of the forces of good, directing the
player's attention to the Romantic literary aspects of the game against the
technology that allows it. The first *Legend of Zelda* game, published in
1986, included a booklet that told the tale of Zelda and Ganon. The story
ends by addressing the reader directly "Can Link really destroy Ganon
and save princess Zelda? Only your skill can answer that question. Good
luck. Use the Triforce wisely."[34] In other words, from its inception, the
game merged printed children's literature with digital games. The commercial announcing the release of *Ocarina of Time* shows Miyamonto's
continued commitment to framing the game within a literary tradition.
Inserted between scenes from the game are phrases that read like a poem,
imitating Shakespearean English presented in gothic font:

A dark time is approaching
Willst thou run?
Or fly?
Willst thou sink?
Or swim?
Willst thou finish?
Or die trying?
And in the end, willst thou soar?
Or willst thou suck?
Have ye what it takes?[35]

This language reveals that the decision to make a connection between
established literary traditions and the new digital technology was a conscious one.
   Discussing role playing adventure videogames as children's literature
allows us to enter into the heart of the definition of the genre. We find
ourselves revisiting questions of the balance between instruction and
amusement, for example, or the ever-present tension between adult
writer and child reader. We examine questions of narrative, speaker, setting, plot, and reader response. We find ourselves analyzing videogames
using the same language we have for literature. As we discuss these digital literary works, we need to understand what is similar to traditional
literature as well as what are the important differences. But the idea that
videogames are texts for children does not endanger the genre; rather, it
reinforces it. *The Legend of Zelda* offers the child playing it connections
between the joy of reading and active co-writing production, between

his actual world and possible world of Hyrule, between being a child and visualizing himself as the hero of time. These connections are so strong, often so much stronger than one most books offer that they persist when the game is stopped.

The child's emotional identification with Link is not easily severed. During the final cut-scene in *Ocarina of Time,* after Ganon has been sealed away, Princess Zelda takes back the Ocarina of Time in order to return Link to his childhood. If the player changed Link's name to his own at the start of the game, she addresses the player by name directly:

> When peace returns to Hyrule it will be time for us to say goodbye. Now, go home, Link, regain your lost time! Home, where you are supposed to be the way you are supposed to be. Thank you, Link. Goodbye.[36]

The language she uses can be understood in two ways. She is declaring the end of the game, but also she is telling the child player to regain the time he has "lost" playing the game. She tells him to leave Hyrule to which he was transported through Link and return to his real home in the Primary world, where he will again be himself rather than the Hero of Time. The ending is bittersweet, but also inevitable. This speech shows Miyamoto's deep understanding of the emotional connections created through his game's narrative and mechanics.

We have come a long way since videogames have been blamed for enticing negative effects on children and encouraging violence. Shiguro Miyamoto's *The Legend of Zelda*, a narrative-based videogame, examined as a text for children, contradicts any prejudice against the medium as being detrimental to children's literary traditions. The Romantics ensured that childhood would forever be seen as the world of imagination, creativity, and integrity. The Victorians' triumph was their ability to invent fantasy, a genre that created possible worlds that validated children's view of their actual world. *The Legend of Zelda*, and other action adventure videogames, continues this evolutionary progress of children's literature as a genre to allow children, as well as adults, to live and inhabit the worlds of their imagination.

Notes

1 Charles Lamb, *The Letters of Charles Lamb* (New York, NY: Macmillen & Co. 1888), 189–191. Accessed October 27, 2019. *Internet Archive.Org.* https://archive.org/details/lettersofcharles01lamb/page/n10.
2 Peter Hunt, Introduction to *Understanding Children's Literature*, ed. Peter Hunt (Malden, MA: Blackwell, 2001), 9.
3 Children's literature as a genre created and published specifically for children as a primary audience began in the 17th century, with Puritan books such as James Janeway's *A Token for Children*, which were strictly dedicated to

religious education. Fairy tales and fantasy for children began in the 18th century with chapbook editions of various fairy tales and nonsense poetry. Original fairy tales and fantasy specifically for children was not published until the early 19th century, with the publication of *Household Tales* of the Brothers' Grimm (1823) with a preface by John Ruskin who praised them as being very much suitable for children and utterly free from faults. [*German Popular Stories*. With illustrations after the original designs of George Cruikshank. Edited by Edgar Taylor. With introduction by John Ruskin, M.A. London: John Camden Hotten (1869) v. Catherine Sinclair's *Holiday House* (1839), which featured a chapter entitled "Uncle David's Nonsensical Story" paved the way for other writers to develop the Victorian canon we know as "The Golden Age" of children's literature. See Mary V. Jackson, *Engines of Instructions Mischief, and Magic* (Lincoln, NB: University of Nebraska Press, 1989) and Michael Levy and Farah Medelson, *Children's Fantasy Literature* (Cambridge: Cambridge University Press, 2016).

4 See Michael Elam's and Anthony G. Cirillia's contributions to this volume.

5 Stephen F. Kuniak. "It's Dangerous to Go Alone: The Hero's Journey in the *Legend of Zelda*," in *The Psychology of Zelda*, ed. Anthony M. Bean (Dallas, TX: BenBella Books, 2019), 23–60.

6 Lamb, 189–191.

7 J. R. R. Tolkien, "On Fairy-Stories," in *Brainstorm Services*, (West Chester University, 2005), 11. http://brainstorm-services.com/wcu-2005/pdf/fairystories-tolkien.pdf.

8 Ibid., 11.

9 Jean-Jacque Rousseau, *Emile, or Education* (New York, NY: E.P. Dutton, 1921), 54. http://oll-resources.s3.amazonaws.com/titles/2256/Rousseau_1499_Bk.pdf.

10 Lewis Carroll, *Alice's Adventures in Wonderland*, in *The Complete Works of Lewis Carroll* (New York, NY: Barnes & Noble Books, 1994), 15–125.

11 Ibid., 119.

12 Tolkien, 19.

13 Thomas G. Pavel, *Fictional Worlds* (Boston, MA: Harvard University Press, 1986), 28.

14 Ibid., 46.

15 Ibid., 57.

16 Ibid.

17 Jennifer Dewinter, *Shigeru Miyamoto* (New York, NY: Bloomsbury, 2015), 14.

18 Françoise Lavocat, "Possible Worlds, Virtual Worlds," in *Possible Worlds Theory and Contemporary Narratology*, ed. Alice Bell and Marie-Laure Ryan (Lincoln: University Press of Nebraska, 2019), 279.

19 Carolyn Sayre, "10 Questions for Shigeru Miyamoto." *Time Magazine*. July 19, 2007. http://content.time.com/time/magazine/article/0,9171,1645158,00.html.

20 Satoru Iwata, "Many Characters, Many Roles: An Interview with Shigeru Miyamoto," *Iwata Asks*, http://iwataasks.nintendo.com/interviews/#/3ds/zelda-ocarina-of-time/4/1.

21 William Wordsworth, "My Heart Leaps Up," in *The Golden Treasury*, ed. Francis T. Palgrave (London: Humphrey Milford, 1875), 7.

22 It seems that this crusade against technology might have bothered Miyamoto. As if aware of the contradiction presented by depicting man-made technology as evil in a videogame, in the latest release in the series, *Breath of the Wild*, Miyamoto makes a further distinction between digital technology and traditional technology. Digital technology, such as the one that powers

the towers and the Sheikah Slate, is visually presented by a glowing blue light that emanates from purified structures and objects. This energy that helps Link infuse traditional technology with goodness and righteousness and affords him an advantage to triumph over adult corruption and old technologies, which are represented by a red, fiery glow.

23 William Wordsworth, "Ode: Intimations of Immortality from Recollections of Early Childhood," in *The Oxford Book of English Verse: 1250–1900*, ed. Arthur Quiller-Couch (Oxford: Oxford University Press, 1953), 73.
24 Carroll, 117.
25 Tolkien, 15
26 Gilbert Keith Chesterton, "XVII: The Red Angel," in *Tremendous Trifles* (1909). *The Project Gutenberg*, March 9, 2018. www.gutenberg.org/files/8092/8092-h/8092-h.htm.
27 Johnathan Erickson, "Embodying the Virtual Hero: A Link to the Self," in *The Psychology of Zelda*, ed. Anthony M. Bean (Dallas: BenBella Books, 2019), 5–21.
28 In *Breath of the Wild*, the player enjoys the full benefit of a sandbox environment, where he enjoys unlimited freedom to determine the direction and intensity of the narrative, make dramatic choices in the plot and create multiple versions of the basic story.
29 Erickson, 11.
30 Shane Tilton, "The Songs of the Ritos: The Psychology of the Music within *The Legend of Zelda*," in *The Psychology of Zelda*, ed. Anthony M. Bean (Dallas: BenBella Books, 2019), 171–190.
31 James Paul Gee, "Good Video Games and Good Learning," *Phi Kappa Phi Forum* 85, no. 2 (Summer 2005): 34.
32 Ibid.
33 Ibid., 35.
34 "The Legend of Zelda: Ocarina of Time Manual," (1987), *Nintendo*, 4. www.nintendo.co.jp/clv/manuals/en/pdf/CLV-P-NAANE.pdf.
35 "Ocarina of Time US Commercial," YouTube Video, 1:02, "GCNOfficial," March 28, 2011, https://youtu.be/iu_nQwZn02E.
36 Ibid.

11 Take Away the Sword

Teaching for Creativity and Communication with *The Legend of Zelda* in Art History

David Boffa

In the original *Legend of Zelda*, released in 1986 in Japan and 1987 in North America, the hero Link (and thus the player) starts the game without a sword in a dangerous world. Only upon entering a cave in the opening screen do you receive your sword from an old man, who warns you, "It's dangerous to go alone! Take this." This iconic beginning of the Zelda universe was not part of the initial game.[1] According to Shigeru Miyamoto—the game's designer along with Takashi Tezuka—the opening was designed in response to players' dissatisfaction with previous drafts of the game. Miyamoto states:

> [...] when I first showed an early prototype of the NES version of Zelda it did not go over well in Japan. People were confused, they didn't know their objective, they didn't know how to move from stage to stage. They couldn't even solve the puzzles. And a lot of people said, look you know why don't you just put, just make one way through the dungeon, no multiple paths.

Simplifying things would seem to be the logical response here—especially if we consider that in the mid-1980s players' videogame literacy was still in its early stages. Expecting players to understand and decipher the workings of a complex open world might have seemed like a step too far. Yet that's exactly what Miyamoto and his team chose to do. He continues:

> Rather than making it easier for players to understand, I decided to take their sword away from the very beginning. [...] I did this because I wanted to challenge them to find that sword. Because I knew that they would think about these problems, they would think before they go to sleep how am I going to do this, or maybe as they're riding to work in the morning.

Here we see one of the great merits of this decision, present in many great games: an expectation that the player can rise to the challenge.

We also start to see, in my view, where game design and game play-ing intersect with the way college and university instructors approach pedagogy, which this essay explores. Instructors must choose if they want to use pedagogical approaches that put students along a single, straight path of consuming and repeating information, or if they want to open students up to the endlessly branching world of deeper learning and research. If it's the latter, which I think more advantageous, then Miyamoto merits imitation:

> And at the same time I wanted them to talk with other Zelda players and exchange information—ask each other questions, find out where to go next, exchange information. That's what happened. This communication was not a competition, but it was a real life collaboration that helped make the game more popular.[2]

This final passage contains a key of both good games and a meaningful educational experience: communication. Although Miyamoto realizes people tend to see the original *Legend of Zelda* game as a solitary expe-rience between the player and the system or game, in reality he designed it with communication in mind—which is precisely why Link starts without his sword.

This emphasis on communication between players stems largely from one of Miyamoto's creative goals: to design games so "that players them-selves will become more creative." Miyamoto understands that commu-nication forms the basis of learning, discovery, and creativity. Moreover, the most creative kinds of communication are not one-way; rather, they are multifaceted and multi-voiced sharing of problems, solutions, and experiences. This is exactly what many instructors hope to share with our students: the idea that learning does not take place in a vacuum, that contributions to knowledge are best done through a sharing of ideas, and that the production of knowledge itself is a creative act. As currently construed, the American higher education system does not always place these ideas at the center of what it offers to students. But if individual educators are more open to broadening the curriculum it can certainly help us move toward achieving these goals.[3] The task, then, is to take away the pedagogical sword to encourage creative, academic learning.

I examine here my course designed around the *Legend of Zelda* se-ries and the decision-making process involved in it. I wanted to teach a course on a topic which would allow me to utilize students' own inter-ests to help them become more active agents in their learning experience; to get them communicating with each other rather than just absorbing information from me or a textbook; and to encourage them to think cre-atively about the production and dissemination of knowledge.[4] In doing so, I wanted to create a better introduction to the study of visual and material culture than the one typically employed at the college level.

Furthermore, the class was an opportunity to advance the value of vid-eogames as valid artifacts worthy of serious art historical study.

The Art History Survey

My *Legend of Zelda* class was part of an ongoing effort to introduce students to studying visual culture without relying on a traditional art history survey.[5] The difficulties faced in designing or teaching an ade-quate and inspiring art history survey have long been noted. In a 1954 article on undergraduate teaching, art historian Albert Elsen claimed, "The most challenging problem is that of the introductory course."[6] Although there are variations, the "classic" art history survey gener-ally consists of a series of slide lectures based primarily around Western visual culture from prehistory to the present. This structure is most of-ten associated with one of the three classic survey textbooks currently in use: Marilyn Stokstad's *Art History* (now in its 6th edition), Helen Gardner's *Art Through the Ages* (currently 15th edition), and H.W. Jan-son's *History of Art* (8th edition).[7] While this format remains popular in many institutions (and is not without merit), critics have long been aware of its problems: an extreme bias toward Western art, the exclusion of underrepresented voices such as women and non-white individuals and culture, implicit statements of what constitutes high and low art (and thus the inclusion/exclusion of objects worthy of study), and a focus on memorization rather than skill building and deep learning, to name just a few.[8] While there have been recent efforts by textbook publishers to address these issues they have often been piecemeal fixes rather than significant departures from tradition. Elsen's assertion from the 1950s— that "the majority of these courses stress the accumulation of vast stores of information"—still holds true today in many, if not most, introduc-tory art history courses.[9]

   At many small liberal arts colleges this type of Western survey remains a central part of the art history experience. In an analysis of 66 insti-tutions conducted by Melissa R. Kerin and Andrea Lepage published in 2016, they found that only 16% of the schools gave equal weight to courses focused on *any* region (i.e., only 16% of schools did *not* explic-itly prioritize Western surveys); the rest all required the Western survey in some capacity (as a standalone requirement or alongside at least one course on a region outside the West).[10]

   While I was at Beloit and in an attempt to approach the material from a new angle, I started to teach courses on different types of visual cul-ture, including videogames.[11] As a Renaissance art historian I am keenly aware of the passion that can be generated through "classic" works of art from the traditional Western survey. But studying a topic like the *Legend of Zelda* series offered an opportunity to parlay student inter-est and excitement around an example of art they engage with in their everyday experience into a better understanding of the discipline of art history.[12] The goal of many visual culture educators—myself included—is not that students walk away from a course with a head full of disassociated images and rote facts about them, but that students develop the facility to interrogate images, to formulate questions *about* objects and their contexts, to search for and debate answers, and to communicate their findings and ideas in a compelling and academically rigorous fashion.[13] With that in mind—and with Miyamoto's inspiration—I wanted to offer students something that would inspire them creatively and develop enthusiasm, not just for Zelda games but for videogame and visual culture more broadly.

Background, Context, and Class Makeup

The class on the *Legend of Zelda* series was my third offering on videogames and art history, although it was the first time I focused on a specific game series. In offering courses on less conventional art history, I was attempting to appeal to a wider and more diverse range of students, and with the *Legend of Zelda* course this aim was particularly successful. Compared to most other art history courses at Beloit College, the student composition of the *Legend of Zelda* class differed in several respects. For one, the gender breakdown was mostly male, which is unusual for intro art history courses: of 18 students in the Zelda class, 13 were male and five were female. In comparison, in my Fall 2015 traditional survey course (ARTH 120: Art, History and Culture to 1300), 14 of 21 students identified as female; in my Fall 2014 survey course, 28 of 31 students identified as female; in Fall 2013, 21 of 25 identified as female. The students in my Zelda course also came from a variety of different majors and concentrations that spanned the humanities (Classical Philology and Comparative Literature), the social sciences (Sociology and Business Economics), and STEM (Biochemistry and Computer Science).

A short student data sheet that students filled out at the start of the semester provided information on their familiarity with the *Legend of Zelda* series. All but one student had significant experience with at least one game in the series; many of them indicated experience with several games. This level of familiarity with the subject matter is unusual for a survey or introductory course, which typically assumes no pre-existing knowledge of the material on the part of the student (most students did not have previous art history experience in this class).

Class Components

Despite its designation as a 200-level course (necessitated by the department's course codes at the time), the *Legend of Zelda* class was structured as an introduction to art history (100-level), and thus did not assume any previous experience with the discipline or familiarity with videogame history. The course had the following goals: introduce students to art history, to the *Legend of Zelda* series, and to videogame history more broadly; provide students with the skills to be more critical and thoughtful media consumers; and teach students about the process of selecting and curating artifacts for a museum setting. To achieve these goals, several types of assignments were used. The first was the critical playing and analysis of games from the series and discussions of their histories. Second was the development of a museum exhibition that explored central themes in the *Legend of Zelda* series. Third was evaluating mythopoeic and related themes in other media, including Tolkien's *The Hobbit*. Additionally, the Zelda series' popularity provided a starting point for discussions central to art history: e.g., the creation of "canons," the status of art and art objects, and the ways that some cultural artifacts and their creators transcend their origins to become themselves the subject of mythologizing—a phenomenon that goes back at least as far as Giorgio Vasari's 16th-century *Lives of the Artists*, in which Michelangelo was declared to be divine.

The course began with a series of short lectures on the history of videogames and the history of the *Legend of Zelda* series in particular. While several students came into the course with detailed knowledge of certain Zelda games, none of the students had studied the history of the series or of videogames more broadly. This demonstrates one of the (potential) challenges noted by Graff: to get students "to see their own interests in an academic way."[14] These lectures and associated discussions were thus an opportunity to fill in some of this information and introduce students to the methods of historical and art historical research—for example, what it means to look at objects critically, using different interpretations of the historical record, rather than as strictly fans or consumers. Furthermore, the historical overview required students to play some early videogames—such as *Spacewar!* and *Zork*—as homework assignments.

These initial lectures and assignments also allowed the class to reflect on what exactly is meant by the term "game." Students read Bernard Suits's essay "What is a Game?" alongside a selection from *Racing the Beam: The Atari Video Computer System* by Nick Montfort and Ian Bogost.[15] Suits's definition of a game—based on specific activities limited by rules whose only purpose is to make the activity possible—was discussed alongside other definitions from game researchers and designers.[16] Questions we considered once we had defined our terms included: What games *do not* fit into this (and other) definitions? What makes a Zelda game a game? And what makes a Zelda game a *Zelda* game, in particular?

The lectures on the history of the Zelda series focused on 9 of the 16 main titles in the series, from *The Legend of Zelda* (1986 in Japan; 1987 in North America) to *Skyward Sword* (2011), which was the most recent console game at the time of the course.[17] Looking at these titles provoked discussions on what—if anything—was the common ludic thread that ran between them. While there are certainly story and visual elements that are retained across many games (e.g., an incarnation of Link as the hero, Zelda as the princess, Hyrule as a setting, etc.), critics like Tevis Thompson have argued that modern (i.e., post-*A Link to the Past* from 1991) Zelda games are not open-world adventures (as was the case in the original 1986 *Legend of Zelda*) but "elaborate contraptions reskinned with a nature theme, a giant nest of interconnected locks."[18] My goal in presenting these histories alongside readings like Thompson's, or selections from Nathan Altice's book *I AM ERROR*, was to get students thinking critically about individual games and the series as a whole, similarly to how in traditional art history you examine single objects and artists' entire oeuvres or the relationship between individual artworks to movements or styles.[19] This meant that by mid-semester, students who counted themselves passionate fans of a game like *Ocarina of Time* (1998) could begin to ask themselves whether they thought it really was a game about exploration and discovery (like the original Zelda) or whether it was just a series of overly mechanistic puzzles with no real opportunity for creative play (as argued by Thompson).

Journal Assignment and Critical Play

Critical play of the Zelda games was fostered through a semester-long journal assignment, in which students played one or two games for the duration of the course and then reflected on their experiences in weekly writings. Readings on related topics were assigned to help them reflect on their gameplay—e.g., Suits' essay "What is a game?" or James Paul Gee's "Playing Metal Gear Solid 4 Well: Being a Good Snake," which considers the player's own identity in relation to player-character identity.[20] Specific instructions were also provided to guide players toward certain topics, including the particular game's (or games') historical context within the *Legend of Zelda* series or game history more broadly and their relationship to other media. It is important to note that this assignment was not looking for only the objective type of analysis advocated by Raph Koster in his essay "How I Analyze a Game."[21] With my students, I was looking for *both* a personal, subjective report of the experience along with more removed, "objective" analysis. Furthermore, I was hoping the journals would prime students for in-class discussions not just with me but with their peers, generating the kind of communication that Miyamoto was after when he designed the first game in the Zelda series.

As could be expected, the quality of the journal assignments varied significantly. In several instances, students did little more than recount what they had done during gameplay: which dungeons they beat, how long they played, where they got stuck, and so on. However, in the most thoughtful journal entries, students would reflect on their status as players, the games' relationship to the readings, and the links between different games in the series. The quotes below illustrate some of the more insightful comments from throughout the semester.

In this instance, a student commented on the nature of difficulty (or lack thereof) in two Zelda games, a theme first raised when the class read Thompson's essay:

> *Ocarina of Time- Ocarina of Time 3D* was definitely more "welcoming" [than the original *Legend of Zelda*] in terms of general game mechanics. I came across no enemies in the fifteen minutes that I played for this session, unless one counts a boulder rolling on a flat surface. The design approach seems worlds different from the NES original: this game is definitely trying to slowly inch the player towards engaging with the game world, rather than dropping them in. As mentioned in a previous entry, this could be an attempt to draw in newer players to the Zelda series. [...] Also, I did not die once. [MB]

This notion of difficulty (or lack of difficulty) was also raised on a number of occasions in class, and the student was thus incorporating material from readings and discussions. Those kinds of connections were precisely what I was after with this assignment.

In trying to unpack the difficulty behind the original game, the same student focused on the particular mechanics of the overworld (the primary environment, distinct from the dungeon stages):

> The mechanics behind the difficulty of staying alive [in the original *Legend of Zelda*] seems to be two things: the grid-based movement and the confined spaces. One could argue that the overworld is very expansive, sure. But, the individual screens of the overworld lend to a noticeable feeling of claustrophobia. If an enemy is onscreen, they are never further away than a few footsteps. Enemies sometimes clump together, further cementing the enclosed nature of most of the screens. *Zelda*'s grid-based movement, as mentioned before, lends to a small amount of player error if left uncompensated for. Couple these with a low heart container count early-game and a short hit-invincibility period, and the difficulty remains old-school hard. [MB]

Some students also applied concepts from the readings about certain games (such as *I AM ERROR*, about the early Zelda games) to later games in the series:

> One last little thing that came to mind after reading *I Am Error* chapter 5 was the amount of waiting in the Zelda games. The chapter mentions the screen transitions of the original game, which took a couple of seconds each, and the descent into dungeons, which took even longer. While it's not something that bothers me very much, waiting in Zelda games seems to be a recurring theme. I'm not sure if you've watched Arin Hanson's (of Game Grumps fame) Sequelitis video comparing *A Link to the Past* with *Ocarina of Time*, and criticizing *OoT* for a lot of things, but in it he mentions the amount of time spent waiting for things in *OoT*—chests, cutscenes, all sorts of things. It's significantly more time than the original's screen transitions, but it made me think about the role waiting plays in the Zelda games. [DP]

In this instance the student was also making a connection between popular analyses of the Zelda series—represented by the Sequelitis video—and more academic studies, such as that of *I AM ERROR*. Putting those two sources in dialogue to then consider "the role waiting plays in the Zelda games" was not something I had planned, and it was encouraging to see this student (like some others) thinking about Zelda studies with sources from a variety of registers.

Students also responded to the details of gameplay and in some cases speculated on why certain aspects—which we often take for granted—may have originally been designed, such as this student who considered the nature of Link's heart containers or health:

> For one hour, all I did was walk around and fight enemies. I had now seven heart containers, which allowed me to take quite some damage before dying. This was when I realised that even though the player can stack up multiple heart containers, which make him longer lasting, it makes it much harder for the player to have all heart containers filled at a time, which in turn prevents them from the shooting sword. In my opinion, the ability to have a ranged attack is one of the most essential things in the game.
>
> [...]
>
> Keeping in mind that the game was released back in 1986, this could be a way for the developers to balance the game. [...] If, for example, a player has ten heart containers, and he's halfway down his health, it'll require a lot of skill to refill all heart containers. [VM]

The first Zelda game (which many students played) was particularly challenging for most of them, perhaps due to the vast difference between it and the modern games students were more accustomed to. In some cases, though, they turned to the type of communication that was exactly what Miyamoto claimed was his intention. One student, for example, after discussing her confusion in the game and repeatedly getting stuck or lost, made this comment:

> Now that I know she's playing it [*The Legend of Zelda*] too, I'm going to make a point to talk to Anna about the game. Even if we're both getting nowhere, I imagine we're getting nowhere in *different* ways, so maybe either of us will have some knowledge that can help the other out. [JR]

In retrospect, the regular journaling was one of the more successful assignments not just in this course, but among all my classes. Not only did it push students to think more critically and thoroughly about their games and readings, it also gave me an opportunity to see the thought processes of quieter students. Furthermore, commenting on the entries (in Google Docs) allowed for a dialogue between me and students outside class time.

The Hero's Journey Exhibition

The exhibition assignment asked students to evaluate where certain traditional art historical methods, such as formal and iconographic analysis, both succeeded and failed in the presentation of game-related media and knowledge to the public. The exhibition also asked students to effectively communicate their viewpoints to a public with varying degrees of familiarity with the topic—a key trait not only for art historians but most academics (even if not all of them do it well). In conceptualizing a museum show using videogames, videogame artifacts, and museum objects, students had to contend with questions of audience, thematic choices, logistical choices, and promotion, among other issues. As a course assignment, the exhibition was a way to address several elements of active learning strategies outlined by scholars like Gasper-Hulvat: in particular, the use of object-based learning and the practices of debate and role playing.[22] It also gave students the chance to engage in the type of persuasive argumentation and debate that is a critical part of academic thinking, as they discussed different approaches to the various elements required for a successful exhibition.[23] Finally, leaving the outcome in students' hands without a clearly defined single path to follow—taking away the sword, so to speak, to call Miyamoto's actions to mind—forced them to develop their own creative strategies among themselves using what they were learning in class.

An object-based approach to the exhibition meant each student was responsible for researching their particular object (or objects)—which were game-related, or artworks from the museum's collection that could be compellingly connected to the game—and writing a short museum label to be displayed alongside it in the exhibition. As nearly all students had no experience writing museum labels, I tried to scaffold the assignment to gradually introduce them to this particular mode of communication. After looking at examples of what they considered to be "good" and "bad" labels, students went through several rounds of writing and revision. The directives for label writing were simple, and asked that students consider their roles as authors, their target audience, and their place within the show theme. In addition, I provided basic guidelines on writing effective labels, such as brevity, accessible language, and having a point and/or telling a story.[24] I also encouraged students to think of ways to incorporate Zelda mythology or ludic elements into their labels—particularly for labels of non-videogame objects from the college's collection, where the connections to the *Zelda* series were not explicit. Below is an example of the ways one student linked the Zelda world with the museum objects in their label:

Objects:
Trickster / 2002
Jeremy Red Star Wolf (b. 1977)
A two-color lithograph
Bishop Theobald's Bestiary of Twelve Animals / 1964
Rudy Pozzatti
Wolves appear as both positive and negative figures in the *Legend of Zelda* series. Several of the games feature yellow-eyed wolf monsters called Wolfos, leaping out of shadowy caves and forests to surround Link. Jeremy Red Star Wolf's "Trickster," the smaller image in which the wolf's orange-eyed shadow stretches toward the viewer, depicts this ominous, dangerous version of the wolf. In *Twilight Princess*, Link is unwillingly transformed into a wolf. This is the doing of Midna, one of his mentor figures. This transformation is the beginning of Link's (and the player's) journey in the game, as he is thrust into an unfamiliar body and environment in order to save his kingdom. The larger image is a reproduction of "Bishop Theobald's Bestiary of Twelve Animals," originally created in 15th-century Rome. It represents Wolf Link—the unsure hero still learning to accept his place within this adventure.

What was interesting from an educational and mythopoeic standpoint was how frequently students crafted Zelda-themed narratives or analyses for the non-videogame objects. By using the museum objects in tandem with the Zelda mythology they became active participants in creating or deriving meaning from works of art. In future courses, exploring the idea of viewers creating meanings independent of the original "authorial intent," would allow for deeper engagement with higher-level art historical theory and methodology.

From an active learning standpoint, the exhibition also gave students the opportunity for significant debate and role playing (even if they did not realize they were engaged in the latter). Although they may not have realized it at the time, students were acting out the roles of museum curators and educators. The project (create an exhibition) and the topic (*The Legend of Zelda*) were a means of entry for students, but when work on the show was underway many of them argued for their particular ideas *not* with the disinterested or forced attitude of someone completing a class assignment but with the enthusiasm of people with a real stake in the outcomes.[25]

Four objects in the exhibition were accessioned by the college museum especially for the show: original Nintendo NES and Nintendo 64 consoles and copies of *The Legend of Zelda* and *The Legend of Zelda: Ocarina of Time*, which raised important issues around videogame preservation and display for the students. These objects were set up at opposite ends of the gallery (a one-room space) and were available for museumgoers to play. For many students, this was their first time seeing the original *Legend of Zelda* game on an NES console, as most of them were playing the original game via an emulator on their personal computers. While an emulator and game ROM image (a file containing a copy of a game's data) can recreate the onscreen game experience, it is misleading to think that a game—especially ones so closely linked to specific hardware, as was the case with the original games in the Zelda series—can be entirely contained within a ROM image.[26] Although "perfect accuracy" is the design goal of an emulated game, "perfect emulation is nearly impossible to achieve."[27]

These objects also meant students—and the museum—had to consider issues of videogame preservation and display. Among the biggest questions raised by these artifacts is how much material to preserve.[28] Deciding on specific games for preservation just brings more questions, including which versions of the games to include and what format to use for preservation—i.e., a physical copy or just the code (and *what* copy, in either case).[29] Beyond the games themselves are their related media, including development materials, promotional items, "feelies," and more.[30] One of the white paper's authors correctly states that "the stuff of game history encompasses far more than the games themselves."[31]

Reading *The Hobbit*

The third major assignment of the course was reading J.R.R. Tolkien's *The Hobbit* and looking at it in tandem with games from the *Legend of Zelda* series, resulting in a paper.[32] *The Hobbit*, a fantasy novel first published in 1937 about the adventures of Bilbo Baggins on what is essentially a treasure quest (although which ultimately culminates in an epic battle), is a classic of the fantasy genre. Reading *The Hobbit* along-side the game provided a means of evaluating how authors present their mythologies to audiences.[33] Myth and story emerge very differently in *The Hobbit* and Zelda games, or at least in early Zelda games—the book experience is linear and determined by the author, for one, while the experience of a game (and its mythology) can take place in sequences determined by the player. The games require effort on the part of the player that is distinct from reading; the player must explore, engage in combat, and prevail against setbacks. Unlike a novel, the game may ac-tively work *against* the player's efforts (via enemies, obstacles, character death, etc.) to unravel the world's mythologies. As one student noted in a journal entry comparing *The Legend of Zelda* to another videogame which they knew from their own game playing, *Dark Souls*:

> Unlike my other games they both do not spoon feed the story to the player, but instead give the player their mission and have them interpret the world around them as they go. I used to find games like this frustrating because I wanted to know more about the story, but I learned after completing the games that I learned far more than I would have, if they told me because I did my own investing in and out of the game to figure out bits and pieces of the game. [DK]

The student here is responding to the ways in which the mythology of the Zelda universe, in the early games, is *experienced* as much as it is presented via text—the story emerges through gameplay.[34] With later games—starting most notably with *Ocarina of Time*—cinematic cutscenes, which further the story narrative and provide context, be-come an integral part of the game experience and thus of how the world's mythologies are presented to the player.[35] As was discussed in class, this form of reception—watching a story unfold—is much closer to the ex-perience of reading a text like *The Hobbit* than the experience of slowly teasing out a mythology via gameplay. Despite the apparent "freedom" in a game like *Ocarina of Time*, the story unfolds linearly, much like a novel or film; the original game, *The Legend of Zelda*, in comparison, has the player craft their own narrative.[36]

Discussing and then having the students write about Tolkien and Zelda in an art history class also allowed for an examination of mythopoeic elements in the discipline itself. One of the first art historical texts—Giorgio Vasari's 16th-century *Lives of the Artists*—is a cosmology of artistic creation and development that was, in many ways, the product of the author's mind.[37] In Vasari's mythology—centered around the rise of art in antiquity, its fall in the Middle Ages, and its eventual rebirth in

Central Italy, which culminated in his own day—the great Michelangelo is conceived of as a type of savior sent down from the heavens. Although the framework is Judeo-Christian, the narrative is wholly Vasarian (influenced by peers and fellow artists and critics). He opens his biography of Michelangelo by stating that the "most benign Ruler of the Heavens," who apparently took pity on the humans working in vain to resurrect the arts, "[...] was moved to send to earth a spirit who was universally skilled in all the arts and every profession [...] to show what perfection looks like in the art of drawing [...]."[38] In this mythologizing of history, Michelangelo became a divine, or near-divine, messiah—the key to Vasari's tale of artistic birth, death, and rebirth.[39]

Vasari also gave us a legacy of artistic genius, and the ways we mythologize that genius, that is still with us in the Western world. Although the *Legend of Zelda* games are collaborative efforts—as are most videogames—we still attach an authorial role to Shigeru Miyamoto.[40] The notion of single figures receiving credit for group efforts is deeply entrenched in art history. Examining the span of Zelda games (some of which had little or no involvement by Miyamoto) was an opportunity to consider notions of authorship and their roots in early modern writers like Vasari.

Student Feedback

Following the end of the semester, student feedback allowed me to evaluate my approach to this class. From a personal standpoint, and regarding my goals of reimaging an art history survey toward something that encourages enthusiasm and creativity, the biggest victory was the fact that students felt like they had been pushed creatively. The question "The course challenged me to do creative work" elicited better responses than other art history courses and college-wide courses. A vast majority of students (72.2%) responded "Very Much" (7 on the 1–7 scale), for an average of 6.61 ($n = 18$, mode = 7, dev = 0.78), compared to 6.38 for art history courses (FA14-SP16; $n = 693$, mode = 7, dev = 1.06) and 5.90 for college-wide courses FA14-SP16 ($n = 13,874$, mode = 6, dev = 1.43). While students in my upper level courses often reported similar experiences, this result was a significant improvement over earlier survey-level classes (and recall that the Zelda class was intended as an introductory course, despite the 200-level designation).[41] If we consider again Elsen's directive for an art history survey—"to create enthusiasm and to stimulate the student to think"—then it seems the Zelda course helped push students in the right direction.

Conclusions

Using the *Legend of Zelda* as the basis of an introductory art history class allowed me to use students' familiarity with and enthusiasm for a topic as entry points into the worlds of academic discourse, creative research, and successful communication. If a major goal of an introductory course is to encourage creative thinking and inspire excitement about a discipline, I consider this class to have been a promising effort toward achieving that end. There is still much room for improvement, but my hope is that art history (and related disciplines) will continue moving away from the survey model that still dominates so much of undergraduate teaching. As educators consider new pedagogies, replacing the "sage on the stage" with a more student-centered approach, we would do well to develop more courses that consider the media landscape our students are familiar with rather than continue to only prioritize long-established cultural hierarchies. Not only does admitting visual culture from outside the usual canon allow us to leverage students' own interests and abilities, but it demonstrates that colleges' and educators' claimed commitment to inclusivity and diversity are serious and meaningful. By bringing more student voices into our conversations we can create the sort of multifaced sharing of problems, solutions, and experiences that was at the heart of Miyamoto's design philosophy in the original *Legend of Zelda*.

Notes

1 The line has its own Wikipedia page (https://en.wikipedia.org/wiki/It%27s_ dangerous_to_go_alone!), has spawned several internet memes, and has been used and reused extensively (including as part of the title of the course I taught).

2 Shigeru Miyamoto, "Keynote Address," Game Developers Conference, 2007, trans. Bill Trinen. Viewable online at: https://youtu.be/jqBee2YlDPg.

3 As Gerald Graff notes, "[...] from an educational point of view, the real opposition should be not between Henry James and the Spice Girls, but between intellectual and nonintellectual discussion of Henry James *and* the Spice Girls or any other subject." Gerald Graff, *Clueless in Academe: How Schooling Obscures the Life of the Mind* (New Haven and London: Yale University Press, 2003), chap. 1, Kindle.

4 Graff discusses this idea at length in chapter 11 of *Clueless in Academe*.

5 For an in-depth look at the survey, see Josh Yavelberg, "Discovering the Pedagogical Paradigm Inherent in Introductory Art History Survey Courses, a Delphi Study" (PhD diss., George Mason University, 2016), especially Chapter One: Introduction and Chapter Five: Strategy Results.

6 Albert Elsen, "For Better Undergraduate Teaching in Art History," *College Art Journal* 13, no. 3 (Spring 1954): 197, www.jstor.org/stable/772552.

7 On the history of the survey text, see Mitchell Schwarzer, "Origins of the Art History Survey Text," *Art Journal* 54, no. 3 (Autumn 1995), www.jstor.org/stable/777579. For the history of the Gardner text in particular, see Themina Kader, "The Bible of Art History: Gardner's *Art through the Ages*," *Studies in Art Education* 41, no. 2 (Winter 2000), www.jstor.org/stable/1320661.

8 See, e.g., the essays in *Art Journal* 54, no. 3 (Autumn 1995) devoted to the topic "Rethinking the Introductory Art History Survey" as well as in *Art History Pedagogy & Practice* 1, no. 1 (2016), on the topic "What's the problem with the introductory art history survey?"

9 Elsen, "For Better Undergraduate Teaching," 197.

10 Melissa R. Kerin and Andrea Lepage, "De-Centering "The" Survey: The Value of Multiple Introductory Surveys to Art History," *Art History Pedagogy & Practice* 1, no. 1 (2016), 3, https://academicworks.cuny.edu/ahpp/vol1/iss1/3. The authors found that at 43% of the schools surveyed the Western survey remained the dominant model; a majority of the institutions also required an alternative to the Western survey, generally as an intermediate level class.

11 In reworking my intro classes I was indebted to and encouraged by the approaches of others who had made similar moves. Sites such as *Art History Teaching Resources* (http://arthistoryteachingresources.org/), which features pedagogical content and essays by other educators, and *Smarthistory* (https://smarthistory.org/) were crucial resources.

12 Encouragingly, scholars in a variety of other humanities disciplines have begun to consider videogames in the *Legend of Zelda* series as worthy of inclusion and study. See, e.g., the essays in Luke Cuddy, ed., *The Legend of Zelda and Philosophy: I Link Therefore I Am* (Chicago and LaSalle: Open Court, 2008) and Jonathan L. Walls, ed., *The Legend of Zelda and Theology* (Gray Matter Books, 2011).

13 Marie Gasper-Hulvat, "Active Learning in Art History: A Review of Formal Literature," *Art History Pedagogy & Practice* 2, no. 1 (2017): 4–6, discusses some of the history of active learning advocates generally and their relevance to art history more specifically.

14 Graff, *Clueless in Academe*, chap. 11.

15 Bernard Suits, "What Is a Game?" *Philosophy of Science* 34, no. 2 (June 1967): 148–156. www.jstor.org/stable/186102; Nick Montfort and Ian Bogost, *Racing the Beam: The Atari Video Computer System* (Cambridge, MA: MIT Press, 2009).

16 Suits writes: "to play a game is to engage in activity directed toward bringing about a specific state of affairs, using only means permitted by specific rules, where the means permitted by the rules are more limited in scope than they would be in the absence of the rules, and where the sole reason for accepting such limitation is to make possible such activity." Suits, "Game," 148. We also looked at: Johan Huizinga, *Homo Ludens: A Study of the Play-Element in Culture*, first published 1944 (reprinted Boston, MA: Beacon Press, 1950), 1–27; Raph Koster, *A Theory of Fun for Game Design* (Scottsdale, AZ: Paraglyph Press, 2005); Ian Bogost, *How to Do Things with Video Games* (Minneapolis: University of Minnesota Press, 2011).

17 The games covered in class included the following (dates indicate earliest release): *The Legend of Zelda* (1986); *Zelda II: The Adventure of Link* (1987); *A Link to the Past* (1991); *Link's Awakening* (1993); *Ocarina of Time* (1998); *Majora's Mask* (2000); *The Wind Waker* (2002); *Twilight Princess* (2006); and *Skyward Sword* (2011). We also briefly looked at two non-canon titles published for the Philips CD-I: *Link: The Faces of Evil* (1993) and *Zelda's Adventure* (1994).

18 Tevis Thompson, "Saving Zelda," published February 10, 2012, http://tevisthompson.com/saving-zelda/.

19 Nathan Altice, *I AM ERROR: The Nintendo Family Computer / Entertainment System Platform* (Cambridge, MA: MIT Press, 2015).

20 James Paul Gee, "Playing *Metal Gear Solid 4* Well: Being a Good Snake," in *Well Played 1.0: Video Games, Value and Meaning*, ed. by Drew Davidson (Pittsburgh, PA: ETC Press, 2009): 263–274.

21 Raph Koster, "How I Analyze a Game," *Gamasutra*, January 13, 2014, www.gamasutra.com/blogs/RaphKoster/20140113/208527/How_I_Analyze_a_Game.php.

22 See Gasper-Hulvat, "Active Learning," 6–15.
23 See especially Graff, *Clueless in Academe*, chap. 1.
24 Some of these elements were adapted from Helen Adams presentation "Writing Effective Museum Text," *Museums, Libraries and Archives South-East (DMCS) Training and Development series, Oxford*, available online at: www.slideshare.net/HelenHales/writing-effective-museum-text-8243677.
25 For the role of identity in learning, and in particular this concept as it relates to videogames, see James Paul Gee, "Learning and Identity: What Does it Mean to Be a Half-Elf?" in *What Video Games Have to Teach Us about Learning and Literacy* (London: Palgrave Macmillan, 2007), 51–71.
26 For an in-depth discussion of the history of and issues around emulation, see especially Altice, "I AM ERROR," chapter 8.
27 Altice, "I AM ERROR," 302. He goes on:

> Emulation is not solely a matter of replicating the target console's CPU, but also any additional co-processors, I/O devices, lower level instruction sets, and so on. In the Famicom's case, that means the CPU, PPU, APU, controllers, light gun, and any number of peripherals, from the FDS to the Game Genie. Each of these core and ancillary components are necessary for complete and accurate emulation.

28 Devin Monnens, Andrew Armstrong, Judd Ruggill, Ken McAllister, Zach Vowell, and Rachel Donahue, "Before It's Too Late: A Digital Game Preservation White Paper," ed. Henry Lowood (Game Preservation Special Interest Group, International Game Developers Association: March 2009), 12.
29 Altice, "I AM ERROR," 335, discusses issues around game versions in his attempt to establish a means of writing videogame bibliographic entries.
30 The Video Game History Foundation is one organization concerned with this task. To learn more, see "What We're Doing," The Video Game History Foundation, last accessed June 30, 2018, https://gamehistory.org/what-were-doing/.
31 Monnens et al., "Before It's Too Late," 12.
32 The links between the *Zelda* series and the works of Tolkien are explored in greater detail in Alicia Fox-Lenz's essay in this volume, "Kindling Hearts with Legendary Fire: The Legend of Zelda's Hyrule as a scion of Tolkien's Middle-earth."
33 For most students the games themselves were the primary source of Zelda mythology, although a few students were also familiar with *Hyrule Historia*, Nintendo's attempt to codify the Zelda universe and timelines. Patrick Thorpe (ed.), *The Legend of Zelda: Hyrule Historia*, trans. Michael Gombos, Takahiro Moriki, Heidi Plechl, Kumar Sivasubramanian, Aria Tanner, and John Thomas (Dark Horse Books, 2013).
34 The opening text of the original NES *The Legend of Zelda* (which can be ignored before playing) reads: THE LEGEND OF ZELDA / MANY YEARS AGO PRINCE DARKNESS "GANNON" STOLE ONE OF THE TRIFORCE WITH POWER. PRINCESS ZELDA HAD ONE OF THE TRIFORCE WITH WISDOM. SHE DIVIDED IT INTO "8" UNITS TO HIDE IT FROM "GANNON" BEFORE SHE WAS CAPTURED. / GO FIND THE "8" UNITS "LINK" TO SAVE HER.
35 For a thorough discussion of *Ocarina of Time* and the player's experience of its mythopoeic world, see the essay in this volume by Anthony G. Cirilla, "The Triforce and Transformational Play in Link's Mythopoeic Journey."
36 In a comment on an earlier draft of this essay Anthony G. Cirilla noted how *Breath of the Wild* gives players even more freedom—a point with which I agree enthusiastically (and this was one of the reasons I found that game so

enjoyable). While *Breath of the Wild* wasn't out when I initially taught this course, it was ultimately incorporated in a later version (Spring 2019).

37 First published as: *Le vite de' più eccellenti pittori, scultori, e architettori* (Florence: Torrentino, 1550; revised and expanded Giunti, 1568). The Italian editions, edited by Rosanna Bettarini and Paola Barocchi and published by Sansoni (1966–87) have been put online by the Scuola Normale Superiore di Pisa: http://vasari.sns.it/consultazione/Vasari/indice.html.

38 Vasari, "Life of Michelangelo," author's translation of the 1550 edition. Available online at: http://vasari.sns.it/cgi-bin/vasari/Vasari-all?code_f=print_page&work=le_vite&volume_n=6&page_n=4.

39 For more on Vasari, see the recent essays in David Cast (ed.), *The Ashgate Research Companion to Giorgio Vasari* (Burlington, VT: Ashgate, 2014).

40 See, e.g., Jennifer deWinter, *Shigeru Miyamoto: Super Mario Bros., Donkey Kong, The Legend of Zelda* (New York, NY and London: Bloomsbury Academic, 2015).

41 In the fall of 2015, for example, only 26.7% of students in my Introductory Survey (ARTH 120: Art, History and Culture to 1300), responded "Very Much" to the question "The course challenged me to do creative work". Most answers were in the 5–6 range ($n = 15$, av = 5.8, mode = 6, dev. = 0.94). Responses to this question for the same class in the following years were similar.

12 Regenerative Play and the Experience of the Sublime

Breath of the Wild

Gerald Farca, Alexander Lehner, and Victor Navarro-Remesal

Introduction

Link and the player encounter Hyrule as a majestic place and natural world. Lush grasslands and towering mountains create an environment for animals to thrive and offer players a *wilderness* to explore and interact with. Vibrant colors and natural sounds merge with the vastness of the gamespace and recall an expressionist painting come to life. This ergodic and imaginative openness fuels players' creative faculties and their desire for exploration, to seek out possibilities the tranquil scenery offers.

Players of *The Legend of Zelda: Breath of the Wild*[1] thus enter a natural space "uncontaminated by civilization…mobilised to protect particular habitats and species…a place for the reinvigoration of those tired of the moral and material pollution of the city."[2] Yet this *imaginary counter-space*, created in the act of play, is also a hostile one and conforms to an idea of wilderness that "combines connotations of trial and danger with freedom, redemption and purity"[3] Despite all its beauty, Hyrule's natural world is dangerous. It confronts players with perilous mountain ranges and weather phenomena, like thunderstorms or hot and cold climates, deep chasms, and a partially dangerous wildlife.

This "outright hostility"[4] of wilderness is juxtaposed to its serene ambiance and evokes both *terror* and *awe* in players. It thus creates a tension between positive and negative affects—when Link and the player scale a dangerous mountain, for example (where failure and death are imminent), but are nonetheless astounded by its magnitude. This primordial affect, known as the *sublime*, makes players feel *petty* in contrast to the wilderness they experience and evokes reflections about life, nature, and culture, giving way to new insights into existence[5] The result is a sentiment for the natural world but also the creation of a *utopian enclave* as "a place of freedom in which we can recover our true selves we have lost to the corrupting influences of our artificial lives."[6]

Yet this notion of Utopia, as a *regenerative counter-space* to the ecological challenges, is at risk in *BOTW*. When Link and the player step into Hyrule, an ancient evil (Calamity Ganon) has disrupted the world's natural and cultural balance. This destructive "pollution"[7] is the cause for hordes of enemies roaming the environment and has cast the four elements (*water, fire, wind, earth*) into strife. Usually, these are "held together by the chains of love (*philia*) [and are] pulled apart through endemic strife (*neikos*),"[8] but in *BOTW* this intricate balance has tipped. Extreme weather phenomena have a negative impact on the game's four races (Gorons, Zoras, Rito, Gerudos), while the world of Hyrule awaits a long-forgotten hero.

As a nature parable, then, *BOTW* involves players in a mythical, dreamlike gameworld where their unconscious desires for an ecological sustainable Utopia and a romantic imagery of nature are evoked, exposed to distress, and saturated. By sending players on the journey of a hero to restore order in a polluted but majestic world, the game evokes a variety of affects in them. These oscillate between positive and negative ones—such as *curiosity/fear, excitement/distress, startle/anger, pleasure/terror*—and are outlined by the game's structural peculiarities (the implied player) in different ways, depending on the region of the gameworld. The players' affective responses culminate in the *tumultuous emotion of astonishment* and in the aesthetic response of the *sublime*. The experience of play—in the interaction between (*eco)game, player,* and *world* (*culture*)—is thus a *regenerative* one on an affective and subsequent aesthetic level. It resensitizes players to the beauty of the natural world, while granting them a different viewpoint on ecosystems and ecological issues that plague their contemporary surroundings.

Clearly, regenerative play can primarily, but not exclusively, be found in ecogames. As such, we will analyze *BOTW* from an ecocritical (cultural ecology) viewpoint influenced by dream theory and the hero's struggle for an ecological sustainable Utopia. Through the lens of Edmund Burke's deliberations on the sublime and affect theory, we will illuminate the form of regenerative play to be found in *BOTW*. This will be conducted through the scrutiny of the game's affordance and appeal structure (the implied player) and in the analysis of how different affects and resulting emotions are outlined by it. By describing four regions of the game (Goron, Zora, Rito, Gerudo domain) and a restorative fifth one (Korok forest) as different types of gardens and their interrelations, we will illuminate how contrary affects and emotions are triggered and result in the aesthetic response of the sublime.

Heroes, Night-Time Dreams, and the Playful Experience of the Sublime

The task of the hero is "to retreat from the world of secondary effects to those causal zones of the psyche where the difficulties really reside, and there to clarify the difficulties, eradicate them in his own case".[9]

With this statement, Joseph Campbell lays the focus of the hero's journey on a reason ingrained in the human psyche. Within the unconscious rest the "keys that open up the whole realm of the desired and feared adventure of the discovery of the self,"[10] and the task of the hero is to exorcise these demons, to come to terms with his hidden desires.

Campbell traces back his claims to Sigmund Freud's interpretation of dreams and to the Oedipal complex that haunts the son's emancipation and diverts this endeavor to the struggle for maternal security.[11] This inert desire runs into first hindrances with the "intrusion of another order into reality into the beatitude of this earthly restatement of the excellence of the situation within the womb."[12] With the appearance of "the unfortunate father,"[13] an "enemy"[14] is introduced, and a first distribution between evil and good is established: between "death (*thanatos: destrudo*) and (*eros: libido*) impulses."[15]

The plot in *BOTW* follows largely the monomyth structure. It has players immersed into the role of the hero (Link) who embarks on a noble quest to fight evil by helping princess Zelda (the heroin) save Hyrule from darkness. Calamity Ganon is depicted as "the tyrant-monster" (11)[16] and a father figure. "He is the monster avid for the greedy rights of 'my and mine',"[17] who is on a selfish quest for power and gain. This "inflated ego of the tyrant is a curse to himself and his world."[18]

Given this constellation, Link's journey could be described as a re-enactment of the Oedipus complex. However, this may only be part of the truth. For *BOTW* connects the hero's struggle and his unconscious desire for a return to the mother's womb to a greater repression. This wish-fulfilment lies in his relation to Mother Nature, her elements and ecosystems, and human and animal cultures. In fact, even Freud is aware that personal dreams, as "*(disguised) fulfilment[s] of a (suppressed, repressed) wish*"[19] can assume a *universalized* form. For when the artist converts their appearance into representational artwork—in creating storyworlds, characters, plots—she makes them accessible to the public by enabling free floating interpretations.[20] These observations chime well with Fredric Jameson's deliberations on two interlinked types of wish-fulfilment: "a repellent purely personal or individual 'egoistic' type, [the artist's] and a disguised version which has somehow been universalized and made interesting, indeed often gripping and insistent, for other people."[21] This wish shows a decisively *utopian form* and strives to undermine forms of repression while upholding the desire for better tomorrow.[22]

Myth seems to work similar in this respect, as Campbell describes the dream as "the personalized myth," and "myth the depersonalized dream; both myth and dream are symbolic in the same general way of the dynamics of the psyche," but "in myth the problems and solutions shown are directly valid for all mankind".[23] Even Tolkien was aware of this facet, who explored how these types of universal stories create "secondary worlds" in acts of imaginative human-making called "Sub-creation." In describing a secondary world, the artist is creating a consistent space the reader can explore and escape to. For Tolkien, the "Escape of the Prisoner" is then the opposite of the "Flight of the Deserter," and the secondary worlds of fairy-stories are variations of "the Perilous Realm." Subcreating storyworlds through imaginative means and escaping to them as readers are forms of confronting danger and thinking of alternative, better worlds. For Tallon, "Escape, in Tolkien's sense, is already connected to *recovery*, in that escape from the world's ugliness and misery can be an escape into a deeper truth about the world."[24]

This regenerative appeal links utopian philosophy to mythology, whose function is "to supply the symbols that carry the human spirit forward."[25] Certainly, each work of art negotiates the utopian impulse differently—and *BOTW* connects the struggle for Utopia to ecological issues and the hero's desire to restore balance in Hyrule: to appease the four elements disturbed by Ganon and have a restorative influence on the land's ecosystems.

To participate in such an activity is a fundamentally *regenerative* experience. It has players engage with a gameworld, its natural wonders, characters, and elements, and sends them on quests where they come to understand Hyrule. Long hikes, for example, have players gain *respect* for the land they traverse, offering them a sense of scale and the duration of time. They will pass landmarks, savor breathtaking vistas, search for food and set up camp, and encounter different wildlife and domesticated animals.

These serene moments familiarize players to a life in balance with nature and trigger positive affects in them such as the *affection* for living beings, the *curiosity* for wilderness, and their *commitment* to preserving it. Yet *BOTW* complements this tranquil experience with the thrills of adventure and the dangers a stroll through the wild entails. Thereby, the *elements* play a vital role. They add to players' possibilities of traversal—using wind and the paraglider to traverse long distances or fire (arrows) to open up passageways—but also expose them to danger. This happens when players run into a thunderstorm and are hit by lightning or when cold temperatures cause hypothermia. Challenge and failure are thus a constant companion, yet these natural perils add to players' experience of wilderness in positive ways. They offer them an escape to simpler times and a refuge from the capitalist world system and its pollution.

This loss of a nature enclave within civilization is also at stake in *BOTW* and fuels the regenerative experience of the hero's task. Thereby, the notion of regenerative play can include all the above-mentioned interactions with the natural world and other creative enterprises such as Michelle Westerlaken's vegan run where she refuses to utilize in-game materials made from animal products or have Link consume meat.[26]

This sort of transgressive stance makes playing *BOTW* more challenging, for certain objects are out of players' reach. Yet it also grants them possibilities to express themselves creatively and in ethical manners—to act out their desires and values, try out different ways of conduct (if one is not a vegan), and experience an aesthetic effect that may challenge one's habitual dispositions.[27]

In *BOTW*, then, regenerative play centers around the hero's ecological journey to restore balance in Hyrule. It involves players in affective turbulences and has the struggle for Utopia find an outlet in their *experience of the sublime*—which alters players' perceptions of nature, its ecosystems, and their relations to animal and human cultures. For Burke, this affective and aesthetic effect is due to the natural world's potential to evoke the sensation of *terror* and the *fear* of death in its observers[28]— when they witness the vastness of mountain ranges, the unknown realm of oceans,[29] or the obscurity of forests and the appearance and sounds of the wildlife.[30]

> Whatever is fitted in any sort to excite the ideas of pain and danger, that is to say, whatever is in any sort of terrible, or is conversant about terrible objects, or operates in a manner analogous to terror, is a source of the sublime; that is, it is productive of the strongest emotion which the mind is capable of feeling.[31]

The sublime can only be experienced if one is not in imminent danger, however, and observes the natural wonders from afar. Then the observer will experience *"delight"*[32] as a result of fearful emotions.[33] For this reason, the sublime can also be experienced with fictions, since participants find themselves in a relation of *proximity* (psychological, imaginative, ergodic) and *distance* (interpretation, reflection, in a safe space without the story- or gameworld) to the work of art.[34] Their fictional venture then culminates in the affect of "astonishment," a "state of the soul in which all motions are suspended, with some degree of horror" and where the effects of the sublime are at its highest; "the inferior effects are admiration, reverence, and respect."[35]

Yet, whereas non-ergodic fictions (film, literature) evoke astonishment in their participants through imaginative means and the power of sounds and images, games go further. Here, players will become astounded not only by the vastness of the gameworld and frightful interactions but also by the underlying processes and system of this world and their own reactions to events. This may occur when players scale a volcano, where flowing lava and falling rocks hinder the ascent, or when they enter a dark forest with creatures that follow their specific routines but may still *surprise* and *startle* players.

Consequently, players' interactions with these systems and their potential to outline different affects becomes of importance to our analysis. Thereby, we will discuss a form of the *ludic sublime* introduced by Daniel Vella. Following Immanuel Kant's conception, Vella argues that the sublime is experienced when one perceives things that our cognitive mechanisms cannot grasp as a whole (meaning we are aware that they extend beyond our perception). So, the ludic sublime pertains to the sense that players know they have not exhausted a game's 'secrets' and are confronted with "the impossibility of obtaining complete, direct knowledge of the underlying system."[36]

Vella uses the sublime in the sense of the moment when players are *astounded* by the opacity of a game system and its forms of indeterminacy—the potential of interaction with it. Players will never have complete knowledge about this system, and this form of indeterminacy arouses *curiosity* and *terror* in them. This sensation of *astonishment* is further reinforced (and composed) by players' sensorial impressions of a majestic gameworld, its structure, characters and objects of terror, and the task of the hero to restore balance in Hyrule.

To analyze the different affects and how they culminate in the experience of the sublime, we will scrutinize the empirical player's dialectic with the implied player: the *affordance and appeal structure* that holds those predispositions necessary for the game to exercise its aesthetic effect. This underlying structure is composed of a perspectival network that includes:

1 a *sensorial perspective* (visual, auditory, haptic);
2 a *world perspective* (the settings, objects, labyrinthine structures, characters);
3 a *plot perspective* (the hero's journey);
4 a *system perspective* (processes, playing styles and actions).[37]

Before coming to this application, the next section will discuss affect theory in relation to cultural ecology. Affects and their entailing emotions are described as originating in the implied player and coming to live in the act of play—resulting in a form of play that can be regenerative in various ways. In the case of ecogames, such *emotionalizing strategies* promote the potential to raise awareness for the environment and encourage a green counter-discourse.

Affect Theory and Regenerative Play as a Form of Cultural Ecology

To lay bare these emotionalizing strategies and the affective impact of the implied player, one needs to differentiate between *affect* and *emotion* (two intertwined phenomena). In this regard, Gregg and Seigworth definition seems useful. They describe affects as those intensities that pass body to body (human, nonhuman, part-body, and otherwise), in those resonances that circulate about, between, and sometimes stick to bodies and worlds, and in the very passages or variations between these intensities and resonances themselves.[38]

Consequently, affects can be understood as a form of bodily reaction—but the difference to emotions remains unclear. Here, James's three-step model becomes important[39] for he inverts the relation of emotion as the cause of bodily reaction. One does not cry/wince/tremble because one is sad but is sad because one is crying/wincing/trembling.[40] Therefore, three steps can be distinguished, which do not happen in a successive or causal manner but are a construct to make the simultaneously happening elements understandable:

1   The perception of the stimulating event
2   The bodily reaction of the recipient (affect)
3   The interpretation of those reactions (emotion)[41]

Connecting this triad to the proposed function of the implied player as source of the affective potential of games, the stimulating events are situated in the game itself and its perspectives whereas the bodily reaction and interpretation of events occurs in players. To give an example, James mentions an encounter with a bear:

> The sight of the bear excites changes in one's muscles, glands, heart, and skin, which are only recursively felt as fear; we may already be running by the time our emotional response identifies and synchronizes with the more instantaneously immediate visceral reaction.
>
> (Ibid.)[42]

Although James's bear is real, this is comparable the players' encounter with a Lynel—a chimera with a vicious and powerful appearance. Players perceive the Lynel as threatening, and this causes change in their body as they begin to act (affect) while realizing that they fear this frightful entity (emotion).

Consequently, one can assume that the structural organization of the implied player's perspectives outline and trigger certain affective responses, which empirical players interpret as emotions. Weik von Mossner describes this form of embodied simulation as "play[ing] a crucial role in our engagement with the world as well as in aesthetic response."[43] She relates this to empathy and to the potential for ecological awareness through simulated actions by "our capacity for an empathic response".[44] This resonates well with the established connections of green games and the ecological awareness on an experiential, affective, and interpretative level,[45] which is best described as a form of cultural ecology.

In Hubert Zapf's terms, "imaginative literature" influences the discourse by "deal[ing] with the basic relation between culture and nature in particularly multifaceted, self-reflexive, and transformative ways."[46] The "'ecological' dimension" is produced by its "semantic openness, imaginative intensity and aesthetic complexity."[47] Literature thus functions as a kind of *regenerative force* within the cultural system, opening up an imaginative space to enable readers to reflect and explore their own perspectives.[48]

Yet "videogames go beyond the mere representational…mode of literary writing." [49] They do not merely work through semiotic means but employ ergodic, spatial, and procedural ones to outline certain experiences. Therefore, Chang claims that games offer "a chance to think procedurally about the consequences of actions on the environment itself as a system with its own particular inputs, triggers, instabilities, affordances and dangers."[50] This means that empirical players consider affects (outlined by the implied player) and connected emotions on a conceptual level in relation to empirical reality. For example, players' affective response to Ganon disrupting Hyrule is to eradicate him and support Zelda—which may connect to greed and longing for power in reality (symbolized in Ganon's part of the Triforce: power) that destroys the natural-cultural environment and needs to be overcome by courage (Link) and wisdom (Zelda).

To explain this diversity of the implied player, the affects it outlines, and how this connects to the notion of the sublime, we will now analyze *BOTW*'s most important regions and their corresponding cultures by describing the structural organization of the previously mentioned perspectives: *sensorial, world, plot, system*.

Death Mountain: Curiosity, Respect, Haste, and Terror

The most obvious source of players' emotional turbulences and the astonishment created by the sublime is the ascent of Death Mountain. The volcano can be seen from different perspectives as players move closer: when they wander the fields of Hyrule and Death Mountain majestically enters their field of view on the horizon. Streams of red lava are flowing downwards, and the permanent ash cloud above its peak reminds players of Ganon's intrusion in its ecosystem (*sensorial, plot*). This experience excites *curiosity* and fuels desires to scale the volcano but also *respect* for an unknown Other.

Death Mountain is well-known to players of *The Legend of Zelda* series and evokes imaginings of an unforgivable wilderness. The mountain is a rocky landscape full of movement, a living entity in itself, and recalls the *Mountains and River Sutra* (1240) of Dôgen in which the Zen Master writes of "mountains flowing".[51] Death Mountain seems to have a terrible will of its own—triggering emotions in players such as *fear* and *terror* yet also *delight* and *anticipation* to explore its bounds.

Once players get closer, the tranquility and openness of the game-world are narrowed down to a unicursal labyrinth that sends players on an intense route toward the volcanic crater, blocked on both sides by large cliffs and lava streams (*world*). Players need to be prepared. Burning enemies and other obstacles—such as falling rocks and flying Sentries—cause *distress* and *terror*. This situation results from the Divine Beast, Vah Rudania, a mechanical lizard causing tremors and the increase in temperature. Even the Gorons, who are usually adapted to their hostile environment, are suffering. They are a friendly race, organized as an industrial culture in social hierarchies, treating Link with *respect* and as one of them. Players may become attached to the Gorons and *admire* their values, serving as an ethical incentive to restore balance in a disturbed ecosystem (*plot*).

To do so, and to scale the mountain, players have to endure the scorching heat and equip the right gear (wooden equipment bursts into flames). They can either buy an elixir at the foot of the mountain that protects them for a certain time-frame or stack up on food, which attenuates energy loss. This results in the emotions of *haste, frustration,* and *distress*, when the game system together with players' interactions and the entrapment of the world's labyrinthine structures evoke *terror*. Yet this sense of *terror* also leads to *delight* and to *excitement* and *joy* the thrill of adventure entails. The result is the emotion of *astonishment*, when the aesthetic effect of the sublime penetrates players' self and has them reflect on nature as a force and system incomprehensible in its entirety.

Thereby, the elements play a vital role and how players negotiate them through play. While *fire* and *earth* are depicted as dangerous, *wind* and *water* come to players' aid. For one, players may use their paraglider and wind streams to ascend the mountain, while hot springs regenerate Link's energy. Although seemingly a didactic juxtaposition, the elements are not depicted as negative or positive but in neutral ways as both perilous and life-giving. For their function changes from region to region.

Zora's Domain: Anger, Excitement, and Wonder

In Zora's Domain, torrential rain and darkness aggravate players' perception and have the element of *water* shine in a different light—as disorienting, mysterious, where danger resides underneath the surface of river streams and vast lakes (*sensorial*). Yet, there is also a sacred element in *Zelda*'s water bodies, an aesthetic presentation that highlights the presence of the divine. Water is important in many religions and cosmologies as a tool for purification and a life-giving source. It is thus both enigmatic and mesmerizing and elicits different emotions and imaginings in players through uncertainty. There are many wondrous things awaiting, without harmful intentions (animals, travelers, the promise of sacred temples), as well as ill-willed monsters hiding underneath its surface—which triggers *curiosity* as well as *terror* in players, leading to the *astonishment* of water's unfathomable appeal.

To outline these emotional turbulences, the game strategies work similarly to those of Death Mountain, yet the elements are configured differently. Travelling to Zora's Domain, players follow a river winding through a narrow valley. Enemies swarm this unicursal labyrinth, where players have only few possibilities to dodge attacks, which creates a *distressful* atmosphere (*world*). The heavy rain contributes to this and functions as a game mechanic that decreases players' ability to climb walls and escape the labyrinthine system. The result is a feeling of *entrapment* within the confines of natural powers, which can become *frustrating* and *enrage* players (*system*).

This sense of hostility is also felt on a cultural level (*plot*). Due to Mipha's death, caused by the Calamity and Link and Zelda's failed mission in the past, the Zoras have started to disdain the Hylians. This racism is exemplified by Trello, the town's priest, who holds a grudge against Link. Therefore, the Divine Beast, Vah Ruta, does not only function as a cause of imbalance due to Ganon's presence but is also a reminder of Mipha's death and the Hylians' guilt in failing to protect her. This creates *anger* in players, since they are facing the Zoras' disdain without causing it (*plot*).

Finally, the elements again play a vital role in the experience of the sublime—specifically *water*. From being conceived as a threat and opaque in nature, which causes *terror* but also *curiosity* of the unknown, players learn to use water to their benefit. The Zora Set, for example, enables players to swim rapidly in currents and up waterfalls, and inside the mechanical elephant they are able to manipulate the waterflow coming from his trunk to solve puzzles (*system*).

Rito Village: Respect, Admiration, and the Thrills of Reflection

The Rito are a proud nature culture of bird-like specimen. Their appearance is colorful, as are their homes, situated on a towering, narrow cliff. Houses are built around the rock structure and wind up alongside a wooden staircase. The location is surrounded by deep chasms, forests, and grasslands. Various platforms are located high above the grounds and allow the Rito to practice their flying and combat skills, but also facilitate their distribution of goods throughout Hyrule. These endeavors are however restrained by Ganon's intrusion: The Rito are suffering from the Divine Beast, Vah Medoh, which is shooting down anything that flies in the vicinity of Rito Village. Link and the player are treated well by the Rito, with *respect*, which may result in *admiration* and the will to help them calm the Divine Beast (*world, plot*).

The Village and its surroundings are different from the other regions in Hyrule discussed here. It is a tranquil hub space surrounded by an open, peaceful wilderness (*world*). The area brings to mind Miyamoto's description of *Zelda* as "a miniature garden that you can put into a drawer and revisit anytime you like" (Paumgarten 2010, np.). Gardens are man-made, recreational spaces made to be looked at as much as traversed (Mehta and Tada 2008, p. 11) and reconfigure nature for a human perspective. It would however be reductionist and even orientalist to analyze *Zelda* as a Japanese garden. Yet, one can assume some local gardening notions have influenced the franchise.

The design of landscapes and vistas in *Zelda* games go beyond the functionality and challenge of mazes and seem to be made to entice players, make them feel *awe*. These landscapes follow the notions of *shotoku no sansui* ("mimicking nature"), *shakkei* ("borrowed landscape"), and *fuzei* ("following the spirit of the environment"). *Shakkei*, in particular, establishes a relationship with the "natural" (or wild) landscape, incorporating "far-away elements in the background" into the design of the garden (Flath et al. 2016, p. XXX). Gardens, and particularly Zen gardens, are reductions of nature to a manageable, human scale made to provide tranquillity and represent nature through simulation.[52] Chaim Gingold also makes this connection between gardens and the more contemplative side of games:

> A garden has an inner life of its own; it is a world in flux which grows and changes. A garden's internal behaviors, and how we understand those rules, help us to wrap our heads and hands around the garden. The intricate spaces and living systems of a garden surprise, delight, and invite participation. Gardens, like games, are compact, self-sustained worlds we can immerse ourselves in. Japanese gardens often contain a multiplicity of environments and places, such as mountains, oceans, or forests that we can look at, walk around, or interact with. Gardens are a way to think about the aesthetic, cognitive, and representational aspects of game space.[53]

This conception of the gameworlds as gardens has consequences on playing styles—which in the Rito area are slower, reflective—and has repercussions on how the sublime exerts its influence. In Rito Village, players experience majestic vistas from high above and ponder the beauty of the untouched wilderness below. They look into deep chasms, which evokes *terror*, and savor the *thrills* of jumping from platforms to glide across stretches of land. The Rito region thus foregrounds the element of *wind* in the use of the paraglider. It culminates in the encounter with Vah Medoh, where Link uses the streams of wind within and outside of the Divine Beast to solve its riddles.

Gerudo Desert: Confusion, Distress, and the Sense of Otherness

The Gerudo Desert is an open space with small oases that astounds players in diverse ways (*sensorial*). Unlike gardens, the scale of the desert is overwhelming, hostile to exploration. The desert is empty, monotonous, hot, and cold. Entering the area, players get lost in this world, filled with sandstorm mazes and only few oases: gardens that provide relief from the wild nature (*world*). Especially the extreme temperatures make traversing the desert dangerous: During the day the sun heats up the terrain, whereas at night it becomes freezing. The alternation between these temperatures becomes a strategy for instilling *distress* and *haste*. For especially badly equipped players cannot hop from one oasis to another to traverse the desert and fail to stay alive (*world*). To survive in this hostile environment, they need to prepare for both conditions, by equipping the proper gear (warming or cooling armor), the corresponding elemental weapons (fire and ice), or bringing cooling or heating potions (*system*).

In addition, *confusion* is achieved by taking away informational resources from players they have conventionalized during play. The quest "The Silent Swordswomen," for example, has them follow directions indicated by statues within a sandstorm maze (an invisible multicursal labyrinth constructed not by its physical arrangement but by its obstacles to sensorial perception), while the Sheika Slate and the mini map malfunction. Consequently, players' interface is reduced to what they see—causing *confusion* and *distress* due to newfound uncertainty (*sensorial, system*).

This sense of *terror* is further propelled by the encounter with one of the four Moldugas—giant creatures resembling whales swimming through the desert, indicating their position by lifting up sand. Players need to decipher the creature's behavior and come up with a strategy to defeat it. Consequently, *terror* is instilled through an uncertain encounter that requires critical thinking and problem solving (*system as player agency*).

Such an encounter with Otherness can also be experienced from a cultural perspective (if one takes the Western World as a reference point). The Gerudos are a conservative race, a matriarchal society of warriors, depicted in an orientalized manner. They are a proud and violent people with a strong hierarchy in a society shaped by women. The emotions created here are *respect* but also the *curiosity* for their culture, or even its *rejection*. This distrust of the Other is instilled upon first entering Gerudo Town, which only females can access. After receiving the female Gerudo Set, Vilia, the seller, warns players of the wind that could expose Link's disguise by lifting his veil. This cannot occur, of course (rendered impossible by the game system). However, players are not aware of this and *fear* being exposed in the Gerudo society. The *fear* of Otherness then becomes the *fear* of becoming the Other, and being punished for being different in a confining ideology (*system, plot*).

Gerudo Desert is a magnificent example of the sublime's fascinating spell. It shows how all game elements come together and subject players to an entity that is ungraspable in its entirety. The opaqueness of the gamespace and its mazes, the Otherness of characters and monsters, and the opacity of the game mechanics and system (limited visibility, the lack of a map, the danger from heat or cold, which means players are never at ease to explore) make the Gerudo Desert a textbook example of how games can evoke the affective and aesthetic response of the sublime. This *astonishment* is also felt for the elements, which again have players renegotiate their functionality. While *wind* and *earth* are clearly depicted as perilous, *fire* and *water* come to players' aid in attenuating the effects of the extreme temperatures or in seeking shelter in the oases.

Korok Forest: Curiosity, Confusion, Panic, and Terror

The last area that deserves attention is Korok Forest, situated at the heart of Hyrule. It interconnects the different game areas discussed above (and Central Hyrule) and functions as a source of wisdom and power: The Deku Tree is located in its center and the Master Sword represents a means to defeat Ganon. Korok Forest can be seen as the ecological epicenter of Hyrule that holds in balance the elements surrounding it, but is also isolated for this reason, protected from the outer Hyrule and its potential pollution (*world, plot*). When players approach the area, they notice that the forest lies on an island covered in deep mist, where only one entrance grants access to its realms. Light and darkness alternate as players move further and experience a place of utter beauty, lush and alive, a home to an open-hearted nature-culture called the Koroks, but also with dying regions (*sensorial, plot*). This evokes a bewildering variety of contrary emotions in players—such as *compassion* and *caution, curiosity* and *distress, excitement,* and *terror.*

Getting to the center of Korok Forest requires overcoming a mystical maze that defies logic and geography. But once players are there, they are received by nature at its most unruly and overgrown. Here, the forest evokes imaginings of the most spiritual aspects of gardens, and particularly Zen gardens. These require a degree of asymmetry, tension, and depth, where the landscapist hides its hand and their work looks natural, as if the garden "grew by itself".[54] There is a sense of lawlessness in this forest that coincides with a calm harmony, evoking both *excitement* and *terror* in players (*sensorial, world*). For contrary to what it may seem, these two former aspects complement each other. Nature has grown widely by itself here (or so this designed simulation wants players to think), but has done so following a hidden order, a "way" not unlike the Taoist *wuwei* or "non-interference," "an effortless way of comporting oneself in the world with supreme harmony or efficacy" (Barrett, 2001, p. 681). The gardener lets nature manifest through its craft, and the level design of the Korok Forest could be compared to this understanding of creation. This landscape is untouched by human hands, a sacred, ancient space for sensitive and courageous heroes. In here, one can see the differences in attitudes between Ganon and Link that define them in every *Zelda* game they face each other: Ganon uses the TriForce of Power "to try and impose himself over the law of Nature," in a manner contrary to Tao and Shintô, whereas Link uses courage "to better explore and interact with Nature, not to control it".[55]

Korok Forests is a place of sanctuary, trial, mystery, and reflection. These different aspects and their resulting emotions are outlined by the implied player and give rise to the experience of the sublime. Specifically, the Lost Woods and their structural arrangement stand out, for they function as a major source of players' *astonishment*. Entering the area, players encounter a multicultural labyrinth they need to pass to find the Deku Tree and the Master Sword (*plot*). An *obscure* and *unsettling* mist lies over the area, while the noises of the wild contribute to the *intense* and *threatening* atmosphere and evoke emotions such as *confusion*, *panic*, and *terror* (*sensorial, world*). What contributes to their intensity—and adds additional emotions, such as *anger* and *frustration*—is the obscurity of the game system: Overcoming this maze is largely based on trial and error, on deciphering its underlying system. There is only one way through it, and going astray leads failure, since players will be surrounded by blinding mist and the screams of spirits. They are then teleported back to the maze's starting point and have to retry (*system*).

In the Lost Woods, then, game elements such as the confusing structure of the world and its gloomy appeal are combined with an oblique game system that makes players *suffer*. Yet these negative emotions are also a source of players' *enjoyment* and the *delight* of experiencing a dark wilderness in the relative safety of their homes. In addition, they are on hunt for loot and treasure, particularly the Master Sword, and enact a plot that will eventually lead to the restoration of balance in Hyrule (*plot*). The function of the Korok Forest is therefore not to be underestimated. It evokes *respect* and *admiration* for this untouched realm, the *desire* to protect it from the outside pollution, and the sheer *astonishment* of its natural wonders.

Conclusion

The Legend of Zelda: *BOTW* immerses players in a mythical realm and a game narrative that employs all of its game elements (*sensorial, world, plot, system*) to create a coherent participatory experience; what Hans-Joachim Backe considers an efficient ecogame that employs both systemic and semiotic means to convey its message (2017). Players are set in the role of the hero Link and his struggle to restore balance and the natural order in Hyrule by defeating Calamity Ganon as a source of pollution. Yet this journey entails more than a quest for peace and addresses a repression fundamental to humankind: the loss of a life in balance with nature and the protective shell of her womb. This wish-fulfillment and unconscious desire is deeply ingrained in *BOTW* and its game structure and comes in the form of the hero's struggle for an ecologically sustainable Utopia. During the act of play, players become sensitized to nature's wonders as they explore its bounds and elements, an untamed wilderness filled with perils and confusing mazes aiming to overwhelm players. Yet these landscapes are also designed and resemble gardens of different sorts, domesticated yet wild, ambiguous spaces to be appreciated sensorially and traversed ergodically.

The gameworld of *Zelda* and players' potential interactions with it are thus constructed and outlined in such a way as to evoke contrary affects and emotions. Suffocating mazes are juxtaposed to the tranquillity of open world areas and hub structures, with their respective processes and systemic (ludic) possibilities that lead to different playing styles. The result are tumultuous emotions triggered in players—such as *curiosity* and *distress*, *delight* and *terror*, and the *astonishment* of a natural world, its cultures and underlying system, which are incomprehensible for players in their entirety. This aesthetic experience of the sublime has players ponder the similarities and differences between the gameworld's ecosystems and cultures and their empirical surroundings—when they connect the pollution caused by Ganon to ecological issues that plague their times and the imbalances with nature caused by humankind's exuberant lifestyle.

Playing *Zelda* is thus essentially a regenerative experience on both an affective and aesthetic level and represents a form of cultural ecology. It occurs when the fascinating spell of fiction grasps players' attention and has them implicitly ideate the meaning behind their interactions in the gameworld, when they connect the virtually enacted to similar situations in the empirical world. In other words, this dialectic between (*eco*) *game*, *players*, and *culture* (*world*) shows the potential of emancipated play and may exert influence on players' self, changing their habitual dispositions and images of nature, culture, and their mutual dependence.

Notes

1 Nintendo, The Legend of Zelda: Breath of the Wild. Nintendo, 2017, Nintendo Switch version.
2 George Garrard, *Ecocriticism* (New York, NY: Routledge, 2004), 66.
3 Ibid., 68.
4 Ibid., 70
5 Edmond Burke, *A Philosophical Enquiry into the Origins of the Sublime and Beautiful* (Calgery: Anodos Books, 2017), 35–37; Garrard, 70–75.

6 William Cronon, "The Trouble with Wilderness; or, Getting Back to the Wrong Nature," in *Uncommon Ground: Toward Reinventing Nature*, ed. William Cronon (New York, NY: W. W. Norton & Company, 1995), 69–90.
7 Garrard, 1.
8 Jeffrey Cohen and Lowell Ducket, "Eleven Principles of the Elements," in *Elemental Ecocriticism: Thinking with Earth, Air, Water, and Fire*, eds. Jeffrey Cohen and Lowell Duckert (Minneapolis: University of Minnesota Press, 2015), 1–26.
9 Joseph Campbell, *The Hero with a Thousand Faces*, Bollingen Series 18, 3rd ed. Novato, CA: New World Library, 2008, 12.
10 Ibid., 5.
11 Ibid., 4.
12 Ibid.
13 Ibid.
14 Ibid., 5.
15 Ibid., 4.
16 Ibid., 11.
17 Ibid.
18 Ibid.
19 Sigmund Freud, *The Interpretation of Dreams*, trans. A. A. Brill. Hertfordshire (Wendsworth, 1997), 68.
20 Sigmund Freud, *Creative Writers and Day-Dreaming*, vol. 9, *The Standard Edition of the Complete Psychological Works of Sigmund Freud*, trans. The Institute of Psycho-Analysis (London: Vintage, 2001), 141–154.
21 Freud, *Creative Writers and Day-Dreaming*, 141.
22 Ibid., 46.
23 Ibid., 53. Campbell, *The Hero with a Thousand Faces*, 24.
24 Philip Tallon, "The Birth of Gaming from the Spirit of Fantasy: Video Games as Secondary Worlds with Special Reference to *The Legend of Zelda* and J. R. R. Tolkien," in *Legend of Zelda and Theology*, ed. Johnathan L. Walls (Hadley, MA: Grey Matter, 2011), 47–70; J.J.R Tolkien, "On Fairy-Stories", *Heritage Podcasts*.
25 Campbell, 7.
26 Michelle Westerlaken, "Self-fashioning in Action: Zelda's Breath of the Wild Vegan Run," in the 11th International Philosophy of Computer Games Conference, Krakow, 2017. Accessed 27 October 2019. https://gamephilosophy2017.files. wordpress.com/2017/11/westerlaken_pocg17.pdf.
27 Gerald Farca, "The Emancipated Player," *Proceedings of the First International Joint Conference of DiGRA and FGD 13*, no. 1 (2016): 301–318, www.digra.org/digital-library/publications/the-emancipated-player/ (accessed October 27, 2019).
28 Burke, 35–56.
29 Ibid., 45–45.
30 Ibid., 37, 50, 52–54.
31 Ibid., 22.
32 Ibid., 21.
33 Ibid., 23, 84.
34 Farca, 188–189, 213.
35 Burke, 35.
36 Daniel Vella, "No Mastery without Mystery: Dark Souls and the Ludic Sublime," *Game Studies* 15, no. 1 (2015): accessed October 27, 2019, http://gamestudies.org/1501/articles/vella.
37 Farca, 210–249.
38 Melissa Gregg and Gregory J. Seigworth, "An Inventory of Shimmers," in *The Affect Theory Reader*, eds. Melissa Gregg and Gregory J. Seigworth (Durnham, NC: Duke University press, 2010), 1–28.

39 Kate Stanley, "Affect and Emotion: James, Dewey, Tomkins, Damasio, Massumi, Spinoza," in *The Palgrave Handbook of Affect Studies and Textual Criticism*, eds. Daniel R. Wehrs and Thomas Blake (London: Palgrave Macmillan, 2017).

40 Ibid., 98–99.

41 Ibid., 99.

42 Ibid.

43 Alexa Weik von Mossner, *Affective Ecologies: Empathy, Emotion, and Environmental Narrative* (Columbus: Ohio State University Press, 2017) Kindle Version, 159–160.

44 Mossner, 711–713.

45 Alenda Chang, "Games as Environmental Texts," *Qui Parle: Critical Humanities and Social Sciences* 19, no. 2 (2011), 57–84; James Parham, *Green Media and Popular Culture: An Introduction* (London: Palgrave & Macmillan, 2016); Alexander Lehner, Videogames as Cultural Ecology: *Flower* and *Shadow of the Colossus*," *Ecozon@: European Journal of Literature, Culture and Environment* 8, no. 2 (2017): 56–71, http://ecozona.eu/article/view/1349/2089 (accessed October 27, 2019).

46 Hubert Zapf, *Literature as Cultural Ecology: Sustainable Texts* (London: Bloomsbury, 2016), 4.

47 Ibid., 4.

48 Ibid., ff.

49 Lehner, 60.

50 Chang, 4.

51 Dôgen, Eihei, *Shōbōgenzō: A Preciosa Visión del Dharma Verdadero*, translated by Dokushō Villalba (Barcelona, Spain: Editorial Kairós, 2015), 176.

52 Yoon Jung Lee, *Inquiry into and Succession to Traditional Japanese Zen Gardens*, Master's thesis (University of Georgia, 2005), 12, accessed 27 October 2019. https://getd.libs.uga.edu/pdfs/lee_yoon_j_200505_mla.pdf.

53 Gingold, 7.

54 Habib Farah, Sara Nahibi and Hamid Majedi, "Japanese Garden as a Physical Symbol of Japanese Culture." *International Journal of Architecture and Urban Development* 3, no 4 (2013): 16.

55 Victor Navarro-Remesal, "Goddesses in Japanese Videogames: Tradition, Gameplay, Gender, and Power," in *Dialectics of the Goddess in Japanese Audiovisual Culture*, eds. Lorenzo Torres Hortelano, 111–134 (London, UK: Lexington Books, 2018), 125–126.

Bibliography

1Up.com. "Classic.1Up.com's Essential 50: 40. The Legend of Zelda: Ocarina of Time." Accessed 26 June 2018. https://archive.is/20120718054136/http://www.1up.com/features/essential-50-ocarina-time.

"2019 Essential Facts About the Computer and Video Game Industry." *The Entertainment Software Association.* Accessed 17th August 2019. www.theesa.com/about-esa/industry-facts/.

Aarseth, Espen. *Cybertexts: Perspectives on Ergodic Literature.* Baltimore, MD: The Johns Hopkins University Press, 1997.

Aarseth, Espen. "Nonlinearity and Literary Theory." In *The New Media Reader*, edited by NoahWardrip-Fruin and Nick Monfort, 51–85. Cambridge, MA: The MIT Press, 2003.

"About." *[R]econstructionist Art.* Accessed 31 December 2018. www.reconstructionistart.com/about.html.

Adams, Helen. "Writing Effective Museum Text." *Museums, Libraries and Archives South-East (DMCS) Training and Development series, Oxford.* www.slideshare.net/HelenHales/writing-effective-museum-text-8243677.

Ahmed, Sara. *Queer Phenomenology.* Durham, NC: Duke University Press, 2006.

Altice, Nathan. *I AM ERROR: The Nintendo Family Computer/Entertainment System Platform.* Cambridge, MA: MIT Press, 2015.

Arduini, Roberto. "Japan: Reception of Tolkien." In *J.R.R. Tolkien Encyclopedia: Scholarship and Critical Assessment*, edited by Michael D.C. Trout, 310–311. New York: NY, Routledge, 2007.

Aristotle. *Poetics.* Translated by Ingram Bywater. New York, NY: The Modern Library, 1954.

———. *Poetics.* Translated by Malcolm Heath. New York, NY: Penguin Press, 1996.

Ash, James. "Teleplastic Technologies: Charting Practices of Orientation and Navigation in Videogaming." *Transactions of the Institute of British Geographers, New Series* 35, no. 3 (2010): 414–430.

Augé, Marc. *Oblivion.* Minneapolis, MN: University of Minnesota Press, 2004.

Augustine. *On Christian Teaching.* Translated R.P.H. Green. Oxford, UK: Oxford Press, 1997.

Backe, Hans-Joachim. "Within the Mainstream: An Ecocritical Framework for Digital Game History." *Ecozon@: European Journal of Literature, Culture and Environment* 8, no. 2 (2017): 39–55. http://ecozona.eu/article/view/1362/2088.

Barab, Sasha A., Melissa Gresalfi, and Adam Ingram-Goble. "Transformational Play: Using Games to Position Person, Content, and Context." *Educational Researcher* 39, no. 7 (2010): 525–536.

Barad, Karen. *Meeting the Universe Halfway.* Durham, NC: Duke University Press, 2007.

Barrett, Nathaniel. "Wuwei and Flow: Comparative reflections on Spirituality, Transcendence, and Skill in the Zhuangzi." *Philosophy East and West* 61, no. 4 (2011): 679–706.

Belk, Russell W. "Extended Self in a Digital World." *Journal of Consumer Research* 40, no. 3 (October 2013): 477–500.

Berg, Peter. "What Is Bioregionalism?" *Cascadianow.org.* 2002. Accessed 30 June 2018. www.cascadianow.org/about-cascadia/cascadia-bioregionalism/what-is- bioregionalism/.

Bitzer, Lloyd. "The Rhetorical Situation." *Philosophy and Rhetoric* 1, no. 1 (1968): 1–14.

Blanchette, Kyle. "Linking the Landscapes of Twilight Princess and Christian Theology." In *The Legend of Zelda and Theology,* edited by Jonathan L. Walls, 17–31. Los Angeles, CA: Gray Matter Books, 2011.

Bogost, Ian. *How to Do Things with Video Games.* Minneapolis, MN: University of Minnesota Press, 2011.

Bogost, Ian. *Unit Operations: An Approach to Videogame Criticism.* Cambridge, MA: The MIT Press, 2006.

Boym, Svetlana. *The Future of Nostalgia.* New York, NY: Persius Book Group, 2001.

Bozon. "Koji Kondo: An Interview with a Legend." *IGN.* 12 March 2007. Accessed 22 February 2018. www.ign.com/articles/2007/03/12/koji-kondo-an-interview- with-a-legend.

Bribitzer-Stull, Matthew. *Understanding the Leitmotif: From Wagner to Hollywood Film Music.* Cambridge, UK: Cambridge University Press, 2015.

Brooks, Peter. *Reading for the Plot: Design and Intention in Narrative.* New York, NY: Knopf, 1984.

Buckler, Mike. "A History of the Videogame Narrative." *Arts & Living in The Amherst Student* (31 October 2012): 142–148. https://amherststudent.amherst.edu/article/2012/10/31/history-videogame-narrative.htm.

Buell, Lawrence. *The Environmental Imagination: Thoreau, Nature Writing, and the Formation of American Culture.* Cambridge, MA: Belknap Press, 1995.

Burke, D.M. "The Necessity of the Triforce in the Defeat of Ganon." In *The Legend of Zelda and Theology,* edited by Jonathan L. Walls, 155–170. Los Angeles, CA: Gray Matter Books, 2011.

Burke, Edmund. *A Philosophical Enquiry into the Origins of the Sublime and Beautiful.* Calgary, Alberta: Anodos Books, 2017.

Buse, Peter and Andrew Stott. *Ghosts.* Basingtoke, UK: Macmillan Press, 2005.

Campbell, Joseph. *The Hero with a Thousand Faces.* 1949. Princeton, NJ: Princeton University Press, 1973.

———. *The Hero with a Thousand Faces.* 2nd ed. Bollingen Series 17. Princeton, NJ: Princeton University Press, 1973.

———. *The Hero with a Thousand Faces.* Bollingen Series 18, 3rd ed. Novato, CA: New World Library, 2008.

Carpenter, Humphrey. *J.R.R. Tolkien: A Biography*. Boston, MA: Houghton Mifflin, 2000.

Carter, Shannon. *The Way Literacy Lives: Rhetorical Dexterity and Basic Writing Instruction*. New York, NY: State University of New York Press, 2008.

Cast, David, ed. *The Ashgate Research Companion to Giorgio Vasari*. Burlington: Ashgate, 2014.

Chang, Alenda. "Games as Environmental Texts." *Qui Parle: Critical Humanities and Social Sciences* 19, no. 2 (2011): 57–84.

Cohen, Jeffrey and Lowell Duckert. "Eleven Principles of the Elements." In *Elemental Ecocriticism: Thinking with Earth, Air, Water, and Fire*, edited by Jeffrey Cohen and Lowell Duckert, 1–26. Minneapolis, MN: University of Minnesota Press, 2015.

Collins, Karen. *Playing With Sounds: A Theory of Interacting with Sound and Music in Video Games*. Cambridge, MA: The MIT Press, 2013.

Compagno, Dario S. "I Am Link's Transcendental Will: Freedom from Hyrule to Earth." In *The Legend of Zelda and Philosophy: I Link, Therefore I Am*, edited by Luke Cuddy, 179–189. Chicago, IL: Open Court, 2008.

Coupe, Lawrence. *Myth*. 2nd ed. New Critical Idiom. London, UK: Routledge, 2009.

Covel, Casey. "Review, The Legend of Zelda: Twilight Princess (Wii)" *Geeks Under Grace*. 8 August 2014. Accessed 16 January 2018. www.geeksundergrace.com/gaming/review-the-legend-of-zelda-twilight-princess/.

Cronon, William. "The Trouble with Wilderness; or, Getting Back to the Wrong Nature." In *Uncommon Ground: Toward Reinventing Nature*, edited by William Cronon, 69–90. New York, NY: W.W. Norton & Company, 1995.

Cuddy, Luke. "Zelda as Art." In *The Legend of Zelda and Philosophy: I Link, Therefore I Am*, edited by Luke Cuddy, 153–164. Chicago, IL: Open Court, 2008.

Dantzler, Perry. "Multiliteracies of the MCU: Continuity Literacy and the Sophisticated Reader(s) of Superheroes Media." In *Assembling the Marvel Cinematic Universe: Essays on the Social, Cultural, and Geospatial Domains*, edited by Julian C. Chambliss, William L. Svitavsky, and Daniel Fandino, 14–31. Jefferson, NC: McFarland & Company, 2018.

Demaria, Rusel, and Johnny Lee Wilson. *High Score! The Illustrated History of Electronic Videogames*. New York, NY: McGraw-Hill Osborne, 2002.

Derrida, Jacques. *Specters of Marx*. 1st ed. New York, NY: Routledge, 2011.

deWinter, Jennifer. *Shigeru Miyamoto: Super Mario Bros., Donkey Kong, The Legend of Zelda*. New York and London: Bloomsbury Academic, 2015.

Dôgen, Eihei. *Shōbōgenzō: A Preciosa Visión del Dharma Verdadero*. Translated by Dokushō Villalba. Barcelona, Spain: Editorial Kairós, 2015.

Drzaic, Kristina and Peter Rauch. "Slave Morality and Master Swords: Ludus and Paidia in Zelda." In *The Legend of Zelda and Philosophy: I Link, Therefore I Am*, edited by Luke Cuddy, 65–74. Chicago, IL: Open Court, 2008.

Dugan, Patrick. "A Link to the Triforce: Miyamoto, Lacan, and You." In *The Legend of Zelda and Philosophy: I Link Therefore I Am*, edited by Luke Cuddy, 203–210. Chicago, IL: Open Court, 2008.

Duncan, Sean C. and James Paul Gee. "The Hero of Timelines." In *The Legend of Zelda and Philosophy: I Link Therefore I Am*, edited by Luke Cuddy, 85–101. Chicago, IL: Open Court, 2013.

Ellwood, Robert. "The Japanese Hobbit." In *Mythlore: A Journal of J.R.R. Tolkien, C.S. Lewis, Charles Williams, and Mythopoeic Literature* 1, no. 3 (July, 1969): 14–17. Accessed 28 October 2019. https://dc.swosu.edu/cgi/viewcontent.cgi?article=2249&context=mythlore.

Elsen, Albert. "For Better Undergraduate Teaching in Art History." *College Art Journal* 13, no. 3 (Spring 1954): 195–202. https://www.jstor.org/stable/772552.

Erickson, Johnathan. "Embodying the Virtual Hero: A Link to the Self." *The Psychology of Zelda*, edited by Anthony M. Bean, 5–21. Dallas, TX: BenBella Books, 2019.

Ermi, Laura and Frans Mäyrä, "Fundamental Components of the Gameplay Experience: Analyzing Immersion." Paper presented at the Digital Research Association Conference, 2005.

Estok, Simon. "Theorizing in a Space of Ambivalent Openness: Ecocriticism and Ecophobia." *Interdisciplinary Studies in Literature and Environment* 16, no 2 (Spring 2009): 203–225.

Farca, Gerald. *Playing Dystopia: Nightmarish Worlds in Video Games and the Player's Aesthetic Response*. Bielefeld, Germany: Transcript, 2018.

———. "The Emancipated Player." Proceedings of the First International Joint Conference of DiGRA and FGD 13, no. 1 (2016). Accessed 27 October 2019. www.digra.org/digital-library/publications/the-emancipated-player/.Fellela, Toni. "Link's Search for Meaning." In *The Legend of Zelda and Philosophy: I Link Therefore I Am*, edited by Luke Cuddy, 45–54. Chicago, IL: Open Court, 2013.

Felski, Rita. *The Limits of Critique*. Chicago, IL: University of Chicago Press, 2015.

Fenty, Sean. "Why Old School is "Cool:" A Brief Analysis of Classic Video Game Nostalgia." In Playing the Past: *History and Nostalgia in Video Games*, edited by Zach Whalen and Laurie N. Taylor, 19–31. Nashville, TN: Vanderbilt Press, 2008.

Fimi, Dimitra. *Tolkien, Race, and Cultural History: From Fairies to Hobbits*. Basingstoke, UK: Palgrave Macmillan, 2010.

Fisher, Mark. 2006. "HAUNTOLOGY NOW". Blog. K-Punk. 17 January 2016. Accessed 2 July 2019. http://k-punk.abstractdynamics.org/archives/007230.html.

———. *Ghosts of My Life*. Alesford, Hampshire: Zero Books, 2011.

Flath, James, Ana Orengaa, Carlos Rubio and Hiroto Ueda. *Sakura: Diccionario de Cultura Japonesa*. Gijón, Spain: Satori, 2016.

Flieger, Verlyn and Douglas A. Anderson. "Editors' Commentary." In *On Fairy-Stories*, edited by Verlyn Flieger and Douglas A. Anderson, 85–121. London, UK: HarperCollinsPublishers, 2014.

———. "When is a Fairy-Story a Faërie Story? Smith of Wootton Major." In *Green Suns and Faërie: Essays on J.R.R. Tolkien*, 65–73. Kent, Ohio: Kent State University Press, 2012.

Franklin, Seb. "On Game Art, Circuit Bending and Speedrunning as Counter-Practice: 'Hard' and 'Soft' Nonexistence." *Resetting Theory* (2009). https://journals.uvic.ca/index.php/ctheory/article/view/14760/5632.

Freeman, Elizabeth. *Time Binds: Queer Temporalities, Queer Histories*. Durham, NC: Duke University Press, 2010.

Freud, Sigmund. "Creative writers and day-dreaming." In *The Standard Edition of the Complete Psychological Works of Sigmund Freud Volume IX*. Translated by The Institute of Psycho-Analysis, 141–154. London, UK: Vintage, 2001.

———. *The Interpretation of Dreams*. Translated by A. A. Brill. Hertfordshire, UK: Wendsworth, 1997.

Frome, Jonathan. "Why Do We Care Whether Link Saves the Princess?" In *The Legend of Zelda and Philosophy: I Link Therefore I Am*, edited by Luke Cuddy, 3–15. Chicago, IL: Open Court, 2013.

Garrard, Greg. *Ecocriticism*. New York, NY: Routledge, 2004.

Gasper-Hulvat, Marie. "Active Learning in Art History: A Review of Formal Literature." *Art History Pedagogy & Practice* 2, no. 1 (2017). https://academicworks.cuny.edu/ahpp/vol2/iss1/2.

Gee, James Paul. "Playing Metal Gear Solid 4 Well: Being a Good Snake." In *Well Played 1.0: Video Games, Value and Meaning*, edited by Drew Davidson, 263–274. Pittsburgh, PA: ETC Press, 2009.

———. *Social Linguistics and Literacies: Ideology in Discourses*. 3rd ed. London, UK: Routledge, 2007.

———. "What Is Literacy?" In *Literacy: A Critical Sourcebook*, edited by Ellen Cushman, Eugene R. Kintgen, Barry M. Kroll, and Mike Rose, 537–544. Boston and New York: Bedford/St. Martin's, 2001.

———. *What Video Games Have to Teach Us About Learning and Literacy*. New York, NY: Palgrave, 2003.

———. *What Video Games Have to Teach Us About Learning and Literacy*. 2nd ed. London, UK: Palgrave Macmillan, 2007.Gibbs, Joshua. "Should Classical Students Play Video Games?" *The Cedar Room*. 12 April 2019. Accessed 31st October 2019. www.circeinstitute.org/blog/should-classical-students-play-video-games.

Glassner, Andrew. *Interactive Storytelling: Techniques for 21st Century Fiction*. Wellesley, MA: AK Peters, 2004.

Graff, Gerald. *Clueless in Academe: How Schooling Obscures the Life of the Mind*. New Haven, CT: Yale University Press, 2003.

Grau, Oliver. *Visual Art: From Illusion to Immersion*. Cambridge, MA: The MIT Press, 2003.

Green, Amy M. *Storytelling in Video Games: The Art of the Digital Narrative*. Jefferson, NC: McFarland & Company Publishers, 2018.

Gregg, M. and G. J. Seigworth. "An Inventory of Shimmers." In *The Affect Theory Reader*, edited by Melissa Gregg and Gregory J. Seigworth, 1–28. Durham, NC: Duke University Press, 2010.

Guattari, Felix. *The Three Ecologies*. Translated by Ian Pindar and Paul Sutton. New Brunswick, UK: The Athlone Press, 2000.

Habib Farah., Sara Nahibi and Hamid Majedi. "Japanese Garden as a Physical Symbol of Japanese Culture." International Journal of Architecture and Urban Development 3, no. 4 (2013): 13–18.

Halberstam, Judith (Jack). "Queer Temporality and Postmodern Geographies." In *A Queer Time and Place*, 1–21. New York, NY: New York University Press, 2005.

Hammond, Wayne G. and Christina Scull. *The Lord of the Rings: A Reader's Companion*. Boston and New York: Houghton Mifflin Company, 2005.

Haraway, Donna. *Staying with the Trouble: Making Kin in the Chthulucene.* Durham, NC: Duke University Press, 2016.

Harris, Zach. "Spectacle." *Theories of Media Online Presentation.* Winter 2007. Accessed 31st October 2019. University of Chicago. csmt.uchicago. edu/glossary2004/spectacle2.htm.

Hayse, Mark. "The Mediation of Transcendence within The Legend of Zelda: The Wind Waker." In *The Legend of Zelda and Theology,* edited by Jonathan L. Walls, 83–96. Los Angeles, CA: Gray Matter Books, 2011.

Hilburn, Kaitlin Elizabeth. "Transformative Gameplay Practices: Speedrunning through Hyrule." Master's thesis, University of Texas at Austin, 2017. https://repositories.lib.utexas.edu/bitstream/handle/2152/62782/HILBURN-MASTERSREPORT-2017.pdf?sequence=1&isAllowed=y.

Holm, Ian. *The Hobbit: An Unexpected Journey.* DVD. Directed by Peter Jackson. Burbank, CA: Warner Bros., 2012.

Homer. *The Iliad.* Trans. Robert Fagles. New York, NY: Penguin, 1996.

Huizinga, Johan. *Homo Ludens: A Study of the Play-Element in Culture.* First published 1944; reprinted Boston, MA: Beacon Press, 1950.

Hunt, Peter. "Introduction: The Worlds of Children's Studies." *Understanding Children's Literature,* edited by Peter Hunt, 1–14. Karachi Digital Library. Accessed 25 October 2019. https://khidiglibrary.weebly.com/uploads/7/0/5/6/7056479/understanding_childres_literature.pdf.

Hunter, Justus. "On Hylian Virtues: Aristotle, Aquinas, and the Hylian Cosmogenesis." In *The Legend of Zelda and Theology,* edited by Jonathan L. Walls, 109–124. Los Angeles, CA: Gray Matter Books, 2011.

Husin, Salehuddin. "The Legend of Zelda: Twilight Princess." *GameAxis Unwired* 42 (February, 2007): 42–43.

Hyvärinen, Matti. "Travelling Metaphors, Transforming Concepts." In *The Travelling Concept of Narrative,* edited by Mari Hatavara, Lars-Christer Hydén and Matti Hyvärinen, 13–42. Amsterdam, The Netherlands: John Benjamins Publishing Company, 2013.

IGN, "Sensei Speaks: IGN64 Talks to Zelda Creator Shigeru Miyamoto. The Full Interview." 29 January 1999. Archived by the Internet Archive Wayback Machine. Accessed 26 June 2018. https://web.archive.org/web/20130820235938/http://www.ign.com/articles/1999/01/30/sensei-speaks.

Iwata, Satoru. "Many Characters, Many Roles: An Interview with Shigeru Miyamoto." *Iwata Asks.* Accessed 27 October 2019. http://iwataasks.nintendo.com/interviews/#/3ds/zelda-ocarina-of-time/4/1.

Jameson, Frederic. *Archaeologies of the Future: The Desire called Utopia and other Science Fictions.* London, UK: Verso, 2005.

Janssen, Anna B. "The Hero with a Thousand Hearts." In *The Legend of Zelda and Philosophy: I Link Therefore I Am,* edited by Luke Cuddy, 55–62. Chicago, IL: Open Court, 2013.

Jauss, David. "'What We See With': Redefining Plot." *Short Fiction in Theory and Practice* 6 no. 2 (2016): 141–159.

Jenkins, Henry. "Game Design as Narrative Architecture." *First Person: New Media as Story, Performance, and Game. Cambridge,* edited by Noah Wardrip-Fruin and Pat Harrigan, 118–130. Cambridge, MA: MIT Press, 2004.

———. *Textual Poachers: Television Fans and Participatory Culture.* London, UK: Routledge, 2004.

Jensen, Graham H. "Making Sense of Play in Video Games: Ludus, Paidia, and Possibility Spaces." *Eludamos: Journal for Computer Game Culture* 7, no. 1 (2013): 69–80.

Joly, Randy. "Video Games: Developing a New Narrative." *Words for Thought Blog. World Literature Today.* 19 December 2016. Accessed 23 October 2019. www.worldliteraturetoday.org/blog/words-thought/video-games-developing-new-narrative-randy-joly.

Joyce, Michael. *Of Two Minds: Hypertext, Pedagogy, and Poetics.* Ann Arbor, MI: University of Michigan Press, 1995.

Jung Lee, Yoon. "Inquiry into and Succession to Traditional Japanese Zen Gardens." Master's thesis, University of Georgia, 2005. Accessed 27 October 2019. https://getd.libs.uga.edu/pdfs/lee_yoon_j_200505_mla.pdf.

Juul, Jesper. "Games Telling Stories? A Brief Note on Games and Narratives." *Game Studies* 1, no. 1 (July 2001). Accessed 31 October 2019. www.game-studies.org/0101/juul-gts/

———. *Half-Real: Video Games Between Real Rules and Fictional Worlds.* Cambridge, MA: The MIT Press, 2011.

Kader, Themina. "The Bible of Art History: Gardner's Art Through the Ages." *Studies in Art Education* 41, no. 2 (Winter 2000): 164–177. www.jstor.org/stable/1320661.

Kerin, Melissa R. and Andrea Lepage. "De-Centering "The" Survey: The Value of Multiple Introductory Surveys to Art History." *Art History Pedagogy & Practice* 1, no. 1 (2016). https://academicworks.cuny.edu/ahpp/vol1/iss1/3.

King, Geoff and Tanya Krzywinska. *Screenplay.* London, UK: Wallflower Press, 2002.

Kirkpatrick, Graeme. "Between Art and Gameness: Critical Theory and Computer Game Aesthetics." *Thesis Eleven* 89 (May 2007): 74–93.

Kocher, Paul. *The Fiction of J. R. R. Tolkien: Master of Middle Earth.* New York, NY: Random House, 1972.

Kohler, Chris. "VGL: Koji Kondo Interview." *Wired.* 11 March 2007. Accessed 22 February 2018. www.wired.com/2007/03/vgl-koji-kondo-/.

Konami. *Siren.* Japan: Playstation, 2003. Playstation 2 version. van Elferen, Isabella. "¡Un Forastero! Issues of Virtuality and Diegesis in Video Game Music." *Music and the Moving Image* 4, no. 2 (Summer, 2011): 30–39.

Koster, Raph. *A Theory of Fun for Game Design.* Scottsdale, AZ: Paraglyph Press, 2005.

———. "How I Analyze a Game." *Gamasutra.* 13 January 2014. Accessed 31 October 2019. www.gamasutra.com/blogs/RaphKoster/20140113/208527/How_I_Analyz e_a_Game.php.

Kuniak, Stephen F. "It's Dangerous to Go Alone: The Hero's Journey in the Legend of Zelda." *The Psychology of Zelda,* edited by Anthony M Bean, 23–60. Dallas, TX: BenBella Books, 2019.

Lafond, Manuel. "The Complexity of Speedrunning Video Games." Ninth International Conference on Fun with Algorithms (2018): 1–27.

Lamb, Charles. "To Coleridge, Letter XCIV. October 23, 1802." *The Letters of Charles Lamb,* edited by Alfred Ainger, 189–191. New York, NY: Macmillen &

Co. 1888. Accessed 27 October 2019. Internet Archive.Org. https://archive.
org/details/lettersofcharles01lamb/page/n10.

Landow, George. *Hypertext 2.0: The Convergence of Contemporary Critical
Theory and Technology*. Baltimore, MD: Johns Hopkins University Press,
1997.

Landow, George. *Hypertext 3.0: Critical Theory and New Media in an Era of
Globalization*. Baltimore, MD: Johns Hopkins University Press, 2006.

Lavocat, Françoise. "Possible Worlds, Virtual Worlds." In *Possible Worlds Theory and Contemporary Narratology*, edited by Alice Bell and Marie-Laure
Ryan, 272–295. Lincoln, NE: UP Nebraska, 2019.

Le Guin, Ursula K. "The Carrier-Bag Theory of Fiction." In *The Ecocriticism
Reader*, edited by Cheryll Glotfelty and Harold Fromm, 149–154. Athens,
GA: University of Georgia Press, 1996.

Lehner, Alexander. "Videogames as Cultural Ecology: Flower and Shadow
of the Colossus." *Ecozon@: European Journal of Literature, Culture and
Environment* 8, no. 2 (2017): 56–71. Accessed 27 October 27 2019. http://
ecozona.eu/article/view/1349/2089.

Lewis, C.S. "Meditations in a Toolshed." In *God in the Dock: Essays on Theology and Ethics*. edited by Walter Hooper, 212–215. Grand Rapids, MI:
Eerdmans, 1972.

———. "Myth Became Fact." In *God in the Dock: Essays on Theology and
Ethics*, edited by Walter Hooper, 63–67. Grand Rapids, MI: Eerdmans,
1970.

Lin, Tung-Chen. "Effects of Gender and Game Type on Autonomic Nervous
System Physiological Parameters in Long-Hour Online Game Players." *Cyberpsychology, Behavior, and Social Networking* 16, no. 11 (2013): 820–827.

Lind, Stephanie. "Active Interfaces and Thematic Events in The Legend of
Zelda: Ocarina of Time." In *Music Video Games: Performance, Politics, and
Play*, edited by Michael Austin, 83–105. New York, NY: Bloomsbury Pub-
lishing Inc., 2016.

Livy. *History of Rome Vol. 2 (Books 3–4)*. Translated by B.O. Foster. Loeb
Classical Library 133. Cambridge, MA: Harvard University Press, 1922.

Lowood, Henry. "High-Performance Play: The Making of Machinima." *Journal of Media Practice* 7, no. 1 (2006): 25–42.

Mackenzie, Louisa and Stephanie Posthumus. "Reading Latour Outside: A
Response to the Estok—Robisch Controversy." *Interdisciplinary Studies in
Literature and Environment* 20, no. 4 (December 2013): 757–777.

Martin, Thomas L. "As Many Worlds As Original Artists: Possible World Theory and the Literature of Fantasy." In *Possible Worlds Theory and Contemporary Narratology*, edited by Alice Bell and Marie-Laure Ryan, 201–224.
Lincoln, NE: UP Nebraska, 2019.

Mayra, Frans. *An Introduction to Game Studies*. London, UK: Sage Publication, 2008.

McCrea, Christian. "Gaming's Hauntology: Media Apparitions In Forbidden
Siren, Dead Rising And Michigan: Report From Hell." In *Horror Video
Games: Essays on the Fusion of Fear and Play*, edited by Bernard Perron,
220–237. Jefferson, NC: McFarland Press, 2009.

Mehta, Geeta, and Kimie Tada. *Japanese Gardens: Tranquility, Simplicity,
Harmony*. Clarendon, VT: Tuttle Publishing, 2008.

Menotti, Gabriel. "Videorec as Gameplay: Recording Playthroughs and Video Game Engagement." *Game: The Italian Journal of Game Studies* 1, no. 3 (2014): 81–92.

Merleau-Ponty, Maurice. *Phenomenology of Perception*. Translated by Colin Smith. London, UK: Routledge, 1989.

Metts, Jonathan. "The Legend of Zelda: Twilight Princess." *Nintendo World Report*. 18 November 2006. Accessed 17 January 2018. www.nintendo worldreport.com/review/12434/the-legend-of-zelda-twilight-princess-wii.

Miyamoto, Shigeru. "Keynote Address." Game Developers Conference, 2007, translated by Bill Trinen. Accessed 31 October 2019. https://youtu.be/jqBee2YlDPg.

Monnens, Devin, Andrew Armstrong, Judd Ruggill, Ken McAllister, Zach Vowell, and Rachel Donahue. "Before It's Too Late: A Digital Game Preservation White Paper." Edited by Henry Lowood. Game Preservation Special Interest Group, International Game Developers Association, March 2009.

Montfort, Nick and Ian Bogost. *Racing the Beam: The Atari Video Computer System*. Cambridge, MA: MIT Press, 2009.

Morton, Timothy. *Ecology Without Nature*. Cambridge, MA: Harvard University Press, 2009.

Muñoz, José Esteban. *Cruising Utopia: The Then and There of Queer Futurity*. New York, NY: New York University Press, 2009.

Murray, Janet. *Hamlet on the Holodeck: The Future of Narrative in Cyberspace*. New York, NY: The Free Press, 1997.

Myers, David. "The Video Game Aesthetic: Play as Form." In *The Video Game Theory Reader 2*, edited by Bernard Parron and Mark J. P. Wolf, 45–63. New York, NY: Routledge, 2009.

Nacke, Lennart E. and Mark Grimshaw. "Player-Game Interaction through Affective Sound." In *Game Sound Technology and Player Interaction: Concepts and Developments*, edited by Mark Grimshaw, 264–285. Hershey, NY: Information Science Reference, 2011.

Navarro-Remesal, Victor. "Goddesses in Japanese Videogames: Tradition, Gameplay, Gender, and Power." In *Dialectics of the Goddess in Japanese Audiovisual Culture*, edited by Lorenzo Torres Hortelano, 111–134. London, UK: Lexington Books, 2018.

Newman, James. *Playing with Video Games*. London, UK: Routledge, 2008.

Nintendo. *The Legend of Zelda*. Nintendo, 1986. Nintendo Entertainment System version, 1986.

———. *The Legend of Zelda: A Link to the Past*. Nintendo, 1991. Super Nintendo version.

———. *The Legend of Zelda: Link's Awakening*. Nintendo, 1993. Gameboy version.

———. *The Legend of Zelda: Majora's Mask*. Nintendo, 2000. Nintendo 64 version.

———. *The Legend of Zelda: Oracle of Ages*. Nintendo, 2001. Gameboy Color version.

———. *The Legend of Zelda: Oracle of Seasons*. Nintendo, 2001. Gameboy Color version.

———. *The Legend of Zelda: Ocarina of Time*. Nentendo, 1998 Nintendo 64 version.

———. *The Legend of Zelda: Ocarina of Time Official Nintendo Player's Guide.* Edited by Scott Pelland. Washington: Nintendo of America, 1998.

———. *The Legend of Zelda: Skyward Sword.* Nintendo, 2011. Wii version.

———. *The Legend of Zelda: Spirit Tracks.* Nintendo, 2009. DS version.

———. *The Legend of Zelda: The Wind Waker HD.* Nintendo, 2013. Wii version Nintendo, 2013.

———. *The Legend of Zelda: The Wind Waker.* Nintendo, 2002. Gamecube version.

———. *The Legend of Zelda: Twilight Princess.* Nintendo, 2006. Wii version.

———. *Zelda II: The Adventure of Link.* Nintendo, 1987. Nintendo Entertainment System version.

NOAA. "What Is a Watershed?" *National Ocean Service.* Last updated, 25 June 2018. Accessed 30 June 2018. https://oceanservice.noaa.gov/facts/watershed.html.

O'Connor, David K. "Tolkien and Nostalgia." *Thomas International Center.* Accessed 1 March 2018. www.ticenter.net/tolkien-and-nostalgia/.

Parham, James. *Green Media and Popular Culture: An Introduction.* London, UK: Palgrave Macmillan, 2016.

Park, Gene. "The Legend of Zelda: Twilight Princess Review." *Gamecritics,* 23 February 2007. Accessed 22 September 2019. https://gamecritics.com/gene-park/the- legend-of-zelda-twilight-princess-review/.

Paumgarten, Nick. "Master of Play: The many Worlds of a Videogame Artist." *The New Yorker,* 20 and 27 December 2010. Accessed 31 October 2019. www.newyorker.com/magazine/2010/12/20/master-of-play.

———. "Master of Play." *The New Yorker.* 19 June 2017. Accessed 31 December 2018. www.newyorker.com/magazine/2010/12/20/master-of-play.

Pavel, Thomas G. *Fictional Worlds.* Boston, MA: Harvard University Press, 1986.

Perron, Bernard, ed. *Horror Video Games: Essays on the Fusion of Fear and Play.* Jefferson, NC: Mcfarland & Company Incorporated, 2009.

Pozderak-Chenevey, Sarah. "A Direct Link to the Past: Nostalgia and Semiotics in Video Game Music." *Divergencepress.* 2 June 2014. Accessed 17 September, 2019. http://divergencepress.net/articles/2016/11/3/a-direct-link-to-the-past-nostalgia-and-semiotics-in-video-game-music.

Pugh, Tison. "The Queer Narrativity of the Hero's Journey in Nintendo's The Legend of Zelda Video Games." *Journal of Narrative Theory* 48, no. 2 (2018): 225–251.

Rancière, Jacques. "Aesthetic Separation, Aesthetic Community: Scenes from the Aesthetic Regime of Art." *Art and Research* 2, no. 1 (2006). Accessed 1 July 2018, www.artandresearch.org.uk/v2n1/Rancière.html.

Rasmussen, John and Rachel Rasmussen. "Freedom versus Destiny: A Hero's Call." In *The Legend of Zelda and Theology,* edited by Jonathan L. Walls, 71–82. Los Angeles, CA: Gray Matter Books, 2011.

Reed, Kristian. "The Legend of Zelda: Twilight Princess Deserves a Spotlight." *Eurogamer.* 3 April 2008. Accessed 21 September 2019. www.eurogamer.net/articles/r_zeldatp_wii.

Reilly, R.J. "Tolkien and the Fairy Story." *Understanding the Lord of the Rings: The Best of Tolkien Criticism,* edited by Rose A. Zimbardo and Neil D. Isaacs, 93–105. Boston/New York: Houghton Mifflin Company, 2004.

Rickert, Matthew. "The Legend of Zelda: Twilight Princess." *RPGFan.* 4 April 2007. Accessed 18 January 2018. www.rpgfan.com/reviews/zeldatp-wii/index.html.

Robertson, Adrien. "Gaming with Ghosts: Hauntology, Metanarrative, and Gamespace in Video Games." Master's thesis. Carleton University, 2014.

Robinson, Rachel. "Shape Shifting and Time Traveling: Link's Identity Issues." In *The Legend of Zelda and Philosophy: I Link Therefore I Am*, edited by Luke Cuddy, 75–82. Chicago, IL: Open Court, 2013.

Rogers, Tim. "The Literature of the Moment: A Critique of Mother 2." https://web.archive.org/web/20131022032055/http://www.largeprimenumbers.com/article.php?sid=mother2.

Rone, Vincent E. "A Case for Twilight Princess: the Music, Part 1." *Zelda Dungeon.* 2 January 2015. Accessed 21 September 2019. www.zeldadungeon.net/a- case-for-twilight-princess-the-music/.

Rousseau, Jean-Jacque. *Emile, or Education.* Translated by Barbara Foxley. Dutton, 1921. *Online Library of Liberty.* Accessed 23 October 2019. https://oll.libertyfund.org/titles/rousseau-emile-or-education.

Rowland, Thomas. "'And Now Begins Our Game:' Revitalizing the Ludic Robin Hood." In *Robin Hood in Outlaw/ed Spaces: Media, Performance, and Other New Directions*, edited by Lesley Coote and Valerie Johnson, 175–188. Abingdon, UK: Routledge, 2017.

———. "Reading Games and Playing Stories: Intromersive Literary Spaces in the Long History of Reading." Ph.D. Dissertation. Saint Louis University, 2014.

Ryan, Marie-Laure, "Beyond Myth and Metaphor – The Case of Narrative in Digital Media." *Game Studies* 1, no. 1 (July 2001). Accessed 31 October 2019. www.gamestudies.org/0101/ryan/.

———. "Fictional Worlds in the Digital Age." *A Companion to Digital Literacy Studies*, edited by Susan Shreibman and Ray Siemens, 250–266. Oxford; Blackwell, 2008.

———. *Narrative as Virtual Reality II.* Baltimore, MD: The Johns Hopkins University Press, 2015.

———. *Narrative as Virtual Reality: Immersion and Interactivity in Literature and Electronic Media.* Baltimore, MD: Johns Hopkins University Press, 2001.

Ryckert, Dan. "Review: Legend of Zelda: Twilight Princess (Wii)." *Lawrence.* 14 November 2006. Accessed 17 January 2018. www.lawrence.com/news/2006/nov/14/review_legend_zelda_twilight_princess_wii/.

Salen, Katie and Eric Zimmerman. *Rules of Play: Game Design Fundamentals.* Cambridge, MA: MIT Press, 2003.

Schott, Gareth and Maria Kambouri. "Moving Between The Spectral And Material Plane." *Convergence: The International Journal of Research into New Media Technologies* 9 (2003: 3): 41–55.

Schwarzer, Mitchell. "Origins of the Art History Survey Text." *Art Journal* 54, no. 3 (Autumn 1995): 24–29. www.jstor.org/stable/777579.

Scodel, Ruth. "Odysseus' Dog and the Productive Household." *Hermes* 133, no. 4 (2005): 401–408. www.jstor.org/stable/4477672.

Scully-Blaker, Rainforest. "A Practiced Practice: Speedrunning Through Space with de Certeau and Virilio." *Game Studies: The International Journal of*

Computer Game Research 14, no. 1 (2014). http://gamestudies.org/1401/articles/scullyblaker.

Serrels, Mark. "Twilight Princess Is A Game Out Of Time." *Kotaku*. 7 March 2016. Accessed 13 September 2019. www.kotaku.com.au/2016/03/twilight-princess-is-a-game-out-of-time/.

Sherlock, Lee. "Three Days in Termina." In *The Legend of Zelda and Philosophy*, edited by Luke Cuddy Cuddy, 131–132. New York, NY: Open Court, 2008.

Shippey, T.A. *J.R.R Tolkien: Author of the Century*. Boston, MA: Houghton Mifflin, 2002.

Sidney, Philip. "The Defense of Poesy." In *Classic Writings on Poetry*, edited by William Harmon, 117–152. New York, NY: Columbia University Press, 2003.

Silber, Joan. *The Art of Time in Fiction: As Long as It Takes*. St. Paul, MN: Grey Wolf Press, 2009.

Snyder, David. *Speedrunning: Interviews with the Quickest Gamers*. Jefferson, NC: McFarland, 2017.

Stanley, Kate. "Affect and Emotion: James, Dewey, Tomkins, Damasio, Massumi, Spinoza." In *The Palgrave Handbook of Affect Studies and Textual Criticism*, edited by Daniel R. Wehrs and Thomas Blake, 97–111. London: Palgrave Macmillan, 2017.

Stitt, J. Michael. "Tolkien's On Fairy-Stories." *Tolkien Fantasy and Literature*. Accessed 1 March 2018. https://faculty.unlv.edu/jmstitt/Eng477/ofs.html.

Suits, Bernard. "What Is a Game?" *Philosophy of Science* 34, no. 2 (June 1967): 148–156. www.jstor.org/stable/186102.

Summers, Timothy. *Understanding Video Game Music*. Cambridge, UK: Cambridge University Press, 2016.

SWE3tMadness. "More Than Just Noise: Nostalgia and Homecoming." *Destructoid*. 9 September 2010. Accessed 21 September 2019. www.destructoid.com/more-than-just-noise-nostalgia-and-homecoming-183290.phtml.

Tallon, Philip. "The Birth of Gaming from the Spirit of Fantasy: Video Games as Secondary Worlds with Special Reference to The Legend of Zelda and J.R.R. Tolkien." In *The Legend of Zelda and Theology*, edited by Jonathan L. Walls, 49–69. Los Angeles, CA: Gray Matter Books 2011.

"The Legend of Zelda." *Video Game Sales Wiki*. Accessed 26th October 2019. https://vgsales.fandom.com/wiki/The_Legend_of_Zelda.

The Mahabharata of Krishna-Dwaipayana Vyasa. Translated by Kisari Mohan Ganguli. 1883–1896. *Internet Sacred Text Archive*. Accessed 31 October 2019. www.sacred-texts.com/hin/m03/m03186.htm.

The Video Game History Foundation. "What We're Doing." Accessed 24 October 2019. https://gamehistory.org/what-were-doing/.

Thomas Aquinas. *Summa Theologiæ*. Translated by the Fathers of the English Dominican Province. Allen, TX: Christian Classics, 1981.

Thompson, Tevis. "Saving Zelda." Tevis Thompson. 10 February 2012. Accessed 31 October 2019. http://tevisthompson.com/saving-zelda/.

Thorpe, Patrick, Dakota James, Kazuyaka Sakai, Mika Kanmuri, Naoyuki Kayama, and Yukari Tasai, eds. *The Legend of Zelda: Encyclopedia*. Translated by Keaton C. White. Milwaukie, WI: Dark Horse, 2018.

Thorpe, Patrick, ed. *The Legend of Zelda: Hyrule Historia.* Translated by Michael Gombos, Takahiro Moriki, Heidi Plechl, Kumar Sivasubramanian, Aria Tanner, and John Thomas. Milwaukie, WI: Dark Horse Books, 2013.

Tillich, Paul. *The Courage to Be.* New Haven, CT: Yale University Press, 1980.

Tilton, Shane. "The Songs of the Ritos: The Psychology of the Music within The Legend of Zelda." *The Psychology of Zelda*, edited by Anthony M. Bean, 171–190. Dallas, TX: BenBella Books, 2019.

Tolkien, Christopher. *Foreword to The Shaping of Middle Earth.* Edited by Christopher Tolkien. New York, NY: Ballantine Books, 1986, vii–viii.

———. *Preface to The Silmarillion.* Edited by Christopher Tolkien. New York, NY: Ballantine Books, 1977, xi–xiv.

Tolkien, J.R.R. "Beowulf: The Monster and the Critics." In *An Anthology of Beowulf Criticism*, edited by Lewis E. Nicholson, 51–103. Notre Dame, ID: Notre Dame Press, 1963.

———. "On Fairy-Stories." *Heritagepodcast.com.* http://heritagepodcast.com/wp-content/uploads/Tolkien-On-Fairy-Stories-subcreation.pdf.

———. *On Fairy-Stories.* Edited by Douglas Anderson. New York, NY: Harper Collins, 2008.

———. "On Fairy-Stories." In *On Fairy-Stories*, edited by Verlyn Flieger and Douglas A. Anderson, 27–84. London, UK: HarperCollins Publishers, 2014.

———. "On Fairy-Stories." In *The Monsters and the Critics and Other Essays*, edited by Christopher Tolkien, 109–161. London, UK: HarperCollins, 2006.

———. "On Fairy-Stories." In *The Tolkien Reader*, 3–84. New York, NY: Ballantine Books, 1966.

———. "On Fairy-Stories." In *The Tolkien Reader*, 33–90. New York, NY: Dell Rey, 1966.

———. *The Hobbit.* London: George Allen & Unwin Ltd., 1937. Reprinted with Note on the Text by Douglas A. Anderson. Boston, MA: Houghton Mifflin Company, 2001.

———. *The Letters of J.R.R. Tolkien.* Edited by Humphrey Carpenter. Boston, MA: Houghton Mifflin Harcourt, 2000.

———. *The Letters of J.R.R. Tolkien: A Selection.* Edited by Humphrey Carpenter with assistance from Christopher Tolkien. London, UK: HarperCollins Publishers, 2006.

———. *The Lord of the Rings: The Fellowship of the Ring.* Boston, MA: Houghton Mifflin, 1965.

———. *The Lord of the Rings: The Fellowship of the Ring.* Boston, MA: Houghton and Mifflin Co., 1994.

———. *Tree and Leaf: Including Mythopoeia.* New York, NY: HarperCollins, 2001.

———. *The Silmarillion.* Edited by Christopher Tolkien. New York, NY: Ballantine Books, 1977.

———. *The Silmarillion.* Edited by Christopher Tolkien. Boston, MA: Mariner Books, 2001.

Toole, John Kennedy. *A Confederacy of Dunces.* New York, NY: Grover Press, 1980.

Totilo, Stephen. "Shigeru Miyamoto Interviews Me about Hardcore Games, Also Talks 'Punch-Out' and 'Mario,' 'Zelda' Shortcomings." *MTV News.* 29

October 2008. Accessed 13 September 2019. www.mtv.com/news/2457976/
shigeru-miyamoto-punchout-mario-zelda-portal/.

Vasari, Giorgio. *Le vite de' più eccellenti pittori, scultori, e architettori.*
Florence: Torrentino, 1550; revised and expanded Giunti, 1568. Reprinted
and edited by Rosanna Bettarini and Paola Barocchi. Sansoni, 1966–1987.
http://vasari.sns.it/consultazione/Vasari/indice.html.

Vella, Daniel. "No Mastery without Mystery: Dark Souls and the Ludic Sublime." *Game Studies* 15, no. 1 (2015). Accessed 27 October 2019. http://
gamestudies.org/1501/articles/vella.

Virgil. *The Aeneid.* Translated by Robert Fagles. New York, NY: Penguin,
2006.

VPRO and Žižek, Slavoj. "Lecture: Living in the End Times with Slavoj
Žižek." YouTube. 11 March 2010. Accessed 1 July 2018. www.youtube.com/
watch?v=Gw8LPn4irao.

Wardrip-Fruin and Pat Harrigan, eds. *First Person: New Media as Story, Performance, and Game.* Cambridge, MA; MIT Press, 2004.

Warner, Michael. *The Trouble with Normal.* New York, NY: The Free Press,
1999.

Weik von Mossner, Alexa. *Affective Ecologies: Empathy, Emotion, and Environmental Narrative.* Columbus, OH: Ohio State University Press, 2017.
Kindle Version.

Weissmann, Jordan. "The Decline of the American Book Lover." *The Atlantic.*
14 January 2014. Accessed 5 March 2017. www.theatlantic.com/business/
archive/2014/01/the-decline-of-the-american-book-lover/283222/.

Westerlaken, Michelle. "Self-fashioning in Action: Zelda's Breath of the Wild
Vegan Run." 11th International Philosophy of Computer Games Conference,
Krakow, 2017. Accessed 27 October 2019. https://gamephilosophy2017.files.
wordpress.com/2017/11/westerlaken_pocg17.pdf.

Whalen, Zach and Laurie N. Taylor. "Playing the Past: An Introduction." In
Playing the Past: History and Nostalgia in Video Games, edited by Zach
Whalen and Laurie N. Taylor, 1–15. Nashville, TN: Vanderbilt Press, 2008.

White, Lynn. "The Historical Roots of Our Ecologic Crisis." *Science* 155,
no. 3767 (1967): 1203–1207.

Whiteman, Natasha. "Homesick for Silent Hill: Modalities of Nostalgia in Fan
Responses to Silent Hill 4: The Room." In *Playing the Past: History and Nos-
talgia in Video Games*, edited by Zach Whalen and Laurie N. Taylor, 32–50.
Nashville, TN: Vanderbilt Press, 2008.

Yavelberg, Josh. "Questioning the Survey: A Look into Art History Survey and
its Pedagogical Practices." *Journal of Mason Graduate Research* 1, no. 1
(2014): 23–48.

Yee, Nick and Jeremy Bailenson. "The Proteus Effect: The Effect of Transformed Self-Representation on Behavior." *Human Communication Research*
33 (2007): 271–290.

Zapf, Hubert. *Literature as Cultural Ecology: Sustainable Texts.* London, UK:
Bloomsbury, 2016.

Index

Note: **Bold** page numbers refer to tables and page numbers followed by "n" denote endnotes.

For Product Safety Concerns and Information please contact our EU
representative GPSR@taylorandfrancis.com
Taylor & Francis Verlag GmbH, Kaufingerstraße 24, 80331 München, Germany

www.ingramcontent.com/pod-product-compliance
Ingram Content Group UK Ltd.
Pitfield, Milton Keynes, MK11 3LW, UK
UKHW021429080625
459435UK00011B/215